# FROM ATHENS TO JERUSALEM

# FROM ATHENS TO JERUSALEM

*The Love of Wisdom and the Love of God*

STEPHEN R. L. CLARK

CLARENDON PRESS · OXFORD
1984

Oxford University Press, Walton Street, Oxford OX2 6DP
London New York Toronto
Delhi Bombay Calcutta Madras Karachi
Kuala Lumpur Singapore Hong Kong Tokyo
Nairobi Dar es Salaam Cape Town
Melbourne Auckland
and associated companies in
Beirut Berlin Ibadan Mexico City Nicosia

Oxford is a trade mark of Oxford University Press

Published in the United States by
Oxford University Press, New York

British Library Cataloguing in Publication Data
Clark, Stephen R. L.
From Athens to Jerusalem.
1. Theism
I. Title
211'.3       BL200
ISBN 0-19-824698-6
ISBN 0-19-824697-8 Pbk

Library of Congress Cataloging in Publication Data
Clark, Stephen R. L.
From Athens to Jerusalem.
Bibliography: p.
Includes index.
1. Naturalism—Addresses, essays, lectures.
2. Relativity—Addresses, essays, lectures.   3. Reason—
Addresses, essays, lectures.   4. Religion—Philosophy—
Addresses, essays, lectures.   5. Neoplatonism—Addresses,
essays, lectures.   I. Title.
B828.2.C55   1984          141'.2          84-4249
ISBN 0-19-824698-6
ISBN 0-19-824697-8 (pbk.)

Typeset by Joshua Associates, Oxford
Printed in Great Britain
at the University Press, Oxford

# Preface

When the University of Glasgow did my colleague Dr. Christina Larner and myself the honour of asking us to give the Gifford Lectures for 1982, we wondered whether to attempt a single theme, but decided that it would be better to work separately. In the event, there was a theme in common, for we were both strongly aware of both the temptations and the perils of relativism. Her lectures were printed, with only a few revisions, as *The Thinking Peasant* (Pressgang, Glasgow 1982): if I have not found specific occasion to refer to them in what follows, this is not because they were not lively, informative, and at times disturbing. Professor Larner has since died young, of cancer bravely borne, and her funeral was conducted in traditional Presbyterian style, 'complete with hobgoblins, foul fiends, and the twenty-third psalm sung to Crimond', as she wished (Larner (1982), p. 85). Her recommendation of 'methodological and other sorts of atheism' is, obviously, not mine, but her courage and good sense remain an inspiration and example to us all.

When I was asked, shortly before Christmas 1981, to produce some Gifford lectures by the following term, I drew heavily upon a work that academic publishers have found too fanciful, and other publishers too academic. In this I had composed papers in a variety of styles, supposed to be read at a conference on Values of Knowledge and Belief, in an alternate history. I had chosen this once-familar genre in order to reveal the manifold ways in which philosophical topics could be handled, and to release in myself those voices which might not be heard in a more linear discussion. The experiment was, for me, a success, a way (as it were) of consulting some of the echoing congregation of voices that constitute the human soul. In transforming and rewriting some of those papers, which now constitute much of the first three chapters of this book, I have sometimes ignored alternatives that deserve

attention. I would not wish it to be thought that I am unaware of these: but what I here present is my most considered view of the presuppositions of scholarship, and the
consequences for our spiritual lives of our increasing knowledge of the social and physical world.

Some readers may be inclined to think that the title, *From
Athens to Jerusalem*, is inaccurate, that it should have been
*From Athens to Alexandria*, since I advocate a return to Neo-
Platonic speculation that has served the theological purposes
of Jews, Pagans, Christians, Muslims, and Hindus, without
offering any final reason for preferring one tradition to
another. I make no apology, sharing Dean Inge's belief that
'it is an error to suppose that Christianity is compatible with
every reasonable philosophical system' (Inge (1926), p. 76);
and Nasr's that it is high time we rediscovered the *philo-
sophia perennis* (Nasr (1981), pp. 70 ff), and stopped sneer-
ing at each other's insights.

My Gifford lectures appear as the first five chapters. Later
chapters return to and expand upon some themes introduced
earlier. I have discussed other topics from a similar position
in Clark (1983*b*, 1983*c*, 1984), and hope to deal with such
topics as St John's use of Logos-theory, the rules of reason,
and political philosophy in more detail at a later date.
Chapter 7, on Consciousness, was read first to a gathering of
philosophers and zoologists funded by the Thyssen Foundation. I am grateful especially to John Maynard Smith, John
MacDowell, and Eva Schaper for their comments. My thanks
also go to my other colleagues at Glasgow, especially Gillian
Clark, Robin Downie, William Lyons, John Riches, Flint
Schier, Janet Sisson, John Skorupski, and Neil Spurway for
their interest and constructive disagreement over the years,
and to Bishop Derek Rawcliffe for helping me to see that
Charismatic Enthusiasm, rightly understood, is compatible
with intellectual honour.

University of Liverpool

# Contents

# Acknowledgements

The author gratefully acknowledges the permission of the following to include copyright material in this book: Faber and Faber Ltd. and Random House, Inc., for eight lines from W. H. Auden, 'The History of Science', in *Collected Shorter Poems 1926–56*, ed. Edward Mendelson, copyright © W. H. Auden 1966; The National Trust and Macmillan London Ltd., for eight lines from Rudyard Kipling, 'We and They', in *Collected Verse: Inclusive Edition*, 1927; Constable Publishers and Dame Felicitas Corrigan, OSB, for ten lines from Boethius, translated by Helen Waddell in *Medieval Latin Lyrics*, first published 1929.

# 1

# Philosophy and the Care of the Soul

In 1885 Adam Gifford, being convinced 'that the true knowledge of God, and the true and felt knowledge (not merely
nominal knowledge) of the relations of man and the universe
to Him, and of the true foundations of all ethics and morals,
when really felt and acted on, is the means of man's highest
well-being', set about establishing what were to be the Gifford
Lectures at the four Scottish Universities.[1] There have been
lectures on God, on knowledge, on religion, morals and the
universe. They have usually been given by Professors, well-
established in their chosen careers. That Glasgow has preferred,
on this occasion and perhaps never again, to ask a mere
Lecturer to perform lays a special burden on me. No one
could stand here and not be conscious of the weight of his
predecessors, but Professors are perhaps used to sitting in the
seat of the wise. I hope that I will not be held to have dis-
graced myself. The Giffords are old and tough enough not to
be dishonoured by an inept performance: I am not.
  'The true knowledge of God . . . is the means of man's
highest well-being.' Lord Gifford did not require of his
lecturers that they agree with his assessment. 'They may be
of any religion or way of thinking . . . or they may be so-
called sceptics or agnostics or freethinkers, provided only
that the patrons will use diligence to secure that they be able,
reverent men, true thinkers, sincere lovers of and earnest
inquirers after truth.' My concern in these lectures is to discover how that reverent love of truth may be related to the
knowledge of God, and to make a case for Lord Gifford's
own belief. The true knowledge of God is the means of man's
highest well-being, and that knowledge is available to those
who sincerely desire it.

[1] See Jones (1970), p. 7.

What can a philosopher know of these things? Isn't philosophy simply the study of words and ideas and arguments, perennially disproving whatever was established by an earlier generation of philosophers?

It's fine to have a share in philosophy far enough for education, and it is not shameful for someone to philosophize when he is a boy. But whenever a man who is older still philosophizes, the thing becomes ridiculous.[2]

Philosophy, for many, is either a trivial or a dangerous word-game. Do grown men really sit around discussing whether treason is wrong? Either they are joking or they are seriously disturbed. What effect could such maunderings have on the impressionable young? Surely they will conclude that philosophical argument is essentially inconclusive, that nothing can be securely demonstrated. And from that discovery they will go away as cynics or as melancholiacs. How do we dare?

Some years ago I was rash enough to write as follows:

Opinions that are generally taken to demonstrate the speaker's lunacy, that he is a machine or that there is nobody behind any one else's behaviour, do not suddenly become reputable, though they become respectable, when uttered by a philosopher in philosophical (i.e. insincere) tones.[3]

And again:

It may seem merely foolish to engage in philosophical, and insincere, discussion, say, of solipsism or of the existence of the material world. Not because these are empty questions, but because those who actually experience their full challenge, for whom they are living options, are unlikely to be assisted by the rhetoric of disputing philosophers.[4]

But perhaps it is more than foolish: perhaps it is dangerous. How do we know how we are affecting those who come to us? If we cause them to doubt themselves, the world, morality, what will they go away believing?

[2] Plato, *Gorgias* 485a5 f. (T. Irwin).
[3] Clark (1975), p. 195.
[4] Clark (1977*a*), p. 1.

> He who shall teach the Child to Doubt
> the rotting Grave shall ne'er get out.[5]

It is not enough to reply that we only wish them to doubt certain things, or that they will learn some more secure way of safeguarding the essentials: not enough, at any rate, if we make no attempt to show what that way may be. And what are the things we should not wish them to doubt? We are not all as bold as Samuel Johnson:

> One evening when a young gentleman teized him with an account of the infidelity of his servant, who, he said, would not believe the scriptures, because he could not read them in the original tongues, and be sure that they were not invented, "Why, foolish fellow, (said Johnson) has he any better authority for almost everything that he believes?" BOSWELL: "Then the vulgar, Sir, never can know that they are right, but must submit themselves to the learned." JOHNSON: "To be sure, Sir. The vulgar are the children of the State, and must be taught like children." BOSWELL: "Then Sir, a poor Turk must be Mahometan, just as a poor Englishman must be a Christian?" JOHNSON: "Why, yes, Sir; and what then? This is now such stuff as I used to talk to my mother, when I first began to think myself a clever fellow; and she ought to have whipt me for it."[6]

In the days of our innocence we did not question common sense, accepted truth. It is when we begin to ask ourselves, or others ask us, how we can be sure of what we have believed, that philosophy begins. But once we have started, how shall we come to a conclusion?

> Demanding formal proof,
> and seeking it in everything, I lost
> all feeling of conviction, and, in fine,
> sick, wearied out with contrarieties,
> yielded up moral questions in despair.[7]

It comes to seem that there are questions which cannot be answered, that we cannot establish what we ought to believe. Nothing is certain; we lose all confidence in our powers.

[5] Blake *Auguries of Innocence*: Keynes (1966), p. 433.
[6] Boswell (1953), p. 361: spring 1766.
[7] Wordsworth, *Prelude* 11. 301 ff.

The way we teach may make this result even more likely. When our students present the arguments for some philosophical thesis, it is common form to challenge them, to require further detail, further argument. Sometimes our victims may be able to respond in kind, to show that they really understand the arguments. Often they may conclude either that they are themselves incompetent, or that philosophic reasoning itself is inconclusive. If we find that despair is setting in, we refer them to a psychotherapist!

To spell out this latter point: if my friend comes to me with a conundrum that purports to show the impossibility of knowing another's feelings, or the essential meaninglessness of life, or the impossibility of drawing any inference from past to future, I may engage her in philosophical debate. But if it is evident that she really means it, I am perhaps more likely to begin to enquire about her diet, her state of health, the progress or otherwise of her affections. 'The analyst will simply not take the question (what is the meaning of life) seriously as a question but only as a symptom.'[8] There are some arguments, after all—we have the word of Sextus Empiricus as well as David Hume—that admit of no answer, but produce no conviction, at least in a healthy and a happy creature.[9] There are some beliefs to which only the melancholiac can give a real assent.

Does it seem then that philosophers spend their time attempting to induce psychotic doubts in the young, and then stepping back aghast when they succeed? Must despair and cynicism be the fruits of philosophy? It is obvious enough that my answer must be 'No': if it were otherwise I would not be here. What responses are available to philosophic doubt?

The first is indeed despair, which comes in at least two forms. Melancholy despair afflicts those who feel themselves wholly inadequate to establish any conclusion. Whatever

---

[8] Collier (1977), p. 109.
[9] Sextus Empiricus, *Outlines of Pyrrhonism* 2. 244 f.: (1933) i. 315; Hume (1888) i. 4. 7.

proof of whatever thesis can be devised serves not to compel belief, but to suggest new doubts, both of the premisses and of the form of argument that links premisses and conclusion.[10] Whatever can be asserted can also be questioned. However much evidence is adduced for a particular claim it will always be logically possible that the evidence be as it is said to be, yet the claim be false. And if it is logically possible how shall we ever tell that it is not the case? How can we find out that the claims which seem best established are actually true? All that we can do is see whether certain 'evidence' is forthcoming: we can never tell that the evidence is of truth. You can't deduce one fact from another, so the principle which says 'When such and such evidence is present such and such a claim is true' cannot be established by reason; but neither can it be established by experience. I do not incontrovertibly *experience* the truth of any claim about the world: my experience could always be conjoined with the falsity of the claim they lead me (psychologically) to make. So the link between evidence and truth seems to be one I cannot establish. I cannot compare two lists: one of claims I am seriously inclined to make, and one of true claims. What should I put in the second list but claims I am seriously inclined to make? I never have two lists, but only one.

Whether my response to this is a melancholy despair perhaps depends on non-rational factors in my personality and circumstances. Perhaps instead I fall into Pyrrhonian scepticism, a form maybe of cynicism. One argument can always be deployed against another; one natural conviction born of beef and backgammon can be set against the melancholy induced by too long a stay in one's study. The Pyrrhonian sceptic acknowledges the sometime force of the argument for total agnosticism I have sketched, but finds this a source of calm. If every argument can be refuted and re-stated and re-refuted let us play the game, bowing to the quadruple compulsion of Nature, sensation, custom, and the rules of such crafts as we choose to practise—

[10] Forder (1927), p. viii; see Lakatos (1976), p. 48.

not that we hold these true, but so as not to be wholly inactive.[11]

True Pyrrhonians are a rare breed, and exasperating company. Whatever is said to them by way of persuasion, they will respond with questions, alternative arguments, outright and outrageous fallacies. If they cannot think of any detailed response they will retort as follows:

Just as, before the birth of the founder of the School to which you belong, the theory it holds was not as yet apparent as a sound theory, although it was really (sc. as you say) true, so likewise it is possible that the opposite theory to that which you now propound is already really 'true', though not yet apparent to us, so that we ought not to yield assent to this theory which at the moment seems to be valid.[12]

This passage, from Sextus Empiricus, really requires lengthy analysis, but its message is clear enough. The true sceptic will not himself be convinced of anything: the tranquillity that others seek in certainty, in a regression to the days of innocence, he has found in a permanently suspended judgement. Systems of philosophy are 'so many plays brought out and performed, creating fictitious and theatrical worlds', as Francis Bacon would have had it.[13] Nor will the sceptic have any higher opinion of Bacon's own system.

But though thorough-going sceptics are rare (it being very hard to put aside our human nature), there is a commoner variety. A confused relativism is one of the commonest intellectual habits of our day. All argument is greeted with the supposed rebuttal, 'Well, that's what you think'; efforts to get someone to think for herself only earn a list of the victim's opinions, which it is considered ill-mannered or impertinent to test for consistency or plausibility. What is that but to impose one's own opinions on another? Even in more sophisticated quarters there is a tendency to confuse liberalism with relativism: those who wish to claim that 'everyone has a right to his or her own opinion' sometimes

---

[11] Sextus, *OP* i. 23: (1933) i. 17.
[12] Sextus, *OP* i. 34: (1933) i. 23.
[13] Bacon (1855), p. 21: i. 44.

imagine that they help their case by saying that there is no single truth, no standard test, but all opinions are true-for-those-who-hold-them. If this were true, of course, it would lend no support to the liberal thesis against the authoritarian: both would be true-for-their-supporters, neither true. Someone who attempts to live out his relativism loses the ability to say that he truly believes anything, for he believes nothing to be true-in-fact. That what he believes he believes to be true-for-him only means that whatever he believes he believes that he believes. His belief is Pickwickian: but for the grace of everyday life, he would end as a Pyrrhonian.

That all relativists are sincere in their claims is unlikely: most do no more than parrot the clichés of their age. But a genuine experience lies behind this absurdity, this refusal to be dictated to by any supposedly objective standard of truth. Chairman Mao's words are perhaps too harsh: 'It should be pointed out that the source of ultra-democracy consists in the petty bourgeoisie's individualistic aversion to discipline.'[14] 'Ultra-democracy', the individual's refusal ever to bend to common or authoritative judgement, may have its political uses. Its effect on epistemology is disastrous. 'The man who betakes himself to feeling, to immediate knowledge, to his own ideas or his own thoughts, shuts himself up in his own particularity and breaks off any fellowship or community with others—one must leave him alone.'[15] It may be that relativists imagine that they can continue to live ordinary lives, to use ordinary language: they are mistaken. They can no longer coherently disagree with the most eccentric judgements of fact or value: they may say that these are not their opinions, but they have forsworn any belief in a common reality, mutually assessible judgements. When they say that Zebedee is married to Rahab, they cannot legitimately conclude that Rahab is married to Zebedee, or that anyone is married to Rahab, or that there are marriages. All the links that bind our speech together are resolved into matters of

[14] Mao Tse-Tung (1967), pp. 163 f.
[15] Hegel: cited by Westphal (1974), p. 39.

personal opinion. But in that case it becomes impossible to know what anyone means by the words they utter.

At other times and places, I would spend more time in analysing relativism and scepticism, seeking some more coherent form of the systems. For the moment it is enough to point out that these attitudes do not stem from the corrupting effects of professional philosophy, though past philosophers have played a part in their dissemination. Scepticism, relativism, and less attractive intellectual habits are endemic in our society. It is not that innocent students lose their faith in truth, justice, and reason when confronted by philosophical arguments. They have already lost that faith, or never had it, or lack the courage to express their real faith in words. For this last factor we must bear some responsibility: fear of being made to seem foolish is a strong motive for concealing real convictions behind a façade of relativism. But the office of philosophers is far more often to encourage people to see the implications of what they say than to destroy their faith in argument, or in their own pre-philosophical convictions.

So far I have described three roads away from our early innocence, the days when we believed in Santa Claus and thought it obvious what was fair, what not. The melancholiac has failed to find proof that life is worth living, or that there is a world of living creatures outwith her mind. Sometimes this takes clearly psychotic forms: one unfortunate, after many attempts at suicide or self-injury, was brought by a therapist of my acquaintance to reveal that he was uncertain whether or not he was a ghost. With a commendable diligence he tried to discover the truth by seeing whether suicidal acts, self-injury had any effect. His tragedy, of course, was that no test could be final: if he hadn't been a ghost before, he certainly might be now. The question always came again, and could receive no empirical answer: it was a metaphysical question, not open to the keys of scientific method, but still a real problem. He had lost faith in the world of common day, and could find no other worthier his esteem.

Such extremities of depression come our way quite rarely, but it is certainly not uncommon to find someone uncertain of his or her own identity or society. These doubts are rarely created by philosophic questioning, but they may be made worse by unskilful attentions, simply because we do not suspect the presence of depression until it is quite far advanced. The other types are more recognizable, the sceptic and the would-be relativist, and these too are not created by philosophical discussion: they are to be found in the world, and we must deal with them, forcing the consequences of what they say upon them, pointing out the difficulties and uncertainties in the very steps that have led them to take such a stance.

Two other common attitudes need to be mentioned, which I will christen 'indifferentism' and 'voluntarism'. These are efforts to avoid despair, particularly the despair induced by thoughts of the deserts of dusty eternity that surround our globe. Where my first three types have wholly despaired of reason, these do not. The indifferentist may at first seem like a relativist: he too is inclined to say, of some sorts of argument, that these are merely matters of 'opinion' or of taste. There are no objective truths in the field of ethics, he supposes, and from this concludes that 'the universe is indifferent to value', that the first principle of action and belief in an age dedicated to science must be 'do not project your values on the universe'. Nothing that happens in the world has any point or purpose, and if we are to understand things as they are we must give up our superstitious habit of attributing moral value to things or to the motions of 'matter in that state known as living'. Facts are facts, but values are only fancies. The reasonable man ignores such phantoms.

Once again, it is rare to find a genuine indifferentist. Most of the muddle-heads who take pleasure in telling moral philosophers that 'they don't believe in morality, don't believe that there are any moral truisms, or that moral disagreement could ever be resolved by rational debate', are honest and honourable enough. Even those who take the

further step of saying that we ought to acknowledge everything as essentially valueless may have hearts a little wiser
than their heads. But indifferentism is still advocated, and
not only by Lao Tzu: 'Heaven and earth are ruthless, and
treat the myriad creatures as straw dogs; the sage is ruthless,
and treats the people as straw dogs.'[16]

Jacques Monod, a Nobel Prize winning biologist, is the
most notable advocate of this incoherent 'ethic for modern
man'.[17] Since, he supposes, human life is the product of
chance and necessity in a universe that is not directed to any
objectively good end, we must acknowledge our absurdity in
thinking that anything really matters. Whatever happens or
is done is a bare event: even our decision to treat the world
scientifically is an arbitrary one, not required of us by any
objective principle. Once made, it requires of us that we
treat everything simply as an occasion for scientific enquiry,
unfettered by any thought of honour, decency, kindness, or
justice. How many of the real consequences of his creed
Monod intended I have no way of knowing; presumably, in
common with other indifferentists, he made exceptions in
favour of his own body, career, family, friends. Hard it is to
strip off human nature! But it is alarmingly easy for people
to drain their world of all emotional affect when it is a matter
of more distant loyalties: the fate of laboratory animals in
the last century, treated as research tools and without serious
regard for their own interests, is a warning of what life would
be like if we were ruled by indifferentists.

Most of Monod's argument is incoherent, as are later efforts
to substitute sociobiology for ethical enquiry, but one
particular step in it deserves our attention: the famous division between 'facts' and 'values'. Facts are what they are
independently of our discovery: values, it is held, are projections of our subjective concerns. Facts can, in principle,
be discovered by some agreed system of enquiry: values can
only be affirmed, and *de gustibus non est disputandum*. The

[16] Tao Te Ching 1. 14: Chan (1963), p. 141.
[17] Monod (1972), pp. 163 ff.

arguments for this distinction are complex, and beyond my present brief: what is worth pointing out is that for a claim to be established as factual we need to show that it ought, consistently with other claims and principles, to be believed. To prove something is to show that it follows from or is the best explanation of some other claim which is currently uncontested. The laws of logic, the rules of inference and probability are moral rules, statements of what ought to be done. Someone who holds that moral rules are all mere expressions of irrational taste, and that we ought (!) to see things simply as they are, as they are revealed to an investigation conducted in accordance with the laws of logic and scholarship, is talking nonsense: to deny morality is in the end to deny any obligation to talk sense, follow an argument, or accept unwelcome conclusions.

A second point worth emphasizing is this: whereas it has become a commonplace that one cannot legitimately deduce an 'ought' from an 'is', cannot prove a moral conclusion purely on the basis of some factual claim, it has been forgotten that this is only an instance of a wider principle. That wider principle is that one cannot legitimately deduce any claim simply from another: that Zebedee is married to Rahab does not, of itself, imply that Rahab is married to Zebedee nor that Zebedee is not married to Tamar. To reach such conclusions we need additional premises, about the institution of marriage. If one claim were enough to establish what had seemed to be a different claim, that would be reason to consider that the second claim really was no other than the first, under some disguise. As I remarked earlier, no amount of evidential claims will enable us to *deduce* the claim for which they constitute the evidence. That Zebedee is married to Rahab is not the same truth as that we have seen their signatures in the registry, that we remember attending the ceremony, that they have lived together now for thirty years, that no long-lost bride or husband has ever sued for bigamy: it would make sense to say that none the less they were not married, even though no sensible person would make such a claim. Similarly, that Zebedee has committed a grave wrong which ought to be condemned is not the same truth as that he has abandoned his wife and children, stolen the life-savings of a family friend, kicked his dog to death, knowingly sold poisoned food, raped a seven-year-old, given the formula of a new biological poison to a psychopathic tyrant, and regularly boasted of his exploits in the Sunday papers. It makes sense, of a sort, to say that all these things are true but no wrong has been done, but no sensible person would take that step. Since I have piled the wrongs so thickly, one rational response would be a sort of desperate laughter, or a feeling that Zebedee is so wicked that ordinary human standards no longer apply. To say that he has been doing what he ought not seems too weak a comment: the man is a devil, a man possessed. One thing he is not is good. That is as secure a conclusion as any ordinarily factual one, and like the factual conclusion about his married state it depends on unvoiced premisses. In technical language such arguments are enthymemes, syllogisms with a concealed premiss. They are not fallacious arguments, but only unexplicit ones.

What these necessary, concealed premisses may be, in ethics and in science and scholarship, is a matter to which I will turn in the next chapter. Enough here to insist that there is no good argument for the claim that there are no ethical truths, or that ethical argument suffers from radically different problems than scientific argument. But suppose that we examine a rather different strand of the indifferentist case: that the universe is not directed by ethical values, that it is indifferent to all our concerns. Suppose that this is so. What can follow from this? Nothing at all of interest to a moralist, unless we add the premiss that we should value all and only what the universe values. And why should we agree to that? Why not proclaim instead our allegiance to values that will perish with us? The pose of heroic despair has its comic side, of course: Bertrand Russell's vision of Omnipotent Matter rolling upon its relentless way is well mocked by Logan Pearsall-Smith:

We were talking of the Universe at tea, and one of our company declared that he at least was entirely without illusions. He had long since faced the fact that Nature had no sympathy with our hopes and fears, and was completely indifferent to our fate. The Universe, he said, was a great meaningless machine; Man, with his reason and moral judgements, was the product of blind forces, which, though they would so soon destroy him, he must yet despise. To endure this tragedy of our fate with passionless despair, never to wince or bow the head, to confront the hostile powers with high disdain, to fix with eyes of scorn the Gorgon face of Destiny, to stand on the brink of the abyss, clenching his fist at the death-pale stars this, he said, was his attitude, and it produced, as you can imagine, a powerful impression on the company. As for me, I was carried away completely. 'By Jove, that is a stunt!' I cried.[18]

If the world is so much at odds with all that we hold dear, perhaps the best response is defiance, despite its comedy. Why should we be concerned about what the universe approves? Of course, if we rest our ethical decisions on some principle of long-term utility we may be in difficulty: for all our plans and programmes, dreams and ideals will perish. Nothing that we can do will long delay the great night coming, and from that moment all our histories, if anyone should look back to see, will seem insignificant. How much do we trouble ourselves about the distress of Egyptian slaves five millenniums ago? How much will the last men worry about our lives? But why should we adopt that universal, long-term perspective on our own doings? If we do, indifferentism looms, but if our lives and decisions are absurd then so would be the decision to live out the last men's vision of things. Why should we not prefer to act as if our moral vision were correct? Consider a children's story: the speaker and his friends are trapped in an underground realm, about to be charmed into forgetfulness by a witch. The witch, by the way, uses some of the cruder tricks of logical positivism. The speaker finally retorts as follows:

Suppose we have only dreamed, or made up, all those things—trees and grass and sun and moon and stars and Aslan himself. Suppose we

---

[18] Pearsall-Smith (1933), p. 81; cf. Russell (1918), p. 56.

have. Then all I can say is that, in that case, the made-up things seem a good deal more important than the real ones. Suppose this black pit of a kingdom of yours is the only world. Well, it strikes me as a pretty poor one. And that's a funny thing, when you come to think of it. We're just babies making up a game, if you're right. But four babies playing a game can make a play-world which licks your real world hollow. That's why I'm going to stand by the play-world. I'm on Aslan's side even if there isn't any Aslan to lead it. I'm going to live as like a Narnian as I can even if there isn't any Narnia. So . . . we're leaving your court at once and setting out in the dark to spend our lives looking for Overland. Not that our lives will be very long, I should think; but that's small loss if the world's as dull a place as you say.[19]

Or if you prefer a weightier authority, here is Dostoevsky: 'If anyone could prove to me that Christ is outside truth, and if the truth really did exclude Christ, I should prefer to stay with Christ and not with truth.'[20]

These are words that may appeal to any believer, but we must be careful of them. Taken one way, this insistence amounts to another version of relativism: Puddleglum the Marshwiggle proposes to live as if Aslan and Narnia were real, even if they are not, but cannot any longer say that others are mistaken if they live otherwise. To be a Narnian is his decision, not a response to some reality. Jacques Monod takes a different path, equally a personal choice, to live as if nothing mattered except scientific knowledge. Such an approach may end by exalting the will as the source of all value, unconstrained by any restriction of decency, order, or sanity. Continental philosophers, for some reason, have been readier than British ones to see that what they were praising, with their talk of autonomy, self-created value, and the like, was an arch-criminal, one who acknowledges no constraint of objective truth in his evaluations.

To disdain the world is a tricky task. If we are creatures formed wholly in the world then our disdain for it is a disdain for what has, even without intention, made us what we are. This must have the same effect as any serious attempt

[19] Lewis (1953), ch. 12.
[20] Dostoevsky (1914), p. 71: March 1854.

to condemn God: to do so is tantamount to saying 'Nothing that I say can be trusted', for it comes from a tainted source. That is why indifferentism might seem plausible, were that not absurd as well. The world cannot be wholly disdained, nor wholly worshipped: either choice leads out beyond the realm of sanity.

But perhaps the voluntarist's credo can be taken otherwise. Puddleglum will live like a Narnian even if there is no Narnia, but this is not advanced as an arbitrary act of will. Instead he acknowledges the authority of an imagined realm that may not, he admits, be actual. It is in the name and power of that imagined realm that he condemns the black pit in which he seems to find himself. Should it surprise us that the Good need not be embodied in the world if it is to be truly good? That it is worth living like a Narnian, a Christian, does not depend on whether anyone has ever succeeded in doing so. We can correctly say that even if the divine has never been embodied still it should have been: it would be a better world if it had, and if our life is to be of a piece with our recognition of what ought to be, we must act out of that recognition.

To be faithful to our 'ideals' even if the world runs counter to them need not be an insistence on the arbitrary authority of our wills: it may be, and in the cases I have cited most probably was, a recognition that what ought to be and what is need not be the same. This is not to say that statements of what ought to be are always false, or mere expressions of personal preference: it is true that we ought to be merciful, not true that we always are. To learn that the universe lacks mercy is not to learn that we ought to.

Surrounded by depressives, sceptics, half-baked relativists, indifferentists, and voluntarists, what are poor philosophers to do? What is the philosophical response to those who have despaired of truth or justice? In a sense, of course, I have been giving those responses throughout this chapter. A philosopher is an explorer, seeking what sense can be made of the various attitudes that human beings adopt. We do not have to create the tensions and terrors that afflict humanity.

We need to be aware how often we may make them worse by using a pedagogic technique which throws people too soon upon their own resources of imagination and technical skill. But our aim is not to destroy innocence, but rather to lead people on to a new understanding of their situation in the world. The resources even of modern philosophy are not so slight that they can usefully be ignored.

Consider, for example, the problem of solipsism. Only the deeply disturbed, those who have lost all confidence in friends and society, are likely to be seriously tempted to suppose that they are themselves the only reality. But in examining that fantastic dream we can understand more clearly what it is for us to be. Our age's single greatest achievement in philosophical enquiry has been the discovery that 'there is no I without a We'. Solipsism, so far from being the most rational of conclusions to a proper Cartesian doubt, cannot even be expressed as a metaphysical thesis. To say anything, even to say that I am the only reality, is to say that something is true, and would be true even if I did not know it. If I was deluded before in thinking that I am not the only reality, that itself was enough to demonstrate that being-true and being-thought-by-me are not the same. So my attempt to express a genuine solipsism founders, and once it is admitted (as I must) that there is a world distinct from my experience of, and my thought about, that world, I can admit the existence of other perspectives also, other minds. Indeed, I must: for to know myself as a continuing person is to recognize myself in others, to see myself as one of the kind I see around me, to be confirmed as the very person that I am by their reports and accusations. I find myself within a social web. I am not an atom of the ancient kind, whose existence is entirely separate from all other atoms: I am constituted as the being I am by my relations with others.

So we may pass from unthinking acceptance of the existence of other minds, through the terror of solitude, to a deeper understanding of what it is to be, to be a person, to be ourselves. The rich metaphor that Plato devised for philosophical exploration can be of service still. His Socrates, you will recall, pictured a cave where people sat in chains, unable to move their heads away from a shadow-theatre. If one of the prisoners were to move she would discover that the shadows were cast by models manipulated by puppeteers: our common understanding of the world is formed in us by the propaganda, which need not be malevolent, of politicians, sophists, schoolteachers. If the prisoner were to halt here she would lapse into despair or cynicism. But the way lies on: there is a path to light, to the world of which those puppeteers have only partial knowledge.[21] And by the constant friction of words and arguments and images, the fire may be kindled in us also. Or so the author of the *Seventh Letter* of Plato said.[22] And then the enlightened must go back to the cave and help their friends.

Philosophy is the record of our explorations. It rests, however we may disguise it, on the conviction that there is a light, that there is something it is worth knowing even though we have to travel far from our homes to reach it. Without that faith, it would seem better to stick with our comfortable shadows, to use such instruments of propaganda and medicine as will keep us without questions. You will recall the unfortunate who sought to prove that he was not a ghost, by tragically inappropriate methods. Philosophical systems often look like the dreams of the psychotic, but they are worth exploring none the less, and the land to which we return when our journeys are done may not be quite the land we started from.

When we consider the obstinate doubts of the metaphysician, 'Can one ever know what's right or wrong? Can one ever know what others think or feel?' they readily remind us of the chronic doubts of the neurotic and psychotic. 'Have I committed the unpardonable sin? Aren't they all against me really?' On the road to Solipsism . . . there blows the same wind of loneliness which blows on the road to the house with walls of glass which none can break. In the labyrinth of metaphysics are the

[21] Plato, *Republic* 7. 515 f.
[22] Plato (?), *Seventh Letter* 341c6 ff.

same whispers as one hears when climbing Kafka's stairs to the tribunal which is always one floor further up . . . We may hurry away and drown the cries that follow from those silent places—drown them in endless talk, drown them in the whine of the saxophone or the row from the stands. Or, more effectively, we may quiet those phantasmal voices by doing something for people real and alive. But if we can't we must return, force the accusers to speak up, and insist on recognizing the featureless faces. We can hardly do this by ourselves. But there are those who will go with us and, however terrifying the way, not desert us.[23]

What is true is what the sane man says, though he says it because it is true rather than its being true because he says it. On that point I am agreed with my own former self, and Aristotle. But that sanity, to be secure, lies on the far side of a careful mania. Philosophy began as the pursuit of wisdom, the care of the soul, and has not wholly lost that office. When we have travelled down the many circles of our madness and insecurity, we may follow our great guide up through the cranny and so see again the stars.[24]

<hr />

[23] Wisdom (1953), p. 281 ff.
[24] Dante, *Inferno* 34. 133 f.

# 2

# The Roots of Reason

In the last chapter I referred several times to the faith which is necessary if we are to avoid a collapse into despair and confusion. But of course people may have faith in many different and incompatible things; some will refuse to admit that what they have is 'faith', preferring to find their world an obvious one, such as no rational being could reject. It is a dangerous moment when we realize that all we hold most dear could intelligibly be denied, that we can give no good account of why we should believe as we do. These moments are particularly common in ages of social change and migration: to learn that others think and see and act quite differently (or so at first it seems) can be taken as a further reason for thinking them barbarians, but the moment comes when all worlds, all views of the world seem arbitrary.

> All good people agree,
> and all good people say,
> all nice people, like us, are We,
> and everyone else is They:
> but if you cross over the sea,
> instead of over the way,
> you may end by (think of it!) looking on We
> as only a sort of They![1]

The despairing response of an incoherent relativism amounts to an abandonment of the intellectual enterprise; so does the Pyrrhonian refusal ever again to be taken in. Two other responses seem to offer some hope: the rationalist and the pragmatist.

Rationalists hope to secure themselves by finding some rationally indubitable principle from which all other important truths can be deduced, 'a principle by which the truth

[1] Kipling, 'We and They': (1927), p. 709.

will be so manifest, so well recognised by all, that no force in the universe, that no probability can ever make the alternative possible'.[2] Put as crudely as that, the programme is bound to seem ridiculous. Even if an ideally competent intelligence could deduce all important truths from a simple set of principles, we are not so competent. To propose that we could deduce all important truths from set principles which could not rationally be doubted, is to deny the surprising quality of the scientific and scholarly programme. Certainly our past efforts to deduce the nature of things from laws of logic have not been very successful. It was once supposed, for example, that a true vacuum, or void, was impossible: a void, after all, is a condition where there is nothing, where there isn't anything. What essentially is-not obviously cannot be. Duhem, the great historian and philosopher of science, pinpointed the decree of 1277 as the starting-point of a new scientific era. In that year the bishop of Paris condemned a variety of propositions deriving from the rationalist tradition in order to safeguard the abilities and exclusive rights of the divine Creator.[3] There are indefinitely many possible worlds that God could have decreed: it is within His power to create voids, to set the celestial bodies travelling in straight lines, to shock every little prejudice of His creatures. However far we draw our systemization we shall always be faced by claims that are brute contingencies, which can intelligibly be denied even though we do so falsely. Why is light from certain galaxies redder than light from other celestial objects? Because those galaxies are accelerating away from us, and the wavelength of the light they emit is correspondingly lengthened. Why are they doing so, and why should light behave like that, and why should light of longer wavelengths strike us as being redder? Every time we answer a question, within the context of our current scientific theories, we are left with other questions.

Descartes's dream of establishing a new science and

---

[2] Castellio, *De Arte Dubitandi* i. 23: Hollis (1973) p. 9.
[3] P. Duhem, *Le Système du monde* vi. 66, cited by Jaki (1974), p. 229.

philosophy on rationally indubitable principles foundered at its beginning. His certainty, following an argument of Augustine's, that nothing could deceive him into thinking that he existed when he did not, seemed to him to establish that there was indeed a thinking thing identical with the real, the inner Descartes. From this, and from his recognition of that thing as finite, he concluded to an idea of God the Infinite, sum of all perfections, who could not be supposed willingly to deceive His creatures. From that assurance in turn Descartes advanced to the postulate, implicit in all his arguments up to this point, that what he clearly and distinctly conceived was to be taken as true.

Descartes's rationalism incorporates such theses as can be clearly and distinctly conceived, not merely those that are logically indubitable. His attempt to derive their reliability from rationally self-evident principles about his own existence and God's is generally reckoned a failure. Those who retreat to pure self-knowledge cannot climb out of their own private pit: 'When the philosopher become solipsist fancies himself about to reap the reward of his logical purity in perfect knowledge, limited indeed but invulnerable, just then the statement he had hoped to make dwindles to the senseless whimper of an elderly infant in the mansions of the dead.'[4] But the theory is worth recalling: Descartes realized that if he were to maintain that his ideas of what was clear and plausible bore on reality he must also suppose that there was a genuine connection between reality and what he thought of it. This is a point to which I shall return.

Another version of rationalism, the belief that we can discover a set of principles which will lead us into an assurance of all truth, incorporates empirical claims. It is admitted that we cannot deduce what is real simply from the axioms of logic or the clear impressions of our hearts. We also need empirical evidence. It is more usual for systematizers to distinguish the empirical from the rationalist tradition, urging that what is crucial in the former is the method of

[4] Wisdom (1953), p. 170.

observation and experiment. They are of course correct. The empirical tradition also blends imperceptibly with the pragmatist. But before discussing that alternative, consider again the status of evidence. I cannot justifiably infer one fact from another, unless I am assured that there is a principle connecting the two. I cannot justly conclude that because a kettle of water is being heated at sea-level, the water will boil, unless I already know that water boils under those conditions. If I know that all water boils when heated thus, then all is well: but how can I know that until I have tried this sample of water, and all others? Nothing is gained by assimilating the boiling of water to the more rapid motion of molecules when thermal energy is applied: I shall still be compelled to infer one event (the turning of water into steam on this occasion) on the basis of past experience. And what licenses me to suppose that this is an event of the same class as any past event?

Such very familiar arguments can be supplemented by the problem to which I referred in the first chapter. Even if it seems to me and all other witnesses that the water has boiled, it is still logically possible that it has not. But if there is no logical link between any amount of evidence and the reality of the situation, the rationalist's conclusion must be that the link is known solely through experience. But such a link cannot be experienced unless we experience both the evidence and the reality together at least once in a while (waiving the Humean difficulty about induction). Sextus distinguished between 'suggestive signs' (as the appearance of smoke suggests the appearance of fire) and 'indicative signs', which purport to lead from appearance to reality, and argued that the latter could not be rationally defended.[5] Nothing can be known to be an indicative sign either by deduction from the laws of logic, or by observation and experiment.

Can we try to evade this conclusion by appealing to probabilities? One proposition $p$ is evidence for another $q$ if (1) $p$ would be more likely to be true if $q$ were true than if it

_____
[5] Sextus, *OP* 2. 102: (1933) i. 217.

were false, (2) $q$ is not intrinsically less likely to be true than $p$ itself in the absence of $q$. There may be other conditions. I would be more likely to see a tabby cat on my desk if there were a cat there than if there were not, and it is not all that improbable that there is a cat there. So my seeming to see the cat is evidence that there is a cat there. Similarly with more recondite historical or scientific claims. The trouble is, of course, that I need some warrant for my belief that I am more likely to see a cat if there is one, that cats-on-desks are not intrinsically less probable than that I should see cats where there are none. How should I know these things without *a priori* knowledge of what is likely to be true?

Consider indeed the following very strong argument for the impossibility of knowledge or justified belief. Take any claim you are sure that you know: say, that you are sitting down. This claim I shall call '$p$'. Now if you know $p$, then $p$ is true, and every claim incompatible with the truth of $p$ is false. Since you know that, and have followed the deduction, you must know that any such claim as $q$ is false. Here is the claim I am calling '$q$': there is a very powerful, clever species of extraterrestrial beings who are currently amusing themselves by deceiving you about the truth of $p$. Clearly, if $q$ were true then $p$ would be false: you know that $p$ is true, so you know that $q$ is false. But of course, you don't. Neither you nor I have sufficient knowledge of the universe to know even how likely it is that there are such hobgoblins. So you don't know that $q$ is false: but if you knew that $p$ was true, you would know that $q$ was false. So you don't know that $p$ is true: you don't know any of the things you were most certain of.[6]

There are various technical problems about this argument, which is a modern, formal version of Descartes's demon argument. Some people are defeated by it, and retreat to scepticism. Those who reject the argument mostly offer one of two responses: the pragmatist and the fideist.

The pragmatic response is one that you may have found

[6] Lehrer (1970–1); Unger (1975); see Clark (1983*b*).

yourself inclined to make when I was speaking of that unruly kettle. I said, you remember, that even if I and all other accessible witnesses were agreed that the kettle had boiled, it would still make sense to suppose that it hadn't. The supposition is not that cold water will emerge from the spout: everything will be 'as if' the kettle had boiled. But in that case what does it matter if it 'really' hasn't? As long as our tea is hot, who cares? On this account all that matters to us is the consistency of appearances. So maybe the extra-terrestrial hobgoblins are manipulating our perceptions: either they are inconsistent in this, and we shall have reason to withdraw our assent from some, but not all, of our previous convictions; or they are consistent, and we shall never have cause to regret what we thought we knew.

Put in its strongest form, the pragmatist's reply to all these issues is that Truth, conceived as what is really the case independently of our investigations and experience, lies too far afield for us. What is the point of a truth which cannot be known as such? Might it not be better to prefer another sort of truth, 'agreement with the result of the most rigorous imaginable intrasubjective, dialectical examination of our most important experiences'?[7] A proposition $p$ is true just if 'the rules of confirmation embedded in the conventions of our current conceptual framework fully authorize our asserting $p$'.[8] Pragmatic truth varies from age to age, context to context. Once it was true that there were witches, though it is true that there weren't! In the end we may hope for that final intrasubjective assessment, which is accepted not because it matches reality, but because it provides appropriate satisfactions to its believers.

The pragmatist avoids many intellectual problems: no longer need we worry whether there is any good reason to suppose that our conclusions are veridical, true-in-fact. It is enough that they are warranted by the rules of our intellectual community. We join ourselves to that community because in

[7] Wolff (1970), p. 545.
[8] Almeder (1975), p. 36, after C. S. Peirce.

its own terms, it works. The penalty is that we lose all right to reckon other communities mistaken in their assessment of the situation: their rules work for them, or so they seem to think. More important still, the pragmatist falls foul of those same paradoxes that afflict the naïve relativist: is this persuasive definition of truth itself warranted by the rules of our intellectual community? Is it true-in-fact, or merely a warranted assertion that the rules of our community bring us satisfactions or will do so in the end? The more we seek to avoid the problem of a truth that is more than warranted assertability or serious belief, the more we seem constrained to use that concept. The pragmatist's last escape is into scepticism. His claim, after all, is that we do not need the concept of Truth-in-fact, that we can follow the appearances, bound to the compulsion of Nature, sensation, custom, and the rules of craft: the Pyrrhonian responds, 'Who said otherwise?'

Are we reduced at last to Hume's dictum?

If we believe that fire warms, or water refreshes, 'tis only because it costs us too much pains to think otherwise. Nay if we are philosophers, it ought only to be upon sceptical principles, and from an inclination, which we feel to the employing ourselves after that manner. Where reason is lively, and mixes itself with some propensity, it ought to be assented to. Where it does not, it never can have any title to operate upon us.[9]

Let me retrace my steps. If we abandon any hope of achieving truth-in-fact there is no difficulty about connecting evidence with 'truth', but we are condemned to relativism, scepticism, despair. All we can hope to do is present our 'fictitious and theatrical worlds'. If we hope to be assured of what the real truth is—not of what is warranted by the system of our day—we need to be assured of a link between what is true-in-fact and what we can seriously believe. We need to believe that if we seek the truth in accordance with certain standing assumptions about probability, about what sort of world this is, we shall be rewarded. Such a claim is not

[9] Hume (1888), i. 4. 7.

an axiom of logic, nor derivable from one. Nor can it be validated by experience, our own or others. Our intellectual life, if it is to have the properties we desire for it, must rest on faith.

Consider this example, which acquired a certain topicality in 1981 when an attempt was made in various American States to require that 'creation science' be given equal time with evolutionary theory in State high schools. Philip Gosse, a nineteenth-century Plymouth Brother and a geologist, wished to show that the fossil-record popularly supposed to prove that modern species had envolved from earlier kinds was actually compatible with the account given in Genesis. His argument has since been gravely misunderstood, travestied as the claim that God had set these fossils in the rocks in order to test the faith of nineteenth-century geologists. Even to this travesty there is no very good reply except the counter-assertion that there is no good reason to believe in a God like that, but Gosse's actual argument is a much more interesting one.[10]

He observed that if God were to create, as He clearly could, a full-grown oak tree which some forester then cut down, the trunk of the oak would carry the usual quota of rings, from which the forester might expect to learn how many years the oak had grown, which were good summers, when the oak was attacked by parasites, and so on. A tree which lacked these features would not be a full-grown oak, would not be constructed as oaks must be to survive and reproduce their kind. Any newly created organism of a kind which is usually, or thereafter, to reproduce by 'natural' methods will have a character which would under usual circumstances provide evidence about its past. But such a newly-created oak tree would not have had a real past. Has God set out to deceive the forester? Maybe, but there is no way in which He could have avoided providing such apparent evidence once the decision to create the oak had been taken. Gosse proposed that the same must be true of any organized universe: it

---

[10] Gosse (1857), especially pp. 123 ff., 335 ff., 345, 351, 369.

would, from the moment of its creation, carry in it signs of the same kind as would thereafter warrant us in speaking of a past (I remark in passing that this perhaps does not hold of the primordial monobloc of modern cosmology whose explosion initiated our universe and from whose original condition nothing can be inferred about any previous event). There will be hills and oceans and deserts of the same kind that erosion and volcanic activity and plate tectonics are to create hereafter. There will be rocks also, containing fragmentary images of creatures that might have been: for that is how rocks will be laid down in the future. Even if God had established His garden upon rocks and soil of a kind never thereafter seen (so that no one could ever tell how those rocks would have had to be laid down, if they were laid down), some extrapolations to the imaginary past would have been possible. Why should God not determine to create His world all of a piece, even ensuring that (as it were) the rings of newly-created trees all tell the same story of what might have been (if they do)? Gosse's conclusion was that fossil evidence does not count against the witness of Genesis that God made and stocked the earth in six days, since what we find is just what we should have expected to find if that story were true.

It is not my intention to defend Gosse's theory at length, except to add that the scornful riposte that God might even have created the universe five minutes ago, complete with memories of earlier days, is wholly irrelevant. Gosse would have agreed that we had no reason to suppose God did anything of the kind, whereas we did have reason (the divine revelation) to think that God made the earth about six thousand years ago. If God had warned the forester that not all oaks could be used as evidence of any genuine past, how should the forester complain?

My point is the more general one: what Gosse's case demonstrates is that historical evidence never determines us to believe in any real past. We need to add some premiss concerning the likeliest way of producing such evidence.

That it can be made to tell a consistent story does not prove the story true. We need a non-empirical premiss about the nature of things before we can begin to argue about the nature of things. We need to have faith, whether in Gosse's God or not.

So to find out anything, or to suppose that we have found out anything, about the world we need some prior belief about the world. If I am to benefit from scientific research I need to believe that my memories are accurate enough, that my colleagues are really human, that a certain mathematical elegance is at least some evidence of the theory's truth. None of these claims can be scientifically established, and the attempt to do so would land us in the same trap as the suicidal unfortunate of my first chapter. We need not just a general faith in what we are doing, but a particular faith that the world is . . . whatever we suppose it is. And this fact offers us the chance to form some better concept of the world.

Whatever the world is supposed to be, we must not suppose that it is a world in which such faith would be impossible, inaccurate, or irrational (by its own standards). We cannot suppose this, because to do so would subvert the very faith on which our supposition rests. I cannot believe myself to have discovered that the world is one which remains wholly inscrutable to our enquiries, or one which guarantees that our faith is vain, or one in which it would be vanishingly improbable that any of us should discover or intuit any serious truth about its structure. If I were to believe these things I should have to abandon the intellectual enterprise.

Accordingly, I cannot coherently believe in the standard account of human evolution, for the following reasons. There may be more, but these two suffice. Nothing that I say denies that some evolutionary story may be true: my motives are not Gosse's. But the standard one we have good reason to dismiss.

Firstly: the existence of consciousness is incomprehensible if we are merely complex, self-replicating kinetic systems selected for their inclusive genetic fitness over some four thousand million years. Consciousness, the subjectivity of being, can play no part in the evolutionary story. It is enough that creatures 'behave' in certain ways, as programmed automata might do. There will be those who claim that the only sort of 'consciousness' that has any real existence is behavioural consciousness, not a subjective reality but a type of public behaviour. The man, the dog, the robot is 'conscious' if it is awake, 'awake' if it responds to certain stimuli in certain distinctive ways. My own judgement is that this discounts a known reality, and renders it impossible to think of scientific or other research as remotely rational. To be genuinely conscious is a necessary condition for experiencing the moral obligations implicit in the intellectual enterprise. Accordingly, a story which renders the most obvious of facts incomprehensible cannot be acceptable. I shall develop this argument at greater length in chapter seven.

Secondly: even if neo-Darwinian evolution had thrown up conscious beings, it could not be expected to produce creatures with a capacity for understanding the workings of the universe. Cleverness, even verbal and mathematical intelligence, are devices which, under some circumstances, might have a genetic advantage: who could have foreseen that such practical skills would have so vast an application, so powerful a thrust? Even working scientists have a tendency to imagine that life on other worlds would have developed a quasi-human intelligence: there seems no good reason, within the neo-Darwinian framework, to expect this, and no good reason to expect even that our intelligence could cope with the universe. 'What peculiar privilege has this little agitation of the brain which we call thought, that we must thus make it the model of the whole universe?'[11] It is not enough to reply that surprising things do happen, that evolution has thrown up a world-spanning intelligence as a by-product of the practical cleverness and linguistic ability

[11] Hume, *Dialogues*, Part 2: (1976), p. 168.

which, gave our ancestors a genetic advantage. For we do not know that it has done so: we do not have good reason to think that our abilities do match reality unless we have good reason to think that creatures like us would have such abilities. The neo-Darwinian story gives us good reason to think the opposite.

Accordingly, the neo-Darwinian account of our history is not one that we can coherently believe: if we attempt to follow through its implications we find that it gives us no right to believe in the theories we form about the world, including the neo-Darwinian story itself. It must also lead to doubts about the consciousness of our fellow creatures, and even (absurdly) our own—a doubt which is fostered by the slovenly habit of saying that silicon-based computers 'think', merely because they can perform certain calculations or say 'I'm sorry, worried, angry, or afraid'.

So what must the world be like if we are to have reason to think that the principles in which we put our trust will lead us to an understanding of the world? One possible modification of the standard view which has been suggested recently, by Rupert Sheldrake, may deserve some mention.[12] Sheldrake has proposed that certain standard difficulties in understanding embryology, evolution, learning, and crystallization can be solved by postulating morphogenetic fields with the particular property of turning in to similar fields. If this hypothesis, for which he has proposed a number of ingenious tests, turned out to be useful, there would also be a reason to think that perhaps the field associated with animal intelligence could reproduce, by 'morphic resonance', the fundamental patterns of the world. At least it would be true that we would have a name for the supposed capacity of human beings to get hold of the world, and other examples of the same sort of 'resonance'. But I don't want to comment further on the Sheldrake hypothesis.

What must we suppose the world to be? We need to think that consciousness is to be expected: 'The only experience

[12] Sheldrake (1981).

we concretely have is our own personal life . . . and the
rigorous belief that in its own essential and innermost nature
this is a strictly impersonal world may . . . prove to be the
very defect that our descendants will be most surprised at
in our boasted science.'[13] There are signs that James's
prophecy may yet bear fruit. Much recent work on 'creativity'
in science has emphasized the role that is played by identification, by social models of event: 'Revolutionary science
may more often that we realize derive its inspiration from a
vision of a socially transacting universe.'[14] Nick Humphrey,
whose words these are, makes no greater claim than that we
have evolved to understand our fellow creatures, to operate
within a social realm, and extend these powers of understanding to the wider world. I am inclined to suggest rather
more. We have an insight into the doings of protein molecules, pi-mesons, and the rest because we can, as it were, get
inside their skins. We can identify with things, and find in
ourselves the powers to be them: to understand something,
as Aristotle knew, is to become it, in a sense.[15] A world in
which this method works must be one that is a complex of
socially interacting conscious beings. In understanding the
world we realize the possibilities of consciousness, we overhear the powers that formed the world, we 'remember' the
principles of things: 'Fundamental laws of motion and of
rest . . . are laws of a mathematical nature. . . . We find and
discover them not in Nature, but in ourselves, in our own
mind, in our memory, as Plato long ago has taught us.'[16]
It is always a slight shock, so used are we to supposing that
Galileo was a martyr to pure observational science, when
we realize that Galileo thought of himself as a Platonist,
and formed his theories not on the basis of observations
but of rational insight. Similarly Einstein: 'There is only
the way of intuition which is helped by a feeling for the

---

[13] James (1897), p. 327.
[14] Humphrey (1976), p. 315.
[15] Aristotle, *De Anima* 429b6 ff.
[16] Galileo: Koyré (1968), pp. 13, 42.

order lying behind appearance.'[17] That feeling for order is explicable in a Platonic universe by the postulate that we, being immortal spirits, saw the pattern to which things were made. We can do without pre-existence: the pattern to which things were made is embedded in us; we do not find the universe wholly alien; we are of a piece with the nature of things.

This is, in some form, an essential item of faith for anyone who seeks to understand anything. Of course the phrases I have quoted may not all mean just the same thing, may carry different implications for our intellectual practice and theory. One version, developed by Fawcett, speaks of the universe as the product of divine imagining, an imagining which we can share. To do so we need to move beyond our private fantasies, to quieten ourselves to hear the pattern of things: 'Private imagining may collide with that cosmic imagining bodied forth in the structure of Nature, as when a geologist, enamoured of a dream, affirms some belief regardless of the testimony of the rocks.'[18] Other versions may require, as well as quietness, a certain passionate involvement, a letting-out of the real knowledge we already have, and can trust ourselves to have because things are the product of something like our minds, at their best and happiest.

On this view thought is not, as Hume's Philo mockingly proposed, 'a little agitation of the brain'. If it were, what grounds could we have for trusting it to confirm the existence of brains themselves? Thought is near the origin of things: our thought is, at its best, a receptivity to the pattern by which things are made. Aristotle said as much: we have a capacity to grasp the forms and natures of things, a capacity which he thought was realized in serious contemplation of nature and our friends. In Plato's view we could also rely on a dialectical investigation of our language and everyday opinions. Another thinker has declared that knowledge

[17] Beveridge (1950), p. 57. Einstein himself understood that our apparent capacity to make sense of the universe was a powerful argument for theism: see Feuer (1983).

[18] Fawcett (1921), p. 7.

will come to those who do the Father's will:[19] by practical obedience we come to see and understand what's what.

If we are to take our own reasonings seriously, it can only be by faith or ungrounded intuition (these terms being interchangeable). If we are to have such faith, we must suppose that the universe is of a kind to allow faith to be rewarded. This condition is met by the belief in a universe founded upon socially transacting intelligences with whom we can identify, by whom we can be inspired. Such a universe will allow an understanding of itself, suited to their station in life, to its members. That understanding comes by the same method as in our personal affairs: we must love to be wise.

And since these are Gifford lectures, it seems appropriate to close by commenting on the words of John's Gospel.[20] The Word that was with God in the beginning is the Logos, the pattern by which all things were made; that is the same light that lights every man. To have faith in the possibilities of human science and scholarship it is necessary to think that there is such a Logos, such a pattern that is present also to the human soul. That pattern, unlike the details of our universe, is not an arbitrary one: it is, in the language of theology, 'begotten, not made'. The universe in which we live is in large measure contingent: God did not need to create it as it is, and the details of His creation can only be learnt by inspection, not simple deduction from timelessly valid principles. But pure inspection can never validate or refute a theory: if we are to get anywhere we need to suppose that some logically possible theories are not real options. So we are to conceive of the universe as founded on a pattern which is not itself an arbitrary one.

In theological terms: if God were to make universes real out of His own arbitrary decision, then any logically possible universe would be possible, and we would have no grounds for denying that it was a matter of pure chance which universe

---

[19] Jesus: John 7: 17.

[20] John 1: 1–14. This is the older interpretation of the Prologue (see Schnackenburg (1968), p. 257); I am aware that later exegetes have held that only those who consciously accept Jesus as the Christ are illuminated.

was real. God, in such a case, is no different from chance. If we live in such a universe, we have no good grounds for expecting future events to be of the same classes as any past events: anything can happen. Security resides in the conviction that God creates by His Logos, and that Logos is 'of one substance with the Father', not an arbitrary judgement but the one and only expression of God's nature.

There are further subtleties in the Johannine theology which I shall not now examine. Nothing that I have so far said constrains us to accept the Christian or any other theistic creed. Historically, there is good reason to believe, it was the faith of orthodox theists which provided the sole context in which science could grow, but it may be that some other attempt to ground our faith is yet to be discovered. What is clear, or so it seems to me, is that the roots of reason lie in faith, and that this fact places definite restrictions on the sort of universe we can reasonably suppose ourselves to inhabit. A universe in which our serious presuppositions were unlikely to be accurate is one we cannot seriously investigate or understand. What stands under the phenomena must be a world that we can understand: all that we can understand is Understanding, the divine imagining, the Word of God.

# 3

## The Value of Truth

I have argued that our epistemological (and ethical) standards rest in the end on principles which can be proved neither by logical analysis nor by observation. These principles are accepted on faith alone. I have argued further that if we are to remain settled in our epistemological faith we must suppose that the universe is not one to which consciousness is alien, but one founded on the very patterns to be found also in our intellect. In theological language, the world was made by the same Logos that enlightens every intellectual creature.

The pattern on which the world was founded is one to which we must awaken from our private imaginings: 'For those who've woken up there is one common world; each sleeper's turned aside to a private one.'[1] Interestingly, there is reason to think that the Greeks associated their word for truth, *aletheia*, with memory, lack of forgetfulness. 'The common, divine Logos is the criterion of Truth.'[2] 'So far as we share a memory of it we speak the truth; where we go private, falsehood.'[3] What Herakleitos meant by any of his apophthegms is a matter almost beyond conjecture, but the association of truth and memory is clear. That man is truthful, Hesiod says, who does not forget the laws.[4]

This perspective on truthfulness offers a contrast to the cult of sincerity which is given a sophisticated expression in Heidegger's association of *aletheia* with 'lack of conceal-ment'.[5] Sincerity of speech and manner is not the same as honesty, and it has traditionally been honesty, living in accordance with remembered laws, that has been esteemed.

---

[1] Herakleitos 22 B 89: Diels and Krantz (1952).
[2] See Sextus, *Adv. Mathematicos* 7. 131: (1933) ii. 73.
[3] Sextus, *Adv. Math*. 7. 133: (1933) ii. 73.
[4] Hesiod, *Theogony* 253 f.
[5] Heidegger (1949), pp. 330 ff.

The honest person remembers and keeps his promises and other obligations, 'though it were to his own hindrance'; reports accurately on what he has observed when he is required to do so; does not lose himself in private imaginings and wishful thinking. Honesty is a virtue: it will be time enough for us to be sincere, openly to express our thoughts and feelings, when we have some secure thoughts and feelings. All too often the injunction to 'say what you really think' produces aphasia or a jumble of half-digested slogans.

The intellectual enterprise is not directed towards self-expression, but to discovery. The question we should ask ourselves is, Why? Why should we set aside our comfortable fantasies, and bind ourselves to remember in accordance with the rules of evidence and our primordial faith in the reasonableness of the universe? In Heidegger's grotesque phraseology: 'Whence does the representative statement receive its command to right itself by the object and thus to be in accord with rightness?'[6] Why should we say and think, of what is, that it is? My question now is not what justifies us in believing that mathematical elegance and observational 'evidence' are real routes to how things genuinely are. Nothing at all can demonstrate the truth of the claim, for we can only rest on faith. We can imagine universes in which we would be quite mistaken in our trust. But all that that amounts to is the hypothetical imperative: if you desire the truth you can only put your faith in the reliability of the pattern of our common intellect. What concerns me now is the categorical imperative: remember how things are.

Heidegger's etymology for *aletheia* suggests that it refers, in origin, to 'what is not concealed', though he detects a connection between 'unforgetfulness' and the Germanic roots of 'thinking'.[7] When people are *aletheis*, accordingly, they are out in the open (recall what I have just said about sincerity). But *aletheia* is not a quality of people, so much as a name for reality. Heidegger suggests that in early Greece

---

[6] Heidegger (1949), p. 330.
[7] See Spiegelberg (1971) i. 340.

the Real was what was Evident, Obvious to all. Only gradually did the consciously paradoxical thought that *aletheia* was un-obvious take shape: 'Really we know nothing, for Truth is in the depths.'[8] 'Either nothing is True, or it's unclear to us at any rate.'[9] With Demokritos the split between appearance and reality is well established: reality is quite unlike the world of common day, to be sought out only by intellectual endeavour.

The Platonic belief that reality was accessible at least to reason found its fruition in the Copernican Revolution, when it was determined that the homely earth was a globe rolling through emptiness. The theory, I emphasize, was accepted on rationalistic grounds, not on any simple correspondence with observational evidence: 'Only men who valued mathematical neatness far more than qualitative accuracy could become convinced and militant Copernicans. The sun-centred universe did not speak to the utilitarian sense of the practising astronomer but to the aesthetic sense of the mathematician.'[10] The only thinker I know of to attempt a reversal of the Copernican Fall was William Blake:

The Sky is an immortal tent built by the sons of Los:
and every Space that a Man views around his dwelling place
. . . is his Universe:
and on its verge the Sun rises and sets, the Clouds bow
to meet the flat Earth & the Sea in such an order'd Space.
As to that false Appearance which appears to the reasoner
as of a Globe rolling through Voidness, it is a delusion of Ulro.[11]

Although there is a place for such a reminder of the role of imagination in the construction of our personal worlds, we could not allow this to tempt us into solipsism. Nor did Blake intend that it should. The Reality which he supposed it necessary to remember was one that allowed for personal, conscious worlds (as the materialist delusion of Ulro does not), but it was not simply identical with the present

[8] Demokritos 68 B 117: Diels and Krantz (1952).
[9] See Aristotle, *Metaphysics* 4. 1009b11.
[10] Shea (1972), p. 110.
[11] Blake, *Milton*, s. 29: Keynes (1966), p. 516.

phenomenal order. Rather was it 'The real and eternal world
of which this Vegetable Universe is but a faint Shadow, & in
which we shall live in our Eternal or Imaginative bodies when
these Vegetable Mortal Bodies are no more.'[12] If that is the
reality which we have forgotten it is clearly worth remembering; details of our phenomenal lives and environment should
be remembered just so far as they help to remind us of 'the
real and eternal world'. In the words of a very different
thinker:

On such a principle depend the heavens and the world of nature. And it
is a life such as the best which we enjoy, and enjoy for but a short time
(for it is ever in this state, which we cannot be) . . . For the actuality
of thought is life, and God is that actuality; and God's self-dependent
actuality is life most good and eternal. We say therefore that God is
a living being, eternal, most good, so that life and duration continuous
and eternal belong to God; for this IS God.[13]

Aristotle's cosmology did not allow for Blake's postulate of
a fall into the realm of appearance. 'Memory' is not quite
the metaphor he prefers for intellectual intuition. But he
shared Blake's conviction that Reality, which Demokritos
had reckoned a world of pure objects in the void, was rather
a life that we could share, whose pattern was discernible in
Nature and the human soul. The truest well-being, *eudai-
monia*, resides in dedication to the service and contemplation
of God, which is also the contemplation of the ultimate
principles of Nature. To love God is to share the divine life.
To seek the order, the beauty of the world is, in part and
momentarily, to feel God within.

In such a world and theory the demands of truth are
clear: those who willingly forgo the truth shut themselves
up in their particularities and lose the worthiest of lives.
But if, *per incredibile*, Jacques Monod's vision of the world
were true, why should anyone seek to discover it? I do not
deny that some particular information might prove useful,
for our more usual ends. I don't even deny that some people

---

[12] Blake, *Jerusalem* 77: Keynes (1966), p. 717.
[13] Aristotle, *Metaphysics* 12. 1072b13 f.

might, as a result of some deviant neuropsychological state, find pleasure in reducing all human endeavour to a flux of elementary particles. What I question is, firstly, how an electrical discharge can as such be either true or false, and secondly, why it should be of any importance whether it, or rather the associated thought, were true or false? Truth-lovers, in Monod's world, are fetishists: it is, after all, the mark of fetishism that desire has been diverted from biologically useful goals to their accidental features. Just so, practical information is something that any forward-looking species might be expected to desire: information about the origin of the universe seems gratuitous. Sceptics may well mock

> that vain animal
> who is so proud of being rational.
> The senses are too gross, and he'll contrive
> a sixth, to counteract the other Five,
> and before certain instinct, will prefer
> Reason, which fifty times for one doth err.
> Stumbling from thought to thought, falls head-long down,
> into doubt's boundless sea, where like to drown,
> books bear him up awhile, and makes him try
> to swim with bladders of philosophy.
> Our Sphere of action, is life's happiness,
> and he who thinks Beyond, thinks like an Ass.[14]

The point here is not merely, as I have argued before, that we have no reason to expect such an animal to be capable of reaching truth, but that there can be no obligation to reach truth in such a universe. There might even be an obligation to suppress the knowledge of truth:

If, per impossible, the mechanistic views of a barbarized science should turn out to be the provable truth of things, this would be a truth by which we as practical, inventive, value- and pattern-oriented beings, could not live, and on which we should have, in all but the lowest instrumentalities, to turn our backs. Truth of this type would neither be worth knowing nor applying, and the suasions of a Nocturnal Council might not be too much in order to secure its suppression.[15]

---

[14] Wilmot, *Satires* 64. 6-11, 18-24, 96-7: (1964), pp. 118 f.
[15] Findlay (1974), pp. 411 f.

Findlay's defence of Plato, and the Inquisition, certainly conflicts with our belief in the value of truth. To deal with it we need to ask ourselves what the world must be like if the truth is to be worth knowing. But before we can do so we must take account of one obvious fact: I have spoken of order and beauty in Nature and the human soul, but that order and beauty is often either broken or ambivalent.

Part of our problem, one of the things which lead to melancholia, is remorse:

Action deadens it, enjoyment drugs it, love lulls it, work dulls it, anxiety covers it up, pain numbs it; but always, in some glacier-crack of the cold night, in some slippery mine-shaft of the hot noon, this devil's drum begins beating again. It is the secret umbilical cord that connects our personal good luck with the ill-luck of all the other sentiencies. It is the scream of the victim in the hands of the police, it is the starvation-groan of the famished, it is the weeping of the lynched, it is the howl of the executed, it is the inert despair of the jobless.[16]

Powys's catalogue could be continued, and his point is clear. For almost all of us our happiness depends upon our not remembering these things. Those few who have given themselves up to conscious cruelty may savour the world's agonies, but most of us are not so malevolent. We live our lives in deliberate and self-deceiving ignorance of what is happening, what is likely enough to happen even to our fortunate selves.

Powys distinguished only two serious alternatives

in adjusting ourselves to this essentially cruel world. The one is to be a Saint. That is to say, to devote your life, by giving up the satisfaction of personal desires, to the alleviation of all sentient suffering—bearing, in fact, that burden which the First Cause refuses to bear! The other is to try to forget the suffering as completely as you can, and to devote your life to a defiant enjoyment of as much happiness, of a certain very especial and particular kind, as you can snatch or create.[17]

The happiness Powys advocates is a dreamy sensuality, fed by the deliberate storing-up of joyous experience, refusal to

[16] Powys (1974), pp. 62 f.
[17] Powys (1974), pp. 251-2.

be shaken by irritating episodes, remembering only what it is a joy to remember. But the saint alone is free from remorse, 'because he has never hardened his heart'.[18] There is at least one other option. Where Powys relies on sensuous experience as the food of a secure happiness, another character might rest instead upon a contemplation of more abstract beauty, more distant horizons. Olaf Stapledon's *Last and First Men* was published in the same year as Powys's *Defence of Sensuality*. In this, and other works, Stapledon offered a vision of human life 'set in perspective': 'The whole duration of humanity, with its many sequent species and its incessant downpour of generations, is but a flash in the lifetime of the cosmos.'[19] His imagined future history, spangled with 'minor astronomical events' like the destruction of Saturn, Earth, and Venus, was designed to raise the human imagination to appreciate the whole tedious brief history of our kind: 'In tracing man's final advance to full humanity we can observe only the broadest features of a whole astronomical era . . . Myriads of individuals, each one unique, live out their lives in rapt intercourse with one another, contribute their heart's pulses to the universal music, and presently vanish, giving place to others.'[20] Other, more scholarly cosmographical exercises direct our attention to the first three seconds of the universe, black holes, or the fate of trilobites. Sometimes we can pretend that these theories are of some relevance to other and more practical concerns, but their real virtue is in diverting us from the thought of agony to a calm appreciation of the way things are. The very immensities which terrified Pascal[21] may serve to ignite a certain ironic passion in some beholders.

This passion is an anodyne for fears, given its most serious philosophical expression by Spinoza. By appreciating our own position as modes of the single rigid universe we can

---

[18] Powys (1974), p. 63.
[19] Stapledon (1963), p. 274.
[20] Stapledon (1963), p. 281.
[21] Pascal, *Pensées*, s. 68: (1966), p. 48. Cf. Pearsall-Smith (1933), p. 154: 'I like my universe as immense, grim, icy and pitiless as possible'.

attain our only equanimity. Its fault, to most of us, lies in the passionlessness which it must bring to everyday phenomena. Is it really so easy to hear the scream of the tortured, the groan of the famished as only episodes, soon to be forgotten, of the unfolding or eternal presence of God and Nature?

The Spinozistic claim is a form of indifferentism, holding that everyday reality is not a matter for which we should be seriously concerned. Only that unique substance which is God and Nature is to be adored. The details of our world, if we could understand the links that bind the world together, would be seen as being exactly what ought to be, for they are, exactly and uniquely, what can be. If we reject this option, we are forced once more upon the question 'Why is knowledge of the truth to be desired?'

As Stapledon himself well knew, the truth of the matter is not only to be found in the long-term perspective of the last men looking back on human life, but also in 'the rapt intercourse' of individuals one with another. To know the truth is to hold the whole truth, compound of all perspectives, steady before us—a trick beyond our mortal intellect. The belief that such a trick would be worth performing, that every increase of knowledge is a step toward that good, sometimes issues in such moral fantasies as George Steiner's claim that Knowledge is the supreme good, sufficient excuse for any experiment, any crucifixion.[22] Steiner was being absurd, but his claim pinpoints the difficulty: if the Whole is supremely worth knowing, complete with warts, then all the episodes that our local perspective finds abominable must shrink into their proper place in the universal economy. Local evil is universal good, the divine artist's cunning admixture of dark colours to increase the beauty of the whole.[23]

That there is a certain profound satisfaction to be gained in contemplating the elegance and beauty not only of the starry heavens but of the liver-fluke's life-cycle is certain.

---

[22] Steiner (1978); cf. Midgley (1981), pp. 320-3.
[23] See Hick (1966), chs. 4, 6.

We seek such theories as reveal elegance, and trustingly suppose that elegant theories are more likely to be true than uglier alternatives. This belief is justified if there is a beauty which the world seeks to embody, a beauty accessible to our human thought. But how can we seek to know things only in that mode? Elegance is not our only value: can we seriously choose not to take the evils of the world as seriously real?

> It is an easy thing to laugh at wrathful elements,
> to hear the dog howl at the wintry door,
> the ox in the slaughter-house moan;
> to see a god on every wind,
> and a blessing on every blast;
> then the groan and the dolor are quite forgotten,
> and the slave grinding at the mill,
> and the captive in chains, and the poor in prison,
> and the soldier in the field
> when the shattered bone hath laid him groaning
> amid the happier dead.[24]

Jeeves once informed that good and wise man, Bertram Wooster, of Marcus Aurelius' dictum, 'Does aught befall you? It is good. It is part of the destiny of the Universe ordained for you from the beginning. All that befalls you is part of the great web.' Bertie properly replied 'Well, you can tell him from me he's an ass', and later mused 'I doubt if Marcus Aurelius's material is ever the stuff to give the troops at a moment when they have just stubbed their toe on the brick of Fate. You want to wait till the agony has abated.'[25] If these evils must be acknowledged as real, and as real evils, what is to be said about knowledge? If we cannot take the Spinozistic option of supposing all to be well, just as it is, what can be said for the mental attitude involved in the pursuit of knowledge? The habits of the ichneumon wasp can be contemplated without horror only if we suppose that its victims are unconscious, and that is perhaps a real possibility. Where it would be clear self-deception to suppose

[24] Blake, *The Four Zoas* 3. 407 f: Keynes (1966), pp. 290 f.
[25] Wodehouse (1957), pp. 42, 86: Jeeves is paraphrasing Marcus Aurelius, *Meditations* 10. 5.

that the victims of predator or parasite are unaware of their fate, how can we take delight in the elegance of predation? David Lindsay's *Voyage to Arcturus*, the most explicit recent evocation of the Gnostic aversion to the world as it is, concludes with a vision of 'how the whole world of will was doomed to eternal anguish in order that one Being might feel joy'.[26] Stapledon's own attempt to reconcile the cosmic and the personal vision concluded in half-nauseated admiration for the Starmaker:

It was with anguish and horror, and yet with acquiescence, even with praise, that I felt or seemed to feel something of the eternal spirit's temper as it apprehended in one intuitive and timeless vision all our lives. Here was no pity, no proffer of salvation, no kindly aid. Or here were all pity and all love, but mastered by a frosty ecstasy. Our broken lives, our loves, our follies, our betrayals, our forlorn and gallant defenses, were one and all calmly anatomized, assessed, and placed. True, they were one and all lived through with complete understanding, with insight and full sympathy, even with passion. But sympathy was not ultimate in the temper of the eternal spirit; contemplation was. Love was not absolute; contemplation was. And though there was love, there was also hate comprised within the spirit's temper, for there was cruel delight in the contemplation of every horror, and glee in the downfall of the virtuous . . . That this should be the upshot of all our lives, this scientist's, no, artist's keen appraisal! and yet I worshipped![27]

Lindsay's firm rejection of the Cosmic Vivisector seems a more humane response, though Stapledon was human and humane enough not to be consistent: 'the cold light of the stars, symbol of the hypercosmical reality, with its crystal ecstasy' was only one light in the darkness, and the hearth-fire of his home, 'our little treasure of community . . . was the solid ground of existence'.[28]

To condemn the sole cause of all our doings is an incoherent enterprise, a way of saying that we have been talking nonsense all along. For that reason alone Lindsay, and traditional Gnostics, have been wise to appeal to what they

[26] Lindsay (1974), p. 286.
[27] Stapledon (1961), p. 217.
[28] Stapledon (1961), p. 219.

have called 'the Great First Light' as independent of the principles and powers on which this world is founded. For Lindsay, the awed appreciation of natural beauty which is one of the sources and goals of intellectual industry is only a device of the Creator-Devil, drawing us to commit more evils and to countenance their commission. The Gnosis, proper knowledge, is not of order expressed in nature, nor an order it is natural to seek and find. Instead, Gnostics gave their hearts to a Wisdom lying outside the natural world, distrusting all the instinctual and conventional norms by which men have sought to understand the universe.

Similar stories are to be found within that vast treasure-house of human thought called Buddhism. Enlightenment is the discovery of a way outside the world. Sometimes this is expressed in ways that sound very like the indifferentist creed: only forget desire and all is well. More often, the Buddhist Way is one of identification with the sufferings of all, what Powys called the way of saints:

The bodhisattva is endowed with wisdom of a kind whereby he looks on all beings as though victims going to the slaughter. And immense compassion grips him . . . So he pours out his love and compassion upon all those unnumerable beings and attends to them, thinking 'I shall become the saviour of all beings, and set them free from their sufferings'.[29]

The complexities of Buddhist philosophy are such, and my ignorance is such, that there is no point in my examining the Buddhist tradition in detail—it covers, after all, two and a half millenniums and four or five separate civilizations. Instead, I shall use this one strand of Buddhist and Christian thought to develop an opposition to the indifferentist, Spinozistic pursuit of cosmic knowledge.

The saint, or the bodhisattva, does not harden her heart. From one point of view that is a very rash programme: which of us is so wise, so strong, so benevolent as to dare to take on board all the world's agonies? It is hard enough for us to attend to our friends. We must also reckon with the power of human self-deception:

[29] *Astasahasrika Prajnaparamita*: De Bary (1969), p. 81.

BOSWELL: 'I have often blamed myself, Sir, for not feeling for others as sensibly as many say they do.' JOHNSON: 'Sir, don't be duped by them any more. You will find these very feeling people are not very ready to do you good. They pay you by feeling.'[30]

Considered as a human programme, remembering the world's agonies seems a futile and probably hypocritical endeavour. But failing to do so, or deliberately setting oneself not to do so, or preferring to think of them as something else than real evils, also seem to be ignoble projects. If we ought to do anything we surely ought to attend to the distress and futility of our fellow-creatures' lives: but how can we do so? Some distresses we could alleviate: far more than we attempt to. But many will be untouched by any charitable hand of ours. Often we cannot even remedy a wrong without inflicting further injuries on someone else. Is forgetfulness, after all, a better plan, except when we are forced to see particular occasions?

We have rejected ignorance. It is the special boast of human beings that they are capable of knowledge, can remember and extrapolate and imagine how the world may be. If ignorance were a better bet, we should prefer to live as animals amongst our peers. And so we are torn: we need to know, but cannot bear to know unless we can convince ourselves that what we know is good. But knowing even what we do, we cannot so convince ourselves. How can the world be bearable to know? We cannot say that all things are all right just as they are; we cannot say that how things are is alien and inscrutable to us; we are moved by what we imagine of elegance and order in the world, but cannot bear to contemplate the cruelties of that elegance.

Consider saints and bodhisattvas once again. We may not dare, we may not be able ourselves to step upon that road, but it has its attractions. What is needed is hope. Hope, indeed, is a necessary virtue even in scientific epistemology: 'the only assumption on which (the scientist) can act rationally is the hope of success'.[31] In this area, hope is a necessity if

---

[30] Boswell (1953), p. 417: 17 March.
[31] Peirce (1931–60), v. 357.

we are to remain sane. To set out upon the road to saintliness we need to be able to hope that the evils of the world can be, will be, remedied. Nor can this be trust in our own powers, which cannot touch the mass of suffering. We also need to believe that it is not ourselves alone who share imaginatively in the distress of things, and set ourselves to heal them. We need to be able to believe that, in some hidden way, something is on our side. To hope is to put our trust in something: 'Hope is a desperate appeal to an ally who is Himself also Love.'[32] Such hope is very easily denigrated as wishful thinking. But consider what it is like to be without it. If we cannot hope for a remedy to evil, we must either sink into deliberate forgetfulness (so that truth is not of itself a value) or else educate ourselves into believing that 'whatever is, is good' (in which case, ignorance also is a good, and 'part of the great web'). If our love of truth is to be maintained, and if it is not to subvert our other convictions, we must be able to bear the thought of all the world's agony, as a real and continuing evil. To do that, we can only hope that there is a remedy which does not depend on us.

I have already argued that if we are to be able to trust our seeming capacity to understand the world, we must suppose that our minds mirror or share in the pattern and life which is the foundation of the world. Can we add that this pattern is one to which the world desires to move, and which (in part) it embodies, but which is not yet in full control of the material? That has been the Platonic response, to suppose that there is a fundamental recalcitrance in things which prevents the perfect embodiment of what we believe there ought to be. That recalcitrance is shown chiefly in natural and moral evil, but may also result in an ineradicable failure of all our most elegant and worthy theories when they attempt detailed predictions. No mathematical theorem is perfectly instantiated in the world; no scientific prediction can ever be exact. Although we have no better route to learning than a trust in our inborn feeling for order and

[32] Marcel (1949): 17 March.

beauty, we cannot expect that we will ever find a beauty wholly without flaw.

The Gnostic blamed that recalcitrance on matter itself: the whole attempt to stamp the divine order on to a physical world was a mistake. Evil arose with the fall of spiritual life into matter, into a world where individual expressions of the primeval order found themselves in competition, with each other and with their own component parts. We may hope for an escape from the cycle of lives, but cannot hope that life in this or any other material world will ever be a full expression of remembered beauty. What we meet in the world will never be more than sweet reminders of the Logos. Knowledge is a good only so far as it leads away from life; knowledge of this world's ways is a reminder or a dangerous irrelevance.

In opposition to this view is the hope that material existence is not of itself an evil, that the world may grow to be a full expression of its founding principle. Things are neither fully good as they now are, nor ineradicably flawed. If we are to believe ourselves to have a reasonable hope, we must suppose that the source of beauty in Nature and in the human soul is capable of victory—which is why the religious quest usually posits an almighty God. In doing so, of course, we create the standard difficulties for ourselves: either God cannot do anything about evil, or He does not want to; either He is not omnipotent, or He is not benevolent. It is on this stone that most would-be believers stumble.

It is easy to accept that God's nature is, in part, inscrutable, but we cannot hold that it is entirely so without subverting the very faith which seems to require a single conscious source for Nature and the Intellect. A Deity wholly beyond our understanding is no different from the unquestionable Fate which failed to give our ancestors a stable basis for their trust in the reasonableness of things. No different, indeed, from Chance.[33] If God is beyond all reasoning, then anything can happen. Accordingly, we cannot evade the challenge

[33] Hume, *Dialogues*, Part 12: (1976), pp. 248 ff.

of evil by claiming that God's purposes and powers are quite inscrutable (however true it may be to say that of particular issues). We need to devise some story which will make it possible to believe in a God both almighty and well-meaning, because our faith is vain if He does not play fair. Efforts to evade the problem by supposing that the evils are not real evils, once considered in the proper tranquil light, fall under Bertie Wooster's rebuke. Efforts to evade it by supposing that the First Cause of things is, after all, not such as we would seriously admire or worship, result in an abandonment of any serious devotion to the truth, and any belief in reason as a way to it. What story shall we tell?

Any story at all, of course, may recall Samuel Johnson's rebuke to the pretensions of Soame Jenyns, who had devised a supposed solution to 'the problem of evil' which merely served to exacerbate the problem:

He thinks it necessary that man should be debarred (from his human perfection), because pain is necessary to the good of the universe and the pain of one order of beings extending its salutary influence to innumerable orders above and below, it was necessary that man should suffer; but because it is not suitable to justice that pain should be inflicted on innocence, it was necessary that man should be criminal. This is given as a satisfactory account of moral evil, which amounts only to this, that God created beings whose guilt he foreknew, in order that he might have proper objects of pain, because the pain of part is, no man knows how or why, necessary to the felicity of the whole.[34]

My own feeling is that all similar efforts to explain suffering and evil away as necessary to some further goal, in whose light we would see that they were not really evil (the moral growth of human beings for example), are as bad as Jenyns's theory. If it were really true that an almighty Creator could devise no other route to His goal than this, we would hold that a genuinely well-meaning being would have abandoned the effort. What achievement, after all, could increase the infinite felicity of God? His felicity can depend on His creatures' suffering only if He is far other than our serious

[34] Johnson, *Review of Jenyns' Free Enquiry*: (1950), p. 372.

standards say. If you doubt this, try and imagine yourself explaining to a mother who has just seen her child die painfully of starvation or disease or war that these things are not evil nor to be regretted.

But though the enterprise is absurd, I think it is not wholly inappropriate to try and articulate a rather different answer. If we attend to the patterns of beauty and justice and kindness that are set in our hearts, we cannot but know many things revealed to us in the world as very great evils. If we are so far attracted by those patterns as to choose to embody the way of life they require, we cannot but oppose those evils, seeking to transform or eradicate them. One of the oldest of religious images is that of light struggling with the dark. We know Good in opposition to Evil: not that it is impossible to have Good without Evil, as some have proposed, but simply that there are real evils, which the Good opposes. Why, if Good is all-powerful, does Evil still remain? Not to attempt the opposition, by witholding all creative energy in that self-dependent actuality we have called God, would be to leave the possibilities forever unredeemed. The life which is God has set itself to face the possibilities, and make good out of them. We are the arena and the agents of that conflict, that would-be transformation. Evil does not exist for a reason, but its realization as something more than fantasy (if God can fantasize) depends on our decision to know both good and evil. Our decision: in the Christian story, the Adam made that choice out of foolish pride, and the Christ out of heroic love. In the myth of the Fall, as it has been amplified by Charles Williams (a better theologian than he was a poet), the Man chose to know what had been known only to God's simple intelligence: the possibility of a privation or deprivation or corruption of the good.

Man desired to know schism in the universe. It was a knowledge reserved to God; man had been warned that he could not bear it—'in the day that thou eatest thereof thou shalt surely die'. A serpentine subtlety overwhelmed that statement with a greater promise—'Ye shall be as gods, knowing good and evil'. Unfortunately to be as gods meant, for the Adam, to die, for to know evil, for them, was to know it not by pure intelligence but by experience. It was, precisely, to experience the opposite of good, the slow destruction of the good, and of themselves with the good.[35]

The story bears within it other 'serpentine subtleties'. Christians have held that the Second Adam did what Adam could not do, and knew the weight of evil but was not overborne. Because the embodied Pattern upon which our trust in the world is founded could bear to know all things of evil and live through them, we can believe that it will prove worth while. More could be said. It is enough for my purposes to suggest only that our pursuit of truth must rest upon the hope that the truth will prove worth knowing, the evil prove to be real evil, really conquered. A universe of evil unredeemed is not worth contemplating; not even worth the effort of sustaining in existence:

Consider how quickly all things are dissolved and resolved; the bodies and substances themselves, into the matter and substance of the world: and their memories into the general age and time of the world. Consider the nature of all worldly sensible things; of those especially, which either ensnare by pleasure, or for their irksomeness are dreadful, or for their outward lustre and show are in great esteem and request, how vile and contemptible, how base and corruptible, how destitute of all true life and being they are.[36]

Consider also how close Aurelius' indifferentism lies to despair.

The ideal of knowledge sometimes called the 'classical' rests on the claim that 'to God all things are beautiful and good and just, but men have thought some things are just, some unjust'.[37] If that were so, we could understand why it was important to adopt that attitude, though in doing so we stepped so far outside the human it would be impossible to see why we should trust our grasp of fact. If the LORD is a lying spirit, what hope have we? If we reject this effort to extinguish evil, we must rest instead upon the hope that there is one who will make all things new, or else retire into our private dreams.

## 4

## The Inwardness of Things

I suggested that we could bear to remember the evils of the world only if we could believe that the pattern towards which the world and our souls are drawn is not yet fully operative in the world. If things as they are are satisfactory to God, then He is so unlike our serious intuitions of what should be, that we can only reckon the universe inscrutable. If we are to think that knowledge of truth is worth pursuing it must be a knowledge that can bear to participate in the world's agony. We have no such strength of ourselves, and therefore need to hope that there is one who will make all things new. The proper attitude to the world is not a reverent contemplation of whatever is, nor a fearful rejection of it, but willingness to be part of the solution. What we must remember are the laws and the promise.

To some, the attitude to life and the world that I have proposed may seem disturbed. It has come to seem a mark of healthy mental attitudes that we should be 'life-affirming', should say 'yes' to the world before we have even heard the question. But though I have no interest in defending the grimmer examples of 'world-denial' and asceticism, which rest upon a profound failure of trust in the powers of Good, I fear that those commentators who speak so easily of the need to say 'yes' to everything, deserve Johnson's rebuke:

Life must be seen before it can be known. [Soame Jenyns] and Pope perhaps never saw the miseries which they imagine thus easy to be born. The poor indeed are insensible of many little vexations which sometimes embitter the possessions and pollute the enjoyments of the rich. They are not pained by casual incivility, or mortified by the mutilation of a compliment; but this happiness is like that of a malefactor who ceases to feel the cords that bind him when the pincers are tearing his flesh.[1]

To say 'yes' to the world, if it means anything worth saying, cannot mean that we do or should accept things as they are. It must mean instead that we accept the challenge, join in the adventure. And let none suppose that this is easy till we have been tried:

If I were to be made a knight,' said the Wart staring dreamily into the fire, 'I should insist on doing my vigil by myself, and I should pray to God to let me encounter all the evil in the world in my own person, so that if I conquered there would be none left, and if I were defeated, I would be the one to suffer for it.' 'That would be extremely presumptuous of you,' said Merlyn, 'and you would be conquered, and you would suffer for it.' 'I shouldn't mind.' 'Wouldn't you? Wait till it happens and see.'[2]

The time is past when even cultured men could seriously think it an obvious and easy thought that all's right with the world. Doubtless Herakleitos was correct to say that 'the real nature of things likes to hide'; we know very little of what is going on, and the truth we must remember is one easily forgotten. But that truth cannot contradict the certainty of evil. William James quotes at length from the writings of an anarchist, Morrison I. Smith:

While Professors Royce and Bradley and a whole host of thoroughfed thinkers are unveiling Reality and the Absolute and explaining away evil and pain, this is the condition of the only beings known to us anywhere in the universe with a developed consciousness of what the universe is. What these people experience is Reality.[3]

Smith gave many examples of such evil: it is easy enough to find more:

On August 22, 1976, according to UPI, a sixteen year old girl, apparently high on LSD, slashed her wrists and arms and then rushed to the steps of a Roman Catholic church, poking a razor to her throat while a crowd of 300 persons cheered and screamed, 'Do your thing, sister!' Police

---

[1] Johnson (1950), p. 357.
[2] White (1939), p. 275.
[3] M. I. Smith: James (1907), p. 30.

called the crowd's cheering 'disgusting' . . . 'They were yelling, Do it, sister!! Right on!' the officers told the detective . . . The crowd cheered when the girl finally fainted and collapsed from loss of blood from her cuts.[4]

All academics who have played any part in the dissemination of a diabolical relativism, please note.

Smith believed that his examples 'invincibly prove religion a nullity',[5] and if religion is the worship of the God of Things as They Are, the attempt to reconcile us to a dreadful world by denying that it is very dreadful, I hold that his case is proved. If the pattern we hold in our hearts of what should be were truly in control, these things would not happen. Even to suggest that evil exists to serve some worthy purpose which we do not know is to insult the victims. Once again, try telling a loving mother that her child *ought* to have been crushed, starved, mangled, burnt alive, diseased: or rather, don't. However, Smith was wrong to suppose that this was true religion—to believe that all is well. True religion is founded on the faith, the hope that Good will conquer, that Evil is of itself unmeaning, that there is War in Heaven. I have argued that the intellectual quest itself, the conviction that we can achieve the truth and ought to try, must rest upon just those beliefs. To take delight in misery is evil: 'The only reason why we should contemplate evil is, that we may bear it better',[6] or that we may share in the travail of defeating it. If there were no hope of ever doing so, forgetfulness would be the better option, and knowledge for the most part vain.

An earlier 'Age of Anxiety', from Aurelius to Constantine, has been described in terms of a 'wave of pessimism': '[A] terrifying rupture between the two orders to which man belongs, the order of Reality and that of Value.'[7] Dodds blames it in part on the manifest insecurity of social and political life in those times:

---

[4] Russell (1977), p. 18.
[5] James (1907), p. 31.
[6] Johnson (1950), p. 367.
[7] S. Petrement, *Le Dualisme chez Platone* (1947), p. 157, cited by Dodds (1965), p. 18.

To identify oneself with such a world, to take it seriously as a place to live and labour in, must have demanded more courage than the average man possessed: better treat it as an illusion or a bad joke, and avoid heartbreak.[8]

The other solution, of course, was to treat it as a battle-ground:

To look at the sum total of things, to treat human miseries with detach-ment—as so many regrettable traffic accidents on the well-regulated road system of the universe—was plainly insufficient. It made no sense of the conflicting emotions within oneself. Hence the most crucial development of these centuries: the definitive splitting-off of the 'demons' as active forces of evil, against whom men had to pit them-selves. The sharp smell of an invisible battle hung over the religious and intellectual life of Late Antique man.[9]

That there are grave spiritual dangers attached to a belief in malevolent non-human forces is clear: at a humorous level, Peter Brown notes that 'one scholar even ascribed bad reviews of his book to demonic inspiration!'[10] But the postulate makes psychological and philosophical sense. A belief in demons as a source of evil, as the enemies of Good Order, so far from increasing anxiety, as Dodds supposed, is a way of relieving it:

[The Christians] focused this anxiety on the demons and at the same time offered a remedy for it. The devil was given a vast but strictly mapped-out power. He was an all-embracing agent of evil in the human race; but had been defeated by Christ and could be held in check by Christ's human agents. The Christians were convinced that they were merely mopping up on earth a battle that had already been won for them in Heaven. The monks treated the demons with the delighted alarm of small boys visiting a lion in the zoo; and the Christian bishops set about their work in the heady frame of mind of many a revolu-tionary—they faced a diabolically organized society that was, at the same time, towering, noxious, and yet hollow, doomed to destruction.[11]

[8] Dodds (1965), p. 12.
[9] Brown (1971), p. 53.
[10] Brown (1971), p. 54.
[11] Brown (1971), p. 85.

The kingdom of God is not of this world: not because it belongs entirely in another world, as Gnostics have supposed, but because it is not established in this age: 'Our fight is not against human foes, but against cosmic powers, against the authorities and potentates of this dark world, against the super-human forces of evil in the heavens.'[12] Those cosmic powers could be discerned in nature as well as in society and the human soul. They were not rivals to the Good, as if there were no single universe at all: they were rebels, for even such existence as they had was derived, as ours is, from the source of all.

That the powers are at once owed obedience, as being ordained by God,[13] and 'made a public spectacle, led as captives in the Christ's triumphal procession'[14] constitutes the fundamental ambivalence of Christian attitudes to Nature and the State. To discuss the latter, openly political, issue, would take me too far afield. Instead I want to compare these two attitudes to Nature, both of which are to be found in the later Christian tradition, with a view to our present environmental crisis. On the one hand Nature is

an admirable creation indeed when we look at the beautiful form of every part, but yet more worthy of admiration, when we consider the harmony and unison of the whole, and how each part fits with every other in fair order, and all with the whole, tending to the perfect completion of the world as a unit.[15]

On the other, 'the whole world is full of angels',[16] including rebellious ones, and the only solution to the problem of imperfection is that 'good will triumph in the end. But no ultimate moral triumph is possible in this present age. It can only be achieved when the ultimate term of the divine purpose for the universe is reached.'[17] Wallace-Hadrill cites Gregory Nazianzen's own consolation of farmers whose crops have been ruined:

[12] Paul, Ephesians 6. 12.
[13] Paul, Romans 13: 1.
[14] Paul, Colossians 2: 15.
[15] Gregory Nazianzen, *Orat.* 38. 10: see Wallace-Hadrill (1968), p. 104.
[16] Origen, *Hom, in Ezek.* 1. 7: Wallace-Hadrill (1968), p. 111.
[17] Wallace-Hadrill (1968), p. 112.

It would be empty comfort indeed to try to persuade them that their distress was imaginary and that in the life to come they would see that the evil they had resented and feared had been only an illusion, a failure to see clearly at the time. What in fact Gregory does is to recognize the evil for what it is and then to assure the sufferers that in the end there is victory.[18]

On the first view Nature is perfect simply as it is, and the knowledge of Nature is knowledge at least of the Good's likeness; on the second, it is not yet perfected, and true knowledge must be to see how best to help it on, how to build the kingdom in the realms of darkness.

In more secure ages it is unsurprising that our thinkers have preferred the stable image. Sometimes humankind itself is included within Nature, sometimes 'only Man is vile'. It is the second variant which lies at the basis of some recent ecomystical rhetoric. The alternative view, that present-day Nature is imperfect and needs our interference, has been blamed for the aggressive exploitation of Nature by Western Man. The question that confronts me is this: can respect for the ecosphere coexist with a view of Nature as a battleground for opposing spiritual forces, or must Christians after all dismiss the ecological imperative as Nature-worship?

'The ecological imperative': this century has seen an enormous increase both in our knowledge of the subtle relationships existing between living things, and in the damage we do to our environment. Long ago, it seems, our ancestors may have destroyed the thronging wildlife of the Pleistocene by injudicious fire-driving.[19] Equipped with increased technological powers and great wealth (mostly taken from less powerful peoples), we have been able to inflict serious wounds on Nature. Deserts spread, the oceans are polluted, and up to forty thousand species vanish from history in each succeeding year. Such damage offers long-term losses even to us: we deplete the genetic potential of the biosphere in ways whose effects we cannot calculate,

[18] Wallace-Hadrill (1968), p. 113.
[19] Martin and Wright (1967).

lose living kinds that already are, or may yet be, of vital interest to us. The plants of Amazonia alone, which may yet succumb to Brazilian forest-clearances, are a reservoir of drugs for the alleviation of our human ills. Even from an anthropocentric point of view it would be well not to be so destructive. A concern for non-human suffering and purposes must also be a factor in any serious moral calculation. But many environmental moralists also hope to remind us of the intrinsic value of living systems, and urge that the Judaeo-Christian injunction 'to subdue the earth' has encouraged a rapist's attitude to the living body of our Mother Earth.

William James, encountering a squatter's hut in the forests of North Carolina, felt at first that 'the forest had been destroyed; and what had "improved" it out of existence was hideous, a sort of ulcer, without a single element of artificial grace to make up for the loss of Nature's beauty.' Then, in one of the sudden insights that make James a great and wrongly neglected philosopher, he saw that 'the clearing, which was [to him] a mere ugly picture on the retina, was to [the settlers] a symbol redolent with moral memories and sang a very paean of duty, struggle and success'.[20] What is out there in the world, as it is presented to us in our human experience, is always rich with meaning. As I have suggested before, even the attempt to construct a 'value-free' universe merely imposes a certain negative significance on things-as-they-are: the theory of a meaningless world is itself a comment on human endeavour. But what felt significance is best relied on? Is the world so much material for human purposes? Or dominated by hostile powers whom it is death either to worship or, in our own strength, defy? Or 'an image of the intelligible, a perceptible god, supreme in greatness and excellence, in beauty and perfection, single in its kind and one'?[21]

Western peoples do not have a monopoly of the view that Nature is fair game, free to be used by anyone who has the

---

[20] James (1964), p. 216.
[21] Plato, *Timaeus* 92c.

strength or the intelligence. An African culture, the Fipa, for example, consider all nature to be open to progressive control, whereby 'the strange and unknown is brought into the light and order of human understanding'.[22] Conversely, some customs which seem to us to embody, even absurdly, a respect for the intrinsic sacredness of certain natural entities, can be given clear economic sense: Hindus hold cows sacred partly because cows are vital to peasant life, sources of fuel and milk and labour.[23] Attempts to show that Westerners are uniquely aggressive towards the natural world, that 'other cultures' embody a respect for it, depend too often on selective quotation from romantic poets and ignorance of what actually has been done by other cultures. Late Roman Paganism, with its gods and spirits of the sacred springs, did not prevent the Romans from making a desert of North Africa. Swinburne's Julian, who mourned the passing of the sacred spring, sacrificed thousands of animals to propitiate Apollo. Japan, despite a background of Nature-worship and Buddhism, has shown little enough respect for Tokyo's air, or the world's whales.

None the less, in a world of arbitrary forces it is well to be careful over any changes that we make: there is some sense in the judgement that experiment is possible only when we can believe that there is a stability about things, and about our relation with things, that cannot be shaken by any act of ours. Danger attends novelty in a demon-ridden universe: who would be fool enough to conduct control experiments to see if rain-dances actually guaranteed the rain? Any attempt to dig a canal, or join an island to the mainland changes an order it is dangerous to meddle with. Such fears may well have placed barriers in the way of experimental science, and of any attempt to improve our environment. At the least, all such changes would have to be undertaken carefully, with due propitiation of the demon-powers. If there are none, the way things are may be

---

[22] Willis (1974), p. 124.
[23] Harris (1975), pp. 11 f.

seen as having no protectors. 'May be': they do not have to be.

Similarly, the view of the world as embodying a perfect order may stand in the way of any attempted alteration. But, of course, human action must also count as part of that order. If a belief in cosmic perfection may stand against over-exploitation of the world, it may also license such exploitation: 'We are natural creatures, and who is to judge whether or not our destructiveness, however we may deplore it, is not an ordained path in nature's road of terrestrial development?'[24] What exactly M. R. Zavon, a consultant of Shell, meant by this reply to charges that overuse of pesticides was damaging our environment, I cannot tell. Probably he meant very little: it is certainly not an obviously consoling reply to someone who fears that our health is being damaged, or chemical resources squandered, or wildlife destroyed. But the remark does point towards a difficulty for all those who find Value embodied in the natural world: namely, that we can no longer believe the natural world unchanging.

In a world conceived as good, apart from the activities of fallen humanity, any alteration is likely to be for the worse:

Before the intervention of men, the great clans of donkeys and horses continued uninterruptedly among themselves. But now, on the contrary, donkeys are crossed with horses, bastardising nature. This is certainly a greater sin than mere fornication, because it is committed contrary to nature: it injures natural affinity, apart from the injury in respect of the person.[25]

That dreadful slogan 'You can't deduce an ought from an is' could hardly be less to the point: the bestiarist is entitled to argue that miscegenation is wrong because it breaches the established order of natural kinds, an order which enshrines the Value we should serve. Modern conservationists also sometimes require us to be 'stewards' of the established order, both by not destroying the pattern set by non-human processes, and by maintaining such near-natural habitats as

[24] M. R. Zavon: Graham (1970), p. 45.
[25] White (1954), p. 205: see Leviticus 19: 19.

would vanish without our help. But the question raised by Zavon's curious remark is this: given the probability that the biosphere has undergone both gradual and abrupt transformations during the last four thousand million years, what is so special about the present order? Most of the species which have ever existed upon earth are already extinct: what harm is done by losing a few more? Either we abandon the whole notion that Value is embodied in the world's order (and so the world ceases to be sacred), or else we suppose that it is embodied over the whole span of history. If we take the latter option, the range of life-forms present at any one time will be only a selection from the beauteous whole, and it would be as foolish to preserve a species past its time as to insist that it occupy all present space. The supremely successful dinosaurs had to pass away before the birds and mammals could proliferate. If we are ourselves living through a crash of Jurassic or Permian standards, maybe that will clear the way for new life-forms, new variations on the age-old themes.

A recent work by Dougal Dixon emphasizes this, as well as providing the beginnings of an answer. 'Evolution', he observes, 'is an on-going process in which new creatures are gradually appearing all the time, while others are becoming extinct.'[26] Evolutionary change has not come to a dead-stop with the emergence of Homo sapiens. Dixon chooses to imagine what new kinds might emerge to fill the niches if humankind itself and a few associated species were to join the list of extinct mammals, and takes a slice across the biosphere of fifty million years ahead. His imagined creatures are not prophecies, but guesses at the sort of thing that might happen. Everyone will have their favourites in this menagerie. My own are the Vortex[27] (*Balenornis vivipera*), a 12-metre long descendant of the Penguin that feeds on plankton; the Common Rabbuck[28] (*Ungulagus silvicultrix*), a hoofed descendant of the rabbit; and the Pfrit[29] (*Aquambulus*

---

[26] Dixon (1981), p. 112.
[27] Dixon (1981), p. 66 f.
[28] Dixon (1981), p. 38 f.
[29] Dixon (1981), pp. 48 f.

*hirsutus*), a tiny shrew with large, water-repellent feet that walks on water.

 The book is a fantasy, though it has the serious object of explaining current evolutionary theory. What it emphasizes, even as it parades its parodies of Linnaean nomenclature, is that our whole modern notion of a species sits very ill with ideas of permanence. Biologists' terminology has gone through something like the same sea-change as physicists': just as an atom is no longer reckoned literally atomic, indivisible, and irreducible, so a biological species is no longer a clear essence which a creature either has or has not. To be 'of the same species' as another creature is to be a member, not of a class of relevantly similar individuals, but of a breeding group—to be child or parent or fertile mate of other members of that particular group. It follows that many creatures are members of 'ring-species', such that they are co-members with two other sorts of creature who are not themselves conspecifics: A-types breed with B-types which breed with C-types, but A-types do not breed with C-types. If evolutionary transformation is a reality, all existing species have interlocking, overlapping relationships with 'other' past and present species. What we see as an orderly assortment of natural kinds is only a 'two-dimensional cross-section of a three-dimensional dynamic system which is constantly changing and continually being modified'.[30]

 It is easy then to represent attempts to 'conserve species' as foredoomed efforts to stave off expectable alterations. Strictly, this has little enough relevance to the detailed arguments for conservation, which rest upon the known and likely benefits to us all of particular species and of a well-stocked biosphere. It also supposes, which is probably false at present, that the rate of speciation is fast enough to replace current occupants of ecological niches. Dixon's fantasy, you will recall, rested on the removal of human-kind from the scene. As long as we exist, and continue our

[30] Dixon (1981), p. 112.

very rapid expansion and cultural change, there is little chance for new kinds to emerge and prosper—except for such opportunists as the sparrow or the rat. Only a very confident person could claim with any conviction that future states of the biosphere will allow us a place, or that the biosphere is forever immune to disaster. J. Lovelock has suggested, despite an underlying optimism, that a human population of ten thousand million, of whom a substantial minority was trying to live at our present standard of energy expenditure, would require so much disruption of established systems as to leave us as inhabitants of 'the prison hulk of Spaceship Earth', rather than of Gaia, the self-maintaining terrestrial biosphere.[31]

None the less, a belief that the natural order, specifically the living order, is an embodiment of value does not require us to be conservationists:

> Are God and Nature then at strife,
>  that Nature lends such evil dreams?
>  so careful of the type she seems,
> so careless of the single life . . .
> So careful of the type? but no,
>  from scarped cliff and quarried stone
>  she cries, A thousand types are gone:
> I care for nothing, all shall go.[32]

Those who make Nature their God must accept that its mode of being is a continual change. It does not follow that we should hurry on that change, nor delay it. Perhaps in adoring Nature we must adore the past as well as the future, and keep in memory the steps by which we have come. Only by recalling where 'we' have been, and what 'we' were, can we cope with the continuing transformation of our world. Aldo Leopold, one of the major thinkers of the ecological movement, based his plea for conservation on a sense of times past and yet to come: '[The crane] is the symbol of our untameable past, of that incredible sweep of millennia which

---

[31] Lovelock (1974), p. 132.
[32] Tennyson, *In Memoriam* 54-5.

underlies and conditions the daily affairs of birds and men.'[33] This may well lie behind much popular and scholarly interest in evolutionary history: the story is a way of locating ourselves in the world, teaching us that we, 'Life-kind', are four thousand million years old. Those short-sighted profiteers who would wipe out the biological record of those ages cast us adrift in time. For the Aranda, as for most other human societies, 'the whole countryside is (their) living, age-old family tree'.[34] So also for us.

Care for the biosphere and its current constituents is of a piece with care for the relics of our human or patriotic past. We do not need to consider Nature wholly worshipful to feel such concern: if we are to respect our selves, feel confidence in the capacities of life, we need such reminders of what we are and have been. The collapse of any strict concept of a species leaves us as members of Life-kind, not merely that temporarily isolated breeding-group called humankind. But there are at least two problems. First, what mode of life is suggested for us by our self-identification with Life-kind, considering what natural life is like? Second, might it not, after all, be right to make a new beginning?

The horrors of the natural world need not be exaggerated. Few living creatures linger in their misery, although their deaths are not always quick. There is some reason to think that creatures developed enough to feel pain may also possess neurophysiologies capable of blanking out all pain in moments of crisis. This device, whose neo-Darwinian explanation would simply be that animals are better able to escape some dangers if they are not in pain, would also serve to anaesthetize the dying. But though 'Life in the Wild' need not be horrible, it is clearly hard. Two things may follow: where so much of Nature rests upon predation, hunger, and disease, how can we spare much energy for distresses closer to home? How can we worry about the victims of hunger or oppression when that is, and perhaps will always be, the way things are?

---

[33] Leopold (1949), p. 96; see Clark (1983c), p. 195.
[34] Strehlow (1947): Williams (1971), p. 92.

We can do nothing about most animal distress: why then should we worry overmuch about the distresses men cause animals, or even each other? Secondly, must we not reckon with the possibility that such distress is not only ineluctable, but needful? That is how kinds are transformed, how Nature moves: if we cut ourselves off from the salutary effects of natural selection, is that not a dead-end? As long as we maintained a liberal faith in the supreme value of human individuals, the likelihood of a world-system which would infallibly and ever after secure all humankind from harm, we could ignore this. Once our hearts are given to the world-system itself, and what we thought of as 'our kind' revealed as a moment within this larger, changing whole, should we not accept the salutary discipline imposed by Nature's God? Even war can be understood within such an evolutionary framework, as a device for disposing of males surplus to the breeding requirements of the primate horde. If we seek peace, we must find something else to do with the young males.

With this sort of background it becomes possible to argue, with Malthus, that humanitarian interference with poverty is bound to do more harm than good. Every improvement in medical care and food distribution is bound to result in an increase of human misery, since it will simply allow the feckless longer time to breed before the ill consequences of their indiscretions are made clear.[35] Such a doctrine is likelier to be held by those who might otherwise feel inclined to help the poor, but it does embody a serious attempt to think of humankind, human society, within the setting 'modern knowledge' prescribes for them. Malthus's predictions were not fulfilled in the West, for Westerners procurred a vast increase of natural resources from elsewhere in the world, as well as improving their technical capacities. It is likely that they will be on a global scale, as long as the rich can salve their consciences with talk of 'Nature's Way'.

An alternative vision, still within the bounds set by a

[35] See Hardin (1969), especially pp. 28, 81.

worshipful respect for Nature-as-it-comes-to-be, might be to emphasize the particular qualities that have been developed within our own genetic line. Humankind has evolved as a species uniquely pre-adapted to co-operate, to share, to understand even the alien. We are the one vertebrate species whose evolution has equipped it to deal empathetically with other species, to be concerned for the health of our environment over the long term, to reason about long-term and abstract possibilities, and to encapsulate our reasonings in spoken or written words. It is not uncommon now to find people suggesting that in us Nature, or at any rate the terrestrial biosphere that Lovelock has called 'Gaia', has grown conscious of itself, that we may turn out to be the leading edge of evolution. If this step is taken, we can no longer simply read our policy off from what 'Nature' has done before. We must ask ourselves how evolution ought to go, not merely how it has gone, and may hope to save more variants from the rubbish-heap than unguided Nature has allowed.

With this, I move on from the first problem posed by self-identification with the multi-millionfold enterprise that is the terrestrial biosphere to the second. It is not as clear as some environmentalists have thought that a worshipful respect for Nature will issue in any gentleness toward those creatures who are fellow-members of Life-kind, or Humankind:

The literature of the movement is marked by a moving reverence for the seamless web of life, accompanied by a shocking indifference to the weaker and less convenient forms of human life and by an almost cavalier readiness to disrupt the carefully woven web of civility and humane values.[36]

Can we not take the careful web of human civility more seriously? The naturalistic myths of the educated Westerner hardly allow us to, if we take them seriously, for we have no grounds in the neo-Darwinian theory to suppose either that our grasp of true value is veridical or that our effort to embody a humane civility will be other than futile, a historical

[36] Neuhaus (1971), p. 188: O'Riordan (1976), p. 32.

episode soon to be replaced by the values of a new hydraulic despotism or post-cataclysmic tribalism. If we do take the values of a humane civility with proper seriousness, it is in faith and hope, expressed in a metaphysics that allows for consciousness and for the search for truth.

The 'classical' view of the world (not that it was ever the only view available to Hellenes) does not guarantee civil treatment of the world, or of our fellow humans. What of the other strand of Christian thought, the 'late classical' view that

> were this world all devils o'er
> and watching to devour us,
> we lay it not to heart so sore;
> not they can overpower us.[37]

Less dramatically (not necessarily more truly): suppose that the world is the arena of a contest between the powers of light and the rebellious powers of darkness, a contest in which it is our office to side with the light. One version of this contest, elaborated by the followers of Zarathustra, is highly favourable to human use of the land: 'he who cultivates barely cultivates righteousness', according to their hymn.[38] Mice and weevils, correspondingly, are creatures of the Evil One, the Lie. The deliberate cultivation and care of land, turning it from wilderness to garden is a tradition of stewardship which has always had its supporters among the great historical religions. It could well be regarded as the inspiration of William James's squatters. Such a tradition certainly could not license the crass destruction of farming land, harmless or useful creatures, but perhaps it ignores a dimension of Value. There have been two aspects of wilderness in our religious tradition: did Jesus go out into the wilderness, amongst the wild beasts, as a sign of desolation, or as a promise of paradise restored?[39] It is at least worth noticing that records of the desert saints, in the East and

[37] M. Luther, tr. T. Carlyle: *Songs of Praise* 436.
[38] A reference drawn from Hume which I cannot now trace.
[39] Jeremias (1971) i. 69.

in Celtic lands, suggest their deep sympathy with the creatures they found there. These two approaches have been called, respectively, the Benedictine and the Franciscan, although it is not clear that even the founders of these orders would have displayed them consistently. The Benedictine's temptation is to suppose that 'useless' or 'harmful' creatures are of the Evil one; the Franciscan's to think that all will run smoothly without any help from us.

It is not surprising that the ecological movement has preferred the Benedictine model: in allowing human cultivation and exploitation of resources, it can seem a politically viable option. Asking, or seeming to ask, people to abandon worldly possessions and follow the One Master, relying on the LORD's bounty, is unlikely to appeal to many. That tradition of the wandering life has been maintained in many cultures, but it has not been possible for the mass of mankind since first we settled down to cultivate the soil. In fact, we need not interpret the Franciscan way so strictly; nor need Benedictines be so unsympathetic. It is, after all, no part of the doctrine that, say, mice and weevils are essentially part of the Lie, even if it is a function of the powers of darkness that creatures are set against each other. Mice are not malevolent, even if demons are. The truly Benedictine approach would take advice from Gaia's way with pollutants, as described by Lovelock. From the first massive pollution of Earth's atmosphere, by free oxygen excreted by early photosynthesizers, to the most recent efforts of the military-industrial complex, Gaia's solution has been, not to fight or restrict the thing, but to incorporate it into some new living system. Amusingly, there are recent reports of bees who collect DDT; presumably they will some day find a use for it, or for its chemical products. Gaia, of course, need operate by nothing more than natural selection. We have, potentially, the wits to find some bearable compromise between the needs of different entities. The wits, but often not the will: 'Shame on you who add house to house and join field to field, until not an acre remains, and you are left to dwell alone in the land.'[40] Isaiah's charge, and similar denunciations by other Hebrew prophets, was directed at the rich, who left neither space nor wealth for the human poor. But the laws of Moses also found room for the wild things: 'What the land produces in the sabbath year shall be food for you, for your male and female slaves, for your hired man, and for the stranger lodging under your roof, for your cattle and for the wild animals in your country.'[41]

The hope of a wholly new order, when 'the wolf and the lamb shall feed together and the lion shall eat straw like cattle',[42] cannot depend on any power of ours. In this age, the whole creation is in labour,[43] and we cannot hasten the birth. But if we think of the world-as-it-is in this way, as in labour with the life of a new age, we need not set ourselves to any destructive remaking of the world. A project based on human wit and aiming at the creation of a world more in accord with our own preferences would be likely to disregard the interests of other creatures. The Franciscan project is founded instead on a strong awareness of the inwardness of things. It is, in a sense, the denial of the practical outlook: 'practical' people look at things with an eye to their usefulness, their function in the agents' plan. Turning aside from such practicalities, it is possible to see things as they are. The price of this is to become aware of agonies. Josiah Royce, whom Morrison Smith attacked in the passage quoted on p. 54, describes the shift:

What then is our neighbour? Thou hast regarded his thought, his feeling as something different from thine . . . He seems to thee a little less living than thou; his life is dim, it is cold, it is a pale fire beside thy own burning desires . . . So, dimly and by instinct hast thou lived with thy neighbour, and hast known him not, being blind. Thou hast made [of him] a thing, no Self at all. Have done with this illusion, and simply try to learn the truth. Pain is pain, joy is joy everywhere, even as in thee. In all the songs of the forest birds; in all the cries of the

---

[40] Isaiah 5: 8; see Black (1970), p. 61.
[41] Leviticus 25: 6 f.
[42] Isaiah 65: 25.
[43] Paul, Romans 8: 21.

wounded and dying, struggling in the captor's power; in the boundless sea where the myriads of water-creatures strive and die; amid all the countless hordes of savage men; in all sickness and sorrow; in all exultation and hope, everywhere, from the lowest to the noblest, the same conscious, burning, wilful life is found, endlessly manifold as the forms of living creatures, unquenchable as the fires of the sun, real as the impulses that even now throb in thine own selfish little heart. Lift up thy eyes, behold that life, and then turn away, and forget it as thou canst; but if thou hast known that, thou hast begun to know thy duty.[44]

A 'true and felt knowledge (not merely nominal knowledge)' of the inner life of other humans, other animals, of Gaia itself, may come on anyone. The sense that all material motions are no more than an outward and visible sign of that inner life need rest on no acknowledged metaphysic. That the inner life is as unquenchable as Royce declared, requires more faith to be quite certain of. But though the price of this awareness is a knowledge of agonies, the testimony of those who experience it does seem to be that it is also an experience joyful in itself:

This unutterable harmony of souls, the phantom of the ideal world, arose in me complete. I never felt anything so great or so instantaneous . . . I shall never enclose in a conception this power, this immensity that nothing will express; this form that nothing will contain; this ideal of a better world which one feels, but which it would seem that nature has not made.[45]

The French novelist that James cites fears the thing a phantom, a merely 'ideal' world. Judged from the perspective of a materialist metaphysics, that must be so. Nature-mysticism of any kind must be some sort of regression to infantile or embryonic life. If we abandon such metaphysical prejudices, the virtual unanimity of the witnesses should give us cause to take them seriously. To be strongly conscious of the inwardness of things is to be joined in that perpetual reaching-out for God on which Aristotle thought the world depended. It is to fall in love.

[44] Royce (1885), pp. 157 ff; see James (1964), p. 220.
[45] De Senancour, *Obermann*, Lettre 30, cited by James (1964), p. 221.

> Wonder not
> if high the transport, great the joy I felt
> communing in this sort through earth and heaven
> with every form of creature, as it looked
> towards the Uncreated with a countenance
> of adoration, with an eye of love.
> One song they sang, and it was audible.[46]

The love experienced for all created things, even in their weak and fallen state, even when the broken reflections of the glory cannot now be pieced together, is the only sure basis from which to care for the world. The Benedictine picture, of humankind as the earth's steward, has its own strengths: Franciscan delight in the experienced inwardness of all things, its recognition of a reaching-forward in however many different and sometimes disparate modes, may enable us to see what our project must be. According to Islamic doctrine, it is because human beings can be saints that they have authority, under God.[47] It is in the saints—a class not restricted to any one religious tradition—that we can see how human life is to be lived in this vast battleground. Really to live with others, in the living world, we must live from that occasional awareness of the life within. To do so is to value all the efforts of our kindred to embody some reflection of the God they reach toward, but not to regret too much the passing of any special shape. To prefer instead either a sterile conservation of the forms there are or else an anthropocentric concentration on what is now of use to 'us' is to ignore the odyssey on which we are embarked, our journey home from exile to the New Jerusalem. That odyssey is moved by love. 'There are three things that last for ever: faith, hope, and love; but the greatest of them all is love.'[48]

---

[46] Wordsworth, *Prelude* 2. 409 f.
[47] Nasr (1981), p. 182.
[48] Paul, I Corinthians 13: 13.

# 5

# Enlightenment and the Holy Spirit

I have argued that our confidence in the powers of human reason to find out the truth, in the worth of truth and the value of the world as we know it, embodies an unadmitted metaphysical system. The natural world is, as it were, a battleground: what of order and beauty it possesses—which we must assume it possesses if we are to trust our theorizing— is the result of Light's endeavour to deal with the Darkness of evil possibilities. The intellectual enterprise rests on faith, hope, and love. Without that grounding it becomes a private fad, a social hypocrisy: 'Objectivity is the faith in the possibility of universal agreement'[1]—a faith which can be coherently maintained only if the world is founded, though imperfectly, upon a principle and order that guarantees the eventual success of honest enquiry. What I have revived is Peirce's doubly 'Neglected Argument': 'The rapid progress in the sciences indicates, as Peirce points out, man's instinctive ability to invent new hypotheses capable of bearing the test of experience, and this must mean that the human mind is "in some deep way attuned to the nature of things".'[2] Our ability to generate new hypotheses that lead us on toward the truth cannot be proved by experience, but it has not been disproved. If it is real, our best explanation for its presence in us is some form of the theistic or spiritualist hypothesis. If it is to be worth exercising in any more than the most tediously practical areas, to form a picture of the truth entire, we must hope for a truth worth knowing, a truth which it is joy inextinguishable to know. To act

---

[1] Knight (1959), p. 20.
[2] Jarvis (1975), p. 160, after Royce (1913) ii. 406 ff; see Peirce (1931–60), vi. 49 ff.

responsibly within the world our musings have uncovered we must appreciate that world's inwardness. To do so is to be aroused by that emotion which I have called 'love': not a desire to possess, but a joyous self-identification with the odyssey, the travail of creation.

In citing such authors as Wordsworth, not unreasonably called a 'nature-mystic', I do not mean to imply that all forms of 'mysticism' are to be identified with each other. Such a banal and ill-informed equation assumes too readily that there is any such thing as 'mysticism' at all. Considered in its most general application, the term means only a reliance on truths that cannot be proved by reason or experience, of which our assurance must be immediate: in that sense every intellectual, every scholar, every scientist is a mystic unaware. Restricting the term's scope a little, we can isolate those who have a 'true and felt knowledge' of those truths, rather than a mere casual adherence to the underlying and forgotten principles of the intellectual craft.

Perhaps, however, there is something to be learnt from the commoner usage of christening as 'mystics' those who seek or have achieved an experience for which they can find no wholly adequate verbal description in terms understandable by the inexperienced. Strictly, this too is an ill-defined group: no experience, of eating chocolate or climbing the Grand Canyon or kissing a friend, is wholly conveyed to the un-initiated by any word of ours. The best we can do is seek out some analogous event and strive to evoke that very imaginative ability on which I have founded my case. We can get the point of verbal descriptions, but that very getting-of-the-point can sometimes be the experience itself, or a reflection of it. That, after all, is the value of poetry, or music, or philosophy, or science: that it sometimes wakens in us that world-spanning devotion, recognition of beauty and the inwardness of things, of that hidden order which Herakleitos thought stronger than the obvious.[3] The total incommunicability of 'mystical experience' has been greatly exaggerated.

[3] Herakleitos 22 B 54: Diels and Krantz (1952).

There is such a mass of 'mystical literature', evocations of the experiences or recipes for 'achieving' them, as well as debates about their proper metaphysical significance, that demands for 'silence concerning that whereof we cannot speak'[4] have a certain Gilbertian flavour about them:

> With cat-like tread, upon our prey we steal,
> In silence dread our cautious way we feel.
> No sound at all, we never speak a word,
> A fly's footfall would be distinctly heard![5]

None the less, there is reason to think that words do sometimes get in the way. Partly, we are diverted into thinking of the words themselves, or the different significances that those words might have, instead of permitting them to evoke our imaginative response. Partly, we are so dedicated to maintaining the structures of our world and our identity, that it is difficult to remember the true being of the world. We maintain our picture of ourselves and of the world by talking to ourselves, naming the things we meet in accordance with our prejudices and purposes, recalling to ourselves the occasions when we did or said or might have done or said something that threw a good or a bad light on us. All manuals to the 'mystical' life, the life imbued with a continual remembrance of our true selves and of the world, begin with exhortations to think rightly: 'If we are full of the noise of our desires and our fears, what else indeed can we see but the innumerably repeated image of our desires and fears?'[6] If we are always telling ourselves that this man is a bully, that women a bore, that car is being driven dangerously, and what we should have said to that pompous ass who disagreed with us, and how foolish we must have looked when . . ., how can we expect to be aware of joy, and of the world-that-is? The words we use to ourselves and to each other fix a picture of the world and of ourselves into our hearts. The effort to

[4] Wittgenstein (1961), s. 7.
[5] W. S. Gilbert, *The Pirates of Penzance*, Act 2.
[6] Satprem (1968), p. 112.

remember may require a disciplined silence—a suggestion that may sound easy if you have not tried it:

> Let the seeker try it for just five minutes and he will see what stuff he is made of! He will find that he lives in a clandestine turmoil, an exhausting whirlwind, but never exhausted, where there is only room for his thoughts, his feelings, his impulsions, his reactions—himself, always himself, enormous gnome who obtrudes everywhere, veils everything, hears only himself, sees only himself, knows only himself (if that) and whose perpetual themes, more or less alternating, can give him the illusion of novelty.[7]

Recipes for silencing that internal chatter include simple dedication to the task, the numbing effect of intellectually irresoluble riddles, concentration on some icon, mandala, or thought, the deliberate surrender of one's verbal powers to what is sometimes called ecstatic utterance.

This last technique, if the word is appropriate, is sometimes known as 'speaking in tongues' or glossolalia, and has had a poor press in academic circles. Why, after all, should one want to talk nonsense? It is usually assumed that such 'effervescent religious revivalism' as is expressed in glossolalia, shaking, and dancing is a form of emotionalism that can appeal only to fringe members of society: the poor and deprived, or else the women of a patriarchal culture.[8] I am in no position to deny the anthropologists' reports that similar behaviour is associated, in the minds of some participants, with spirit-possession, a loss of deliberate control. Nor do I wish to dispute that *some* shamans or spirit-mediums are in a troubled psychological state, diagnosable by Western standards as some form of psychosis. The cosmology which I have been sketching precisely allows the existence of rebellious and hostile spirits. But to assimilate all enthusiasm to this single model is quite unrealistic. Shocking as it may seem to honest academics, enthusiasm is not restricted to the fringes of society, although it may be well represented there. Nor do glossolalia and the other features of charismatic

---

[7] Satprem (1968), p. 33.
[8] Douglas (1973), p. 114.

or pentecostalist revivalism demonstrate psychotic attitudes or involve a loss of personal identity. That grave dangers surround enthusiasm is admitted: that it is essentially a very horrid thing, lacks evidence.

If I were to stop here, with the suggestion that pentecostalism is a set of psychological techniques which can fulfil many functions, honest academics might find no difficulty in agreeing, even if they reckoned that the techniques were not for them. Such enthusiasm could be said to release trapped energies, to relieve depression, even to secure that longed-for inner silence when we cease to think how splendid or how stupid we and others are. Perhaps it involves a spiritual catharsis like that described by Aristotle, a performance in which anyone, however untalented by social standards, may participate. The anthropologists' comment that enthusiasm is engaged in by those marginal to their societies, however false in detail, may hint that here we have an effort after egalitarianism. All participants are equal; any may be the momentary voice of God; none have any natural claim to superior status. So charismatic revivalism can be seen, correctly, as a demonstration against social or ecclesiastical or academic hierarchy, even if (being human) the revivalists are likely enough to establish their own hierarchies in the end.

But though this psychologizing, politicizing account of enthusiasm has its merits, it is clear that participants cannot be approaching things in this manner. When Staal[9] proposes that there should be an attempt to investigate the variety of 'mystical' traditions from within, he assumes that it is possible to create certain experiences in oneself, the very same ones that believers have, without adopting their beliefs about the matter. Even psychologically this is a very dubious assumption, and begs a serious question: namely, what is it to have the 'same' experience, if it is not to encounter the same reality in ways that carry implications for future conduct and belief? Genuine participants are doing something, performing

[9] Staal (1975), pp. 123 ff.

acts and making responses which carry a meaning for them: they are, subjectively, praising and thanking God in communion with their fellow believers, not working away at their theses. To interpret enthusiasm simply as a set of techniques is to ignore its distinctive subjective feature: whereas some varieties of mystic or self-realizing psychotherapist emphasize a need for personal effort, the enthusiast has found her problem solved by someone else.

This feature too has its parallels in other religious and philosophical traditions. It is, for most of us, impossible to achieve inner silence by any act of will, impossible to get rid of the complaining, worrying, angry voices that besiege our equanimity. The very attempt to do so creates more strain, more quarrelling voices. Enlightenment is not to be achieved by careful building up of knowledge, careful control of the mind's acts, but by a certain sort of surrender:

When you strive to gain quiescence by stopping motion, the quiescence thus gained is ever in motion . . . Wordiness and intellection—the more with them the further astray we go; away therefore with wordiness and intellection, and there is no place where we cannot pass freely. When we return to the root, we gain the meaning; when we pursue external objects, we lose the reason.[10]

Selective quotation from Buddhist texts can leave false impressions, if they leave any at all. So it would be unhelpful to cite many such passages, particularly as the Buddhist tradition as wide and varied as the Christian. Some Buddhists can be made to sound like Herakleitean indifferentists; others proclaim the original and lasting unity of the one Mind and all ordinary minds; others again find their enlightenment in the realization of the non-existence of the self. What these doctrines mean in any particular school, to any particular Buddhist is at least as puzzling as attempts to disentangle the definitions of Chalcedon. What accounts of enlightenment do have in common is that it consists in 'true and felt knowledge' of things stumblingly expressed in the scriptures: the writings do not convey this knowledge, but can be recognized

[10] Seng-t'san: Suzuki (1960), pp. 77 f.

(after the event) as attempts to describe it. Nor can argument lead us to such a real knowledge. Although it may provide us with a range of concepts to articulate the experience, even this use of argument is suspect, since the Reality experienced is one that transcends or defeats or ignores all ordinary dichotomies.

Strangely, it is Christian enthusiasm that has a reputation for anti-intellectualism, rather than the paradoxical efforts after enlightenment, the wild rejections of the law of non-contradiction that characterize most of the Buddhist tradition. It has even been almost respectable to be a Zen Buddhist, a school especially noted for its contempt of intellectual strivings, while Christian enthusiasts are assumed to be bigots incapable of serious thought. This is probably due partly to the social factors: though enthusiasts are not found only on the fringes of society, they may certainly form groups which cross class-barriers. Westerners who sympathize with Zen Buddhism are likely to have a secure social position— a point which is no way intended as a criticism of them. But it is worth asking whether Christian enthusiasm is any more opposed to intellectualism than is Buddhism, or whether it is opposed for other reasons. If the opposition is a serious one, what shall a Christian enthusiast who is also a philosopher and intellectual suppose? Tertullian's mocking question 'What business has Jerusalem with Athens?'[11] is the thought from which I began: how shall I respond?

Enlightenment dawns, or so the Buddhists say, when we stop trying to dichotomize, to distinguish me and not-me, pleasant and unpleasant, fair and foul, Nirvana and Samsara. The Suchness realized by the Tathagata, the Buddha, is beyond dichotomy, and of it we can only say 'It is'. Psychologizing commentators sometimes try to write the Buddhist doctrine as an account of self-realization (as they also do the Christian experience of salvation), but we can reasonably doubt that this is how most Buddhists, or most Christians, have regarded it. Buddhists hope to realize their union with

[11] Tertullian, *De Praescriptione Haereticorum* 7. 9.

the One Original, and from that point of rest bring salvation to all creatures:

I must so bring to fruition the root of goodness that all beings find the utmost joy, unheard-of joy, the joy of omniscience. I must be their charioteer, I must be their leader, I must be their torchbearer, I must be their guide to safety . . . I must not wait for the help of another, nor must I lose my resolution and leave my task to another.[12]

The bodhisattva's vow to save all creatures from the cycle of distress in which we live can sometimes be interpreted in Gnostic fashion: the material world is a mistake, from which all need release. But the particular twist provided in Buddhist tradition is that even that dichotomy must be transcended. Nirvana is not somewhere else: it is possible to manifest the uncreated light within the world. Again: it is very often asserted that, in accordance with the final sentence of the above quotation, the Buddhist can rely on no one but herself, whereas the very theme of Christian doctrine is the presence of a Saviour. But this is confused thinking: in a sense, the steps can be taken only by the seeker herself, but this is not to require any form of ego-control, as if the ordinary self had yet another project to its name. 'Whatever Samadhis, psychic faculties and teachings are realized by the Bodhisattvas, they are made possible only by the sustaining power of the Buddhas.'[13] This theme is sometimes made the centre of the Buddhist life, in such strands as Pure Land Buddhism: merely to call on the name of Amida Buddha is to secure help from the secret place. But the theme is not only present there, in what may be regarded as a popular religious cult rather than 'true' Buddhism. The *Lankavatara Sutra* again:

Each must follow the path of study and meditation by himself gradually and with effort, but because of the original vows of the Bodhisattvas and all the Tathagatas who have devoted their merits and identified their lives with all animate life that all may be emancipated, they are not without aid and encouragement . . . The good non-outflowings

[12] Shantideva: De Bary (1969), p. 85.
[13] *Lankavatara Sutra* 9: Goddard (1970), p. 328.

that come with self-realization of Noble Wisdom is a purification that comes instantaneously by the grace of the Tathagatas.[14] Correspondingly, the Christian declaration that it is by the grace won through Jesus that believers are set upon the right way, and endowed with the gifts of the Spirit, does not deny that it is by personal choice and dedication that the way is walked: 'You must work out your own salvation in fear and trembling; for it is God who works in you, inspiring both the will and the deed, for his own chosen purpose.'[15] Far too much conversation between Christians and Buddhists is at cross purposes, with both sides regularly suspecting the other of identical errors. Buddhists suppose that the term 'God' can refer only to the powers whom Gotama defeated, the self-complacent principalities by whom injustice is sanctified and suffering increased. Christians suppose that Nirvana is a nihilistic concept, a wholesale rejection of personal existence. To the Christian, the Buddhist life is a selfish retreat; to the Buddhist, the Christian life is a childish clinging to forms which ought to be understood only as partial images of the One Original. Both sides are inclined to boast that they are the most 'materialistic' of the great religions, the most concerned with ordinary life. There seems little hope of sensible conversation between bearers of these different traditions before we have tried to sort out what we all mean by 'personal existence', 'God', or 'Buddha-nature'.

That there is some congruence between the traditions is confirmed by what they take to be the core of the spiritual life. In the Mahayana tradition enlightenment comes with the realization that it has come already, that there is nothing more to be obtained. The Christian is urged, when she prays, to believe that her prayer is already answered. There is, admittedly, a clear problem for both traditions: on the one hand, if the world as it now is is the best we can hope for our condition is poor indeed; on the other not everything that we pray for is, in our experience, received. But it remains true in

---

[14] *Lankavatara Sutra* 8: Goddard (1970), p. 326.
[15] Paul, Philippians 2: 12 f.

experience that there is a change in our mode of consciousness, in our mood, in the quality of our life-world, if we can
only bring ourselves to thank God for His presence, or
acknowledge the Buddha-nature in the things around us. It is
by thankfulness, acceptance, that our eyes are opened to a
source of life that never thereafter wholly vanishes (though
there may be dry spells in waiting for us all). Whether this
is the 'same' experience for Buddhist and Christian is a
matter that cannot be settled here, chiefly because we have
no clear account of what it ever is to be 'the same experience'.
I remain convinced that both sides are attempting to deal
with the same reality, and making the same discovery about
it, that there is an Unborn and Indestructible, a quality of
life which is that of the Only-Begotten of the Father, full
of grace and truth. The fully enlightened may be in a position
to discriminate more accurately, to say that Milarepa or
St. Francis, Nagarjuna or Aquinas after all knew better: the
rest of us, on the foothills of the eternal mountains, must
find what friends we may.

One psychologizing interpretation of these two modes of
the 'spiritual life' would hold that neither God nor Nirvana
are anything but ideals, projections of human aspirations,
whose actual existence a sensible religiosity ought not to
require. Don Cupitt has travelled, via doubts about the
divinity of Christ, to a final rejection of the existential claims
of any theism. The religious or spiritual life is understood as
its own reward, a particular human project that does not
require (and in Cupitt's view would be damaged by) the real
existence of such ideal forms and figures. 'There cannot and
must not be any religious interest in any extra-religious
existence of God; such a thing would be a frivolous distraction.'[16] I shall not now discuss Cupitt's arguments for this
conclusion, which rest (in my view) on a series of logical
errors, and on uncritical acceptance of a materialist metaphysics. My point here is twofold: on the one hand, such an
interpretation of God and Nirvana could receive seeming

[16] Cupitt (1980), p. 9.

support from some idealistic strands of Buddhism. The principal effort of some Buddhist monks is to visualize the image of some god or Buddha with such strength and in such detail that the thing seems to stand there with as much presence as any item of consensus reality. It is then to be realized that all the phenomenal world is as much the product of creative imagination as that image: that neither the gods nor the world have any existence outside the Mind. It is easy to slip from this to a psychologizing claim such as Cupitt's, but the point (even here) is not the same. The Idealist school of Buddhism seeks to brings its scholars to a real understanding of the One Original by showing, as Berkeley tried to show, that the world of phenomena is held in being by Spirit, of the same kind as the spirit we can come to know ourselves to be. It did not intend Cupitt's sad reduction of the spiritual to a way of life, adopted for no clear reason by a bunch of hairless primates in a world destined for the fire: a vast pretence, a game for children. That world, the world defined by materialist science, is as clear a projection as the world of angels.

The second point worth emphasizing is that psychologizing interpretations of the great traditions must define them as innately opposed to each other. There is no such single thing as 'the spiritual life' when we consider merely human practices and ideals: there is the Islamic or the Theravadin or the Madhyamika or the Protestant or the Catholic life, between which we choose purely temperamentally, but which we cannot expect to agree. A realist interpretation is more ecumenical, since it postulates that all these traditions may be gesturing at the One Original. If this is so, we can consider whether Buddhist and Muslim and Christian and Sioux Indian may not have something to teach each other. We can compare and collate their reports, if we suppose that they are all about the same thing: the relation that our present consciousness should have to the powers of the spiritual realm, and the nature of those powers. As there is good reason to think that such a spiritual cosmology is really true, it would seem better to interpret both God and Nirvana realistically. How else shall we learn but by comparing the insights of our various traditions?

In taking this ecumenical line, of course, I am parting company with a long tradition of mutual vilification. I see no reason always to assume that non-Christians are devil-worshippers (consciously or unconsciously), non-Muslims idolaters, or non-Buddhists ignoramuses. But I do not wholly reject the thought that some spirits are not our friends: there are spirits whom it is death to worship or let into our lives, and their victims are to be pitied, whether they are solitary neurotics or whole societies dedicated to cruelty or vice. In making such a judgement, we must acknowledge also that our own lives, our folk-religion, even the faith of saints may fall into the power of just such demons. The dangers of the spiritual life are very great: so great that it is not surprising that honest men have sought to erect strong barriers against the possibility of ruin. If we devote ourselves to the duties of everyday life, and do not think too hard about the basis for our everyday beliefs we may be spared much trouble— unless that life and those beliefs are themselves the work of devils.

I have come back to the same difficulty that I faced in my first chapter, now cast in a new mode. Serious philosophers attempt to interrogate the 'featureless faces' who raise doubts about our capacities, the nature of the world, the grounds of our judgements. It is not unknown for philosophers to be trapped in one or other insane opinion, not seeing how to escape it. Similarly those who set themselves to remember their own spiritual nature, or to get in touch with those presences that make the world. If I am right, then our every effort at scientific understanding involves such an attempt to overhear the powers, and our social orderings embody or reflect those powers that Paul called angels and elemental spirits.[17] If, as seems most likely, these powers are not altogether our friends, it is necessary

[17] Paul, Galatians 4: 9; Ephesians 6: 12; Colossians 2: 10, 15.

to tread warily. Scholar and scientist and would-be saint all take the risk of being mistaken in the powers they follow. That risk we can believe is less if we can also believe that the One Original is something we can reach towards, that It assures us of Its help. But it is correspondingly easy to worship instead our image of the One Original, to make it a reflection of our wants, instead of being conformed into Its image. In such a trouble we can only pray to be assisted, hope that we are following the right way, confirm or correct our vision by careful hearing of our fellows' visions. 'I take refuge in the Buddha; I take refuge in the Dharma; I take refuge in the Sangha.'[18] The Buddhist's declaration of her faith, in her enlightened Lord, in the Doctrine or Law of Righteousness he preached, and in the community of those who have 'entered the stream', is not merely a formal analogy to the Christian confession. It defines the particular spiritual route through danger that Buddhists take: by spiritual discipline and moral action and faith in the Buddhas (or the single multiply-manifested Buddha) we may hope to achieve enlightenment, to become fountains of that joy for all creation. Similarly, Christians put their faith in the Father, in Jesus, in the Spirit that must animate the fellowship of all believers. In those I take refuge, not denying that another may be led to joy through her devotion to the Way made known by Gotama, and her honest prayers to that which lies beyond all appearance.

Belief, whether it is the commitment of scientists and scholars to the way of reason, or that of Christian enthusiasts, is a social phenomenon. To follow the way is to join with others, to share a form of life. Those who retire into their own particularities have no further share in the right way. The new life, whether for Christian or Buddhist, involves a real recognition of the lives of others, an understanding that one's own identity is not a solid and independent thing, set over against all others. The office of sound philosophy, as I have been urging throughout this work, is to counteract the

[18] Suzuki (1960), p. 14.

arguments of despair. Scepticism, relativism, indifferentism, reductivist materialism, solipsism, and the rest are not rationally inescapable options. On the contrary, serious attempts to think them through reveal that they constitute the death of reason. But the new life is not solely the product of argument, for argument can only lead to notional assent, not to the motion of the whole soul which Cardinal Newman named 'real assent'.[19]

It may seem strange to suggest that many people can summon up no more than a notional assent to such doctrines as the existence of other minds, or of a world not wholly alien. Surely our everyday affairs reveal that we are 'true believers'? David Hume, commenting on Pyrrhonian scepticism, was perhaps naïve in reckoning that no one could ever act out truly Pyrrhonian principles: 'All discourse, all action would immediately cease; and all men remain in a total lethargy, till the necessities of nature, unsatisfied put an end to their miserable existence. It is true; so fatal an event is very little to be dreaded. Nature is always too strong for principle.'[20] Hume was being naïve, both because true Pyrrhonists base themselves precisely on the compulsions exercised by Nature, 'so as not to be wholly inactive',[21] and because it is not unknown for people to sink into just such a lethargy:

For three days and three nights, Phaedrus stares at the wall of the bedroom, his thought moving neither forward nor backward, staying only at the instant. His wife asks if he is sick, and he does not answer. His wife becomes angry, but Phaedrus listens without responding. He is aware of what she says but is no longer able to feel any urgency about it. Not only are his thoughts slowing down, but his desires too. And they slow and slow, as if gaining an imponderable mass. So heavy, so tired, but no sleep comes.[22]

Whether Pirsig's account of his former self's descent into psychosis is to be explained as the effect of sceptical lethargy,

---

[19] Newman (1870), pp. 72 ff.
[20] Hume, *Concerning Human Understanding* 12. 128: (1962), p. 160.
[21] Sextus, *OP* 1; 23: (1933), p. 17.
[22] Pirsig (1974), p. 395.

solipsism, or indifferentism hardly matters. It is at least a state of mind to which only some of us come, though we may encounter moods like that. So was Hume right to think that most of us, at any rate, do genuinely believe in other minds, in the world, in the rules of reason?

When [the Pyrrhonian] awakens from his dream he will be the first to join in the laugh against himself, and to confess that all his objections are mere amusement, and can have no other tendency than to show the whimsical condition of mankind, who must act and reason and believe; though they are not able, by their most diligent enquiry, to satisfy themselves concerning the foundation of these operations, or to remove the objections, which may be raised against them.[23]

If Hume is correct, of course, in founding our conduct upon 'certain instinct',[24] then those who find themselves unable to disbelieve in God, though they lack any conclusive argument for the truth of their belief, may at least take comfort that no one else is in much better a case by rationalist standards. Someone who sets herself to believe only those propositions which are analytically true or which afford the 'best' explanations for the 'immediate' deliverence of sense-experience is adopting an incoherent epistemological project that may land her in the same state as Phaedrus. But I am not sure that Hume was right to suppose that most of us, most of the time, do genuinely believe.

The extremes of depression, when the victim may think she is being persecuted by other humans or by unseen spirits, or else that she is spreading a pollution, or has been abandoned, or has lost control of all her limbs, are distinctive and alarming enough for anyone who has ever encountered them not to forget. To argue someone out of such a state is wasted breath, however important it may be to explore such circles of our mania with true philosophic care. But it is not only the clinically depressed who live under a cloud. Most of us, or so I suspect, are familiar enough with the sense that everything

[23] Hume, *Concerning Human Understanding* 12. 128: (1962), p. 160.
[24] Wilmot, *Satires*, 64, lines 10–11: 'And before certain instinct will prefer Reason, which fifty times for one doth err . . .': (1964), p. 118.

we see is living behind a glass barrier, that we never really encounter anyone else, that our belief in other minds, in the past or the future, or the worth of reason is no more than a notional assent. If we were asked whether we believed in our friends' real existence, we would of course say that we did; probably we behave in acceptable enough ways towards our friends—though as Royce observes we very rarely behave as if we thought them as real as ourselves. Even our own existence is not so secure a thought as common sense would have us say. Most of us live in a mildly depressed state most of the time. If we always did, if we had never experienced any other life, we should not notice. So anyone who is inclined to deny what I have said should perhaps wonder whether this is because he is permanently in full appreciation of his neighbour's full reality, or whether perhaps he never has been!

Those who have never had the experience of waking up to feel the genuine reality of other minds, of the familiar world, of that One Original we worship, may agree with everything that the enlightened say (or some of it). No one who is not far gone in melancholia is likely to deny that there are other minds. Only those brave explorers of the soul called philosophers are prepared to spend much energy in analysing or expounding common truths. But assent remains merely notional without that overpowering presence to which we sometimes awaken. The experience of waking up is what is called enlightenment: I do not mean to suggest that there may not be many stages on the way, many partial awakenings, many other things which even the twice-born have not seen. Those who have, at some time, woken up to have a real sense of those truths to which we may have given a notional assent can we tell the difference.

Paradoxically, the enlightened may sometimes sound like solipsists, for they may say that they see everything as their own body. They feel everything with the same immediacy as we sometimes (not always) feel the bodies we usually consider ours. It is as if they were there in other minds and places. 'If you are awakened, the worlds in all directions, grass, trees, lands are perfected and at once are the true body of the pure light of the Tathagata.'[25] Traherne, speaking of his remembered infancy, seems to express something like the same point:

All things abided eternally as they were in their proper places. Eternity was manifest in the Light of the Day, and something infinite behind everything appeared . . . The streets were mine, the temple was mine, the people were mine, their clothes and gold and silver were mine . . . The skies were, and so were the sun and moon and stars, and all the World was mine; and I the only spectator and I enjoyer of it. I knew no churlish properties, nor bounds nor divisions: but all properties and divisions were mine: all treasures and the possessors of them.[26]

Berkeley too remarks, out of a similar awakening to the glories of the created universe, that he is the true possessor of a thing who enjoys it, not he that owns it.[27] Metaphors of possession, embodiment, or copulation abound in the literature of enlightenment. The enlightened have a real sense of what we can all, in some sense, know: that this body here, this individual cannot be broken from the greater whole.

This is not to deny the reality of persons, to say that what we experience of ourselves and our friends is an illusion: it is to reach a deeper understanding of what it is to be a person, to be a part of the creation. Shut up in our own particularities we are not persons at all.

Because the enlightened have a real sense of this, what they say may sound like a denial of reason: Buddhist writings in particular apparently reject the laws of non-contradiction and excluded middle—laws which are the condition for any intelligible discourse. Sometimes this must be read indeed as the reminder that a real awareness of the world may be impossible to convey in human speech—we are all, I hope, familar with those moments when words fail us—which is one of the sources of glossolalia, as well as of the remarkable

[25] Yampolsky (1971), p. 128.
[26] Traherne 3. 3: (1960), p. 110.
[27] Berkeley, *Essay on Pleasures*: (1948–56), vii. p. 195.

incoherence of lovers' conversation. But we should also be ready to see apparent rejections of the laws of logic rather as denials of some common application: when the Buddha refuses to say whether Nirvana does exist or doesn't, whether there are selves or there aren't, he is not merely refusing to deal with issues that do not lead to edification, but pointing to some obscurity or confusion in the concepts of existence or selfhood. It is not the formal laws, but our concepts that are doubtful.

With this warning, I turn to the major issue between the Buddhist and the Christian traditions of enlightenment, as these have been commonly understood. Is the One Original to be found wholly in our awakening to a sense of unity with all the world, or is there something else to which that union points? Traherne again: 'Had any man spoken of it, it had been the most easy thing in the world, to have taught me, and to have made me believe that Heaven and Earth was God's House, and that He gave it me.'[28] Traherne did not claim that he was aware, in childhood, of the LORD Jehovah, but only that it would have been an easy and natural step to grasp the whole world of his possession as a present from One still greater. Buddhists are commonly supposed to rest content with the 'monistic' vision, unaware that Cosmos and Creator are eternally distinct. It is supposed that only in the theistic vision is a genuinely personal life preserved, a confrontation between separate spirits. But it is far from clear that this contrast is correct. On the one hand, Buddhists need not be understood as denying the reality of personal existence: the new life is the life of sharing, the realization that 'there is no I without a We',[29] that the Self is not a solid. Similarly, there is no assertion that the One Original has no other being than the life of this world. On the other hand, Christian theories of the Trinity or the Atonement must cast doubt on any attempt to make our individuality a solid thing, or to identify the LORD with a particular

[28] Traherne 3. 8: (1960), p. 114.
[29] See Clark (1975), p. 193.

existent. If both sides are agreed that the One Original is strictly incomprehensible, known to us only in metaphor and in obedience to Its way, it seems a little strange that either side should then insist that It is 'really' more like a Person than a Place, more like a Place than a Person. The best that can be said is that the experience of unity points toward that thing.

More could undoubtedly be said about Buddhists and Christians. I hazard no opinion here, for example, whether Christians can regard the Buddhist Way as an alternative path to salvation, or must instead suppose that it is only by the grace of our LORD Jesus Christ that Buddhists, Muslims, animists achieve the end. Nor do I offer any opinion as to whether Buddhists might regard Jesus of Nazareth as at least a bodhisattva. I am sure only that it is time we talked seriously to each other, without assuming too readily that we understand each other's slogans, and that the Ways are not as unlike each other as propagandists have contended.

Instead, I wish to consider why it is that Enlightenment, the Holy Spirit, visionary knowledge of this world and the next, should so often be assumed to stand in opposition to the way of academic reason. Why is it that those who, with good reason, believe that they have been touched by the Spirit, given grace by the Buddhas, shown the truth, are so often assumed to have rejected 'reason'?

The first reason might be this: that the metaphysics required to make sense of such an event are themselves beyond rational belief. Anyone who seriously thinks that an emotional spasm, even if it issues in a change of life, can be regarded as a message from the Spirit-world, must believe in that world. But it is now commonly assumed that such a belief is unreasonable, and that the mere experiences of the visionary cannot be adequate evidence for it. Better regard them as moods, spasms, delusory experiences, to be explained by neurophysiologists when the science is mature. But, if I am right that materialist metaphysics of the kind now popular amongst the half-baked is self-destructive, and that the real existence of the Spirit-world constitutes a good, perhaps the best or only, explanation of our epistemological success (and a good reason to believe that we are successful), then we can no longer dismiss inspiration as a freak event. The metaphysics required to make such inspiration credible is not itself unreasonable.

A second, related charge against the Spirit-filled, is that they adopt other beliefs that seen absurd, whether it be in the existence of evil spirits or the inerrancy of Scripture. Once again, not all these beliefs can be so easily dismissed. A belief in evil spirits, for example, seems to me a far more rational response on any theist's part than plaintive references to the mysteriousness of life. Others of these supposed beliefs are not, in fact, inspired in many of the Spirit-filled. They may be found there, and they may be errors (we have no assurance that enlightenment immediately drives away all error). If they are errors, and can be shown to be such, there seems no reason in principle not to enlighten those who are in error: but it would be exceedingly arrogant to suggest that one such error invalidates all the knowledge claimed by the enlightened.

A third and more important charge is this: that the supposedly enlightened have adopted utterly abhorrent moral attitudes. If it can be shown that a considerable number of those who believe themselves to have undergone a spiritual transformation also believe that women should never take positions of authority over men, that races should not inter-breed, that the earth and its non-human inhabitants are there to be despoiled, that unbelievers are damned or that it is proper to try and exorcise someone who expresses an honest disagreement with the group—then there should at least be some doubt as to what spirit it is that is moving amongst them. The beliefs I have mentioned, of course, are to be found amongst a sizeable number of Christian enthusiasts. Belief in black magic, the possibility of cancelling one's sins by appropriate ritual action, in the inferiority of women, Muslims, and dogs may also be found amongst a sizeable number of South-East Asian Buddhists who have stepped 'into the stream'. It would not be all that difficult to devise similar lists of strange and rationally abhorrent moral beliefs to be found amongst middle-of-the-road Anglicans, Soviet bureaucrats, or biological scientists. We are all subject to judgement, and as likely as anyone to have unthinkingly adopted the morals of our tribe. The abhorrent beliefs that are to be found amongst the 'twice-born' are not held by all of them; I have some doubt whether they are even held by a very much higher proportion than of the population at large (particularly when account is taken of class-distinctions, age, and education). But it must be admitted that the new confidence that comes to the enlightened may spill over into other areas of their life, not altogether to a good effect. Those who have made a real assent to one thing, may incline to feel that anything which they strongly feel (or which they suppose is strongly felt by others) is a message of the LORD. That is one very good reason for insisting that we do not go apart into our own particularities, nor into schism. We must check our convictions, bring them up before the judgement of our fellow-believers, praying that we be guided to a true enlightenment.

And that introduces the fourth, and crucial, claim: it is supposed that those who think of themselves as enlightened or as Spirit-touched, are prepared to go against the rules of reason. Those are well enough for the ignorant, but true knowledge lies in overpassing human reason. We need not be afraid to speak in contradictions, nor do we need any longer to apportion our belief to the evidence. The laws of logic and of sound epistemology alike are scorned. Is this not unreason, and must it not be rejected?

Laws of non-contradiction and excluded middle are necessary to any programme of intelligible speech. Without their aid they cannot even be denied: one who doubts that the assertion of $p$ entails the denial of non-$p$, cannot even deny the law of non-contradiction and expect it to stay dead; But two points need to be made: (1) as I remarked earlier, it is difficult to apply the law—what seem like a pair of contradictory statements may turn out to be compatible under some hitherto-unimagined condition; (2) adherence to the law rests upon the faith that reality is indeed amenable to human discourse. This belief, like other fundamental intellectual postulates, cannot be demonstrated. Reason rests on faith.

Epistemological rules are also difficult to articulate or prove: 'Clifford's Rule'[30] that one should never believe anything without adequate evidence, turns out to be self-defeating as well as sceptical in effect—since no statement can be accepted without showing that it is the best explanation for some datum, and neither the claim nor the datum can be accepted without further evidence, and so for ever. 'Chisholm's Rule',[31] that we should continue to believe what we naturally do until sound evidence turns up to the contrary, is a better bet—although it rests uneasily upon the concept of a natural belief. In short, as I have been arguing, the life of reason (including philosophical reason) rests upon convictions that we cannot further justify. It is the mark of reason to know that not all things can be proved by reason: 'The starting point of reasoning is not reason itself but something greater. What then could be greater than rational knowledge or the human intellect but God?'[32] The practice of enlightenment which the great pagan enthusiast from whom I have just quoted called the theoretic life rests upon our being enlightened, awakened, illuminated, transformed into our proper selves by the light from outside: 'Those being brought to their completion need not to learn but to suffer something.'[33] The twin paths of *pathein* and *mathein* are only with difficulty disentangled, for even learning rests upon interior convictions brought about in response to the attraction exercised by God on all the cosmos. The Master of them that know, Aristotle of Stageira, whom I have been

---

[30] Clifford (1901), ii. 163 ff. See chapter six.
[31] Chisholm (1957), pp. 9 ff.
[32] Aristotle, *Eudemian Ethics* 8. 1248a27 ff.
[33] Aristotle, fr. 45 Rose: see Clark (1975), p. 190.

quoting and paraphrasing, knew very well that Reasoning could not manage by itself.

Philo, so it seems, went further: the path of learning was a second best, and the best way to know God is through direct inspiration.[34] That may be so, although we need to follow also those laws of carefulness that God has set in our hearts. But my conclusion here need only be that the path of inspiration, real assent, is not at variance with the life of reason. The faith of philosophers, unexpressed and ironical as it may sometimes be, is this: that God and the World are not alien to us, and that we are called to follow out our intuitions, to explore the possibilities as members of a continuing tradition.

A close study of early Greek intellectual history divulges that rational philosophy, in which the Greek philosophers put their trust, ultimately derived its impetus from inspiration: sages, prophets and poets. It is illuminating also to note that the inspired prophet-poet-sage was the prototype of the first philosophers, a point modern philosophers and historians of ancient philosophy do not always seem to cherish.[35]

Reasoning does not bring us to a real assent, but real assent is only possible or proper where our intellect also consents. Logic and the laws of evidence are, as it were, the chastity of the intellect: but our intellectual virtue is not tarnished by a lawful marriage to its rightful Lord.

The Gifford Lectures were established in the hope of encouraging the spread of a 'true and felt knowledge' of the One Original. Nothing that I have said can be expected to have induced such real assent. Probably, even your nominal assent cannot be counted on. I hope, at any rate, that I have persuaded you that there are sound reasons to expect that something like the Spirit-world is real, and that purported experiences of enlightenment or rebirth or baptism are not to be dismissed too lightly. Philosophy is not the enemy of faith: if we permit it, it will lead us to that place from which we see that Love which moves the sun and other stars.

---

[34] Dey (1975), pp. 31 ff.
[35] Chroust (1978), p. 54.

# 6

# The Rules of Reason Revisited

My Gifford lectures, which form the first part of this book, were an attempt to show the epistemological and other advantages of a serious, metaphysical theism. I have argued that the scholarly and scientific enterprise depends, in practice, on the assumption that the universe is built according to principles that we can understand, of which we have some prior awareness, and that the truth about things is worth discovering. I have, on the other hand, opposed the ancient tradition of vilifying those who 'disagree about an iota'. It is important that we should seek to understand the terminology and methods of those traditions within which human beings have sought enlightenment. By doing so we may at last, with God's good help, come to understand our own. 'It cannot be that there is one way only to so great a mystery', said Symmachus[1] in opposition to the bigots of his day, and it is in that proposition itself that we may find a further clue to the real nature of intellectual virtue.

At the same time I have poured some scorn on those investigators who have imagined that it is easy to set out the rules of evidence, to define what sort of thing ought to be believed by 'reasonable people'. In the following chapter I shall discuss this problem more fully, and hope at least to lay the foundations for a reputable ethics of belief. Before doing so I should re-emphasize that any merely materialistic or naturalistic metaphysician must have considerable difficulty in accommodating any rules of evidence. If what I think is the echo or epiphenomenon merely of material processes, so that my thought is what it is because my neural chemistry is what it is, it seems very difficult to see

[1] Symmachus, *Relatio* 3. 10: (1883), p. 282.

how that thought can be one that I ought to have or ought not to have. It might of course be better (because more accurate?) if I did, or if I did not, but I can be under no obligation to have it, whether because it is true or because it 'follows' from other thoughts of mine, any more than I have an obligation to cause my heart to beat. My thoughts 'follow' from other thoughts only in the sense that the causal processes which accompany them, or which (on the strictest materialist interpretation) we misdescribe as 'thoughts', take place in ways that can be duplicated in test-tubes, and partially understood. True and consistent materialists ought not to claim that their arguments are ones which anyone ought to accept, or which anyone has any reason to think are true-in-fact. Materialism generates pragmatic relativism, and this in turn renders the materialist hypothesis a mere fable.

My concern here is with the rules of reason, with what we are inclined to reckon that reasonable people ought to believe —leaving aside the question of how they can be obliged to believe or do anything. The swiftest, most rigorous answer, is that we ought to believe what we have good reason to believe is true—but what does that mean? On one inter-pretation it merely says that we ought to believe to be true what we have an obligation to believe to be true—which is probably correct, even if it constitutes a null-class! What is it to believe, and what is it to have good reason to believe? Is the fact, or my fancy, that I shall be, or that everyone will be, happier if I believe $p$ a good enough reason for believing $p$? This must, presumably, be the real opinion of utilitarian thinkers, who ought to acknowledge that we have no good reason to accept their supposed arguments for the truth of utilitarianism unless it is likely that we shall thereby maxi-mize happiness. Nor should we accept that this is likely unless so doing so maximizes happiness, and nor should we accept this unless . . . A more credible variety of utilitarian thought might decree that we ought to adopt those rules of evidence whose adoption and application would in general serve to maximize happiness: we should not believe *p* merely because doing so will make everyone happier, but because it is required by rules general obedience to which will make everyone happier (or obtain whatever net increase in happiness the utilitarian requires).

Such utilitarian argument at least takes the problem seriously and it is possible to devise some argument for the thesis that it would, by and large, be better if people tested their beliefs for truth and accepted them only in so far as they were rationally preferable (whatever that means in detail) to the available alternatives. Failure to do this will accumulate potentially misleading beliefs that may someday cost us dear. But it is notorious that there are imaginably true beliefs which ought, for the sake of happiness, to be suppressed. Those who have travelled with me so far may consistently believe that no truth should be the occasion for despair, for giving up all hope of happiness. But without such a metaphysical and mystical backing there seems no 'good reason' to expect that all truths, all the claims validated by the procedures of rationalist or empiricist enquiry, will prove to be bearable. Is it really obvious that those communities that test their beliefs, or affirm only what follows from prior beliefs, with a view to 'truth', are generally happier than those communities which maintain established creeds by subterfuge and propaganda and poetry? Tribesmen may believe only what they have good reason to believe—but their 'good reasons' may simply be that they were instructed in their initiation ceremonies, or that they have dreamt, or that 'everyone agrees'. The question whether they could have been instructed so, or dreamed, even though the creed was 'really false' probably does not arise—any more than most people in our society are much exercised by the thought of extra-terrestrial demons who delight to deceive us. The question doubtless occurs to some believers, who must then seek out some story which explains why initiation ceremonies or dreams can be expected to match 'the truth', or else admit that they were not really interested in the truth, but in social security.

Such an admission as the latter, of course, involves a certain perversity, To say that one does not care whether what one says is really true is not merely a request that no one else ever again take one's words seriously: it is to abandon reasonable speech entirely. That truth matters (even if it is not the only thing that matters) is one of the central values of any language-user. Imagine for a moment what it would be to deal with a race of creatures who did not aim at truth in their speaking, for whom language was merely 'verbal music'. We would not understand their speech as speech at all. This is not to say, as Kant seems to have said,[2] that all deliberate failures to speak truth and nothing but the truth are treasonable. It does mean that if we are to continue on the way of reason we must acknowledge truth as a value independent of the greater happiness (unless this latter is so understood as to incorporate the value of knowing and speaking truth).

Accordingly, we have to admit that a good reason for believing $p$ is that it is true, and that the procedure by which we have come to believe that it may reasonably be expected to 'track' truth:[3] the procedure would not have led us to this belief unless it really was true. This is not to deny that there may be other good reasons not to believe that very thing, or not to have engaged upon that procedure. If a jealous husband were to investigate his wife's career he might come to believe, might even accurately and properly believe, that his wife was or had been unfaithful: it might still be the case, and he might hold it to be the case, that he ought not to start the investigation, and ought (if at all possible) to forget the result.

So perhaps we can rephrase the first rule of epistemological ethics as follows: 'we ought, unless there are countervailing reasons of prudence or charity or fidelity or the like, to believe all and only what is confirmed by procedures that we have good reason to believe do track the truth'. What

---

[2] Kant (1949) pp. 346 ff.
[3] This is a term we owe to Nozick, though the concept is one that is implicit in much epistemological work.

those procedures might be is a problem to which I shall return. Before doing so, I should point out some of the oddities of this claim, which is of course considerably weaker than 'Clifford's Rule'. The latter allows no other duty to stand in the way of pure truth-seeking, pure reliance on the established procedures. To this, William James made the appropriate retort:

If we had an infallible intellect with its objective certitudes, we might feel ourselves disloyal to such a perfect organ of knowledge in not trusting to it exclusively, in not waiting for its releasing word. But . . . if we believe that no bell in us tolls to let us know for certain when truth is in our grasp, then it seems a piece of idle fantasticality to preach so solemnly our duty of waiting for the bell.[4]

Sometimes we have to act either on the assumption that $p$ is true, or that not-$p$ is true, and have no final or perfect ground for dismissing either option. We must choose which proposition we intend to follow, without restricting the intellectual right of our fellows to choose the contrary. Sometimes, as in the case of the overly jealous husband, we had better not find out what would be believed by a disinterested enquirer: it is not always right to be disinterested; it is not always right to expose ourselves to the risk of despair or anger.

If the search for truth in obedience to established procedures is only one value we cannot reasonably demand that it be pursued at all times and places without regard to other values, whatever they may be. With this necessary proviso, Clifford's Rule seems more plausible. But what is its own status? If we ought (*ceteris paribus*) to believe all and only what is confirmed by procedures that we have good reason to believe do track the truth, ought we to believe this modified version of Clifford's Rule? Is it confirmed, by just such procedures, that those who follow it are likely to track the truth, to believe more true claims and fewer false claims than they would if they followed some other rule? It may seem obvious that this is so: if they follow procedures which they

4 James (1897), p. 30.

do not have good reason to believe do track the truth, the number of accurate 'guesses' they make will be a matter of chance. Only by finding out which procedures track the truth can we have any confidence (as far as their truthfulness goes) in the procedures we use. But this is a confusion: that a procedure does track the truth is not the same fact as that we have good reason to suppose that it does. Many procedures may track the truth that we have never thought of, or that we have dismissed. If we follow unusual procedures it may well be that we will end by affirming genuine truths that could not be confirmed by the established rules. If we keep to these latter we may be spared errors at the expense of losing truths. The sceptic who will never agree that a claim has been finally established may think that she has made no positive mistake, for she has never risked error: she has also lost the chance to find a truth.

Following all and only those procedures which are already established as truth-tracing may well be a recipe for intellectual stagnation even if the procedures genuinely do track truth (that is, they confirm only what is true-in-fact, although they fail to confirm other truths).[5] But how shall we establish that they do? We are to accept only what is confirmed by procedures with the property of expectably confirming only what is true: that is, we are to accept only what is confirmed by procedures with the property of expectably confirming only what is confirmed by those same procedures. This is either unhelpful (for all procedures can presumably be counted on to confirm what they themselves confirm) or arbitrary (for what have these procedures done to be selected as the standard of excellence?). Slightly more content can be built into the rule if we suppose that what is required is not merely coherence at a given time (the procedure should not simultaneously confirm and disconfirm the claim being tested), but consistency over time (the procedure should not dismiss today what it confirmed yesterday)—but if we build this requirement into our epistemology, stagnation

[5] Feyerabend (1975), pp. 41 ff.

is certain. We should be reduced to procedures that never rejected what they had once affirmed, never determined that the Earth went round the Sun or that chemical elements were transmutable.

If the modified version of Clifford's Rule is to have any usable content we must build a neutral description of the recommended procedures into it. We ought, *ceteris paribus*, to accept all and only what is confirmed by rational deduction from established truths or empirical investigation of explanatory hypotheses (i.e. proposed explanations of established truths that have further, investigable, consequences). This Rule, of course, is not itself a claim that can be confirmed like this: rather, it establishes the framework, it expresses an epistemological policy that differs from certain imaginable other policies. These latter include the following: (1) accept all and only what is confirmed by the Azande poison-oracle; (2) accept all and only what can be clearly and coherently conceived; (3) accept all and only those naturally-arising beliefs that have not yet been finally disconfirmed (as that there are other people in the world and events before our births).

The last option in this list approaches what I have called Chisholm's Rule, and has its own weaknesses: what, for example, is to count as a naturally-arising belief? Before examining it in more detail, what more can be said about Clifford's Rule, as I have expanded it here? Two general modes of confirmation are allowed: the deductive and the inductive (where the latter involves a search for the 'best explanation' of other established claims—and how neutral is that notion?). Clearly, neither mode can get started without some initially established claims to serve either as the first premises of the deduction or as the explananda of the induction. Whence do they receive their warranty? Aristotle, not unreasonably, concluded that not everything can be a matter for proof, that some things are perceived or intuited without further evidence. Unfortunately, neither logical self-evidence nor indubitable sense-perception seems sufficient to generate the starting-points of reasonable enquiry. We cannot deduce much of interest about the world merely from logical truism, and we cannot even (so it turns out) express what it is we 'immediately perceive' without recourse to concepts and beliefs that are not strictly self-evident. I would certainly be inclined to say that I am now perceiving certain things-in-the-world (as a video monitor, a computer keyboard, a small turquoise frog, a pickled gherkin), but generations of empiricists have taught us that what I 'really' see are coloured shapes for which I find the 'best' explanation in a story about the material universe (though how any material events at all can strictly explain the mental is a matter on which I shall be commenting in my next chapter). This phantasmagoria of coloured shapes has, in its turn, been worn away: how can any of the words I use to describe things-in-the-world be reapplied to momentary images? To be red is to be the colour of blood and British pillar-boxes as these are regularly perceived by creatures of my kind: 'red' is not the name of a private sensum, the ineffable somewhat that I sometimes have and am inclined to associate with the sight of pillar-boxes.

The apparent impossibility of either describing phenomena as they ineluctably appear to me or of moving from claims about them to claims about the common world has convinced most philosophers that knowledge cannot be founded on the sort of indisputable self-evidence that Clifford's Rule seems to require. We cannot restrict ourselves to those beliefs that are either 'self-evident' or deduced from what is 'self-evident', or offer the 'best' explanation of what is 'self-evident'. The attempt to do so results either in self-deception or in total scepticism. Even if we acknowledge that some claims are such that no one who understands them can rationally deny them (as that it is impossible for any complete proposition to be simultaneously true and false), nothing can usefully be deduced from claims like that: in so far as they are true in all possible worlds they are compatible, precisely, with any possible state of affairs, and cannot tell us which possibility is realized in fact. Even if we agree, for the sake of argument, that phenomena can be accurately described without making any additional hypotheses about their causation the attempt to do so would, precisely, result in descriptions that would be compatible with indefinitely many imaginable explanations, and would therefore not allow us to select any one of those explanations as 'the best'.

Most philosophers, accordingly, have come to suggest that we can only begin our enquiries from within the shared world of our common experience. We do not have to (for we cannot) deduce or rationally infer what is the true state of things: we are already equipped with a complex theoretical understanding of bodies, and times, and causes, and intentional acts. If we are to follow the path of rational enquiry at all we have to begin from where we are: as higher animals whose ancestors equipped themselves with models of reality that enabled them to reproduce their own kind. Other creatures, imaginably, have other realms and understandings: we are mammals, primates, tool-users, and social individuals. Our grasp of what is to be believed includes far more than the merely logical or the merely phenomenal. Even infants have some grasp of such unobvious truths as the continuity of material existence (that material objects do not exist discontinuously) or the personal benevolence of their huge parents. We can only advance if we take this framework as a secure home, something to be repaired and modified, but not something that needs to be rebuilt from scratch.[6]

So Clifford's Rule can only work on the assumption of a shared theoretical realm, such that we seek explanations and make inferences only within the broad context provided by mammalian evolution. Briefly, it must be modified into agreement with Chisholm's Rule: we ought to abandon only such beliefs as turn out to be incompatible with central tenets of our common universe of theory. We ought to accept naturally-arising beliefs until there is sound reason to reject them (they form inconsistent triads, or engender

[6] See Clark (1982a), pp. 1 ff.

regularly disappointed expectations, or strike us as sufficiently inelegant as to be at odds with our inmost theories even if not strictly incompatible with them). On this account we need not establish that there really are no extraterrestrial demons before we can reasonably claim to know anything: the onus is on those who would dispute our ordinary convictions to show that there is good reason to think that there really are such bogles.

Unfortunately, this epistemological model has its troubles too. Are we really so sure that there is one shared world of theory, one set of beliefs that we can regard as 'natural' even for all creatures with whom we have some chance of conversing? Some may hold that

to humanity God is a fact as primitive, an idea as inevitable, a principle as necessary as are the categorical ideas of cause, substance, time and space to our understanding. God is proven to us by the conscience prior to any inference of the mind; just as the sun is proven to us by the testimony of the senses prior to all the arguments of physics. We discover phenomena and laws by observation and experience; only this deeper sense reveals to us existence.[7]

Others may reckon this idea a product of priestcraft, or acknowledge that it is a 'natural' one, one that creatures of our mammalian kind might be expected to have, but one that is so clearly a projection of the social experience in which young mammals come to be as to be easily dismissed.

Others again may find it 'natural' to think the external female genitalia ugly, dirty, and dangerous. It is indeed alarmingly clear that large sections of the human race think exactly that, and respond by excising them. It is supposed that the only way to preserve female 'chastity' is to protect women against their own ungovernable urges by cutting out their root. Once such a tradition is established it becomes a part of the 'way of our ancestors', to be defended against 'Western liberal' interference, and all too often forced upon the young by older women who have, for their own sanity's sake, to believe the operation vital to personal purity and

[7] Proudhon (1970), p. 72.

social order.[8] Psychoanalytic or sociological explanations for this syndrome may, in their turn, imply that this is a perverse or 'unnatural' belief, one that requires some special explanation, one that human beings 'as nature meant them to be' would not develop.

In brief, the notion that we must take our start in epistemology from a set of unprovable but not self-evident propositions that are the ones 'anyone would take for granted' either dissolves into social relativism of the familiar kind or else rests upon a strong notion of 'the natural' which cannot be equated simply with 'what happens'. Finding a secure base for epistemology in 'the natural' seems as forlorn a hope as to find it in the logically indisputable or in the ineluctable testimony of the senses. Westerners tend to think it 'natural' or 'obvious' to believe that there are separable material substances that cause us to perceive the world as made up of separate, individual beings. This notion is itself vulnerable to philosophical attack,[9] but the least that can be said against it is that not every human being nor every human society finds this so natural a thought. Westerners used to think it 'natural' and 'obvious' that there was a God, as even David Hume acknowledges.[10] If even these central dogmas of our tribe are suspect, and optional, how can we require that investigators stay within the bounds of common sense?

One answer is to abandon any such requirement. Investigators are entitled to any hypothesis they care to adopt, and no rules can be given for what should or should not be believed. Feyerabend has argued at length that what is generally regarded as scientific progress would have been severely curtailed if investigators had been confined by any of the standard rules. His 'solution' is simply to acknowledge the strength of Mill's argument for liberty of thought and expression: 'anything goes', and all investigators must stake their lives and fortunes on their gratuitous preference for

---

[8] Tevoedjre *et al.* (1980), pp. 6 ff.
[9] See Clark (1983*b*).
[10] Hume, *Dialogues* Part 12: (1976), pp. 244 f.

this project or for that.[11] What the world is becomes, for this perspective, as unfathomable a question as what the world ought to be (on modern assumptions about the irrationality of morals). There is a pleasing irony about this proposal, whereby the notion of 'facts' or 'scientific facts' that has been employed in deliberate contrast to the supposedly fluid and inarguable realm of 'values' itself dissolves into the sea of dreams. If there are no good grounds for finally preferring one policy to another, then there are no good grounds for preferring one research programme or one theory to another. What is to be believed is a matter of private decision —and so nothing is strictly to be believed at all.

This latter conclusion follows very easily: if we agree that there is no final reason to prefer one theory to another, that what is to be believed is as personal a matter as half-baked relativists believe 'what is to be done' to be, then we agree that there is no final reason to believe even this much. To believe something, strictly speaking, is to believe that it is true: to believe, that is, either that it is true-in-fact or, at the very least, that it is a thing to be believed (assuming the anti-realist account of truth to be acceptable). But if we deny that there is any final reason to believe anything, or any of the first-order claims we normally affirm, we are denying that these claims are things to be believed—and so we can no longer coherently claim to believe them. I cannot coherently say 'I believe $p$, but not that it's true'.

So long as we are unaware that there are any alternatives to the present consensus about life, the universe, and everything, these problems need not concern us. We can swim within our little pools and not wonder if there are oceans out of sight. Once the thought has occurred to us it will do no good to insist that we have no choice, that there is a particular set of beliefs that 'all of us' would accept if only we were not corrupted by false philosophy. We cannot retrieve our innocence, though we can pretend to it. On the other hand, if we follow Feyerabend into the

[11] Feyerabend (1975, 1981).

trackless wastes it seems that we must cease strictly to believe anything, including this whole tale of trackless wastes.

Epistemological rules cannot require us to believe all and only what is 'proved by reason' or established by 'the testimony of the senses', both because the rule is pragmatically self-refuting and because nothing worth believing can be proved by reason or the senses. At first sight it seems plausible to suggest that we are entitled to believe what comes naturally, a set of 'basic beliefs', unless and until some argument is produced against them. But there seems to be no agreed list of such basic beliefs, and though we might be able (question-beggingly) to argue that some beliefs are just what would be expected in (say) terrestrial mammals (and therefore 'natural' to us), this very argument leads to a profound suspicion of those very same beliefs. Unless we have reason to believe that 'naturally arising beliefs' are likely to be largely accurate, we can feel no reasoned confidence in the beliefs we find it natural to have. Pantheism, of course, is in practice the conviction that what comes naturally is right (and so leads to Protagorean relativism, that declares all appearances accurate). Naturalists of the modern kind, who hold that of the indefinitely many possible universes there happens to be one that allows for our existence and that things happen 'as chance would fall', have provided no such reason. Terrestrial mammals and (for example) hydrocarbon arachnoids from Jupiter could not be expected to have any thought in common,[12] and neither could have any grounds for thinking themselves in tune with truth. The only honest course is therefore to promote sceptical relativism, and so abandon reasoned speech.

Naturalism begets sceptical relativism, and this in turn begets silence. If there is to be any escape we must find some acceptable guidance in the sea of dreams, some way of discriminating between one thought and another, some ground for thinking that the rules of reason are not wholly false (though they may not be mechanically applicable).

[12] Cf. Clark (1975), p. 25.

One possible answer can be drawn from meta-ethical philosophy: in the absence of clear, finitely-statable moral rules of any plausibility whatsoever, moralists have proposed that we should not act 'as the rules dictate' but 'with a view to the good' or 'out of virtuous motives'. The former variant is usually no more than a cloak for the advocacy of one of the least plausible of general principles (that one should act so as to create the maximum amount of happiness), and the latter does find it difficult to isolate what it is to be a virtuous motive without recourse to the notion of action in accordance with the right rule.[13] There is, all the same, something to be said for their intuition, both in the strictly ethical and in the epistemological sphere. Rules describe, but do not determine the good life.

I emphasized in the last chapter the extent to which 'our thoughts' are an exhausting whirlwind far beyond our power to control. What we think, considered merely as the thoughts we have, often does not bear examination. Only those who have never attempted to organize their thoughts find it easy to believe that they themselves own those thoughts, or that they themselves are the very stream of thought. The self that awakens in me when I seek to contemplate the thoughts that arise in me, or float across me, is something other than the sea of thought in which I drown. Unless my life is wholly incoherent I must choose among those thoughts, and sometimes think that I bring new thoughts into being—but most of my thinking (where this means more than the mere having of thoughts) rests in selection, not in creation. If I were to write down all the thoughts that float momentarily across the inward eye the result would be nightmare (although it would also, I suspect, be very boring). So the question of what I am to believe (what anyone in my position is to believe?) amounts to the question, what route shall I follow or what thoughts allow to grow?

The discovery that in a real sense one's thoughts are not one's own, that they usually float in from some vast 'outside',

[13] Aristotle, *Nicomachean Ethics* 2. 1106b36 f.

need not of course be taken too literally (though I shall argue that it is more nearly accurate than naturalists allow). It is enough that our job is not to create new thoughts, but to select old ones, to follow 'the argument' where it leads, to refuse thoughts that have the wrong flavour. Following the argument, hunting down the trail, are metaphors familar to readers of Plato:[14] he meant them, I suspect, more literally than we might suppose. His travail was not the mechanical application of fixed rules, but the search for a half-remembered beauty, the bringing-to-birth of a new life (or the elimination of a still-birth).[15] Socrates' Daimon that warned him what not to do, what line not to follow, was how Socrates (it seems) experienced what all honest thinkers recognize in Clifford's splendid phrase: 'the still, small voice that whispers "Fiddlesticks!".[16] But daimons differ: how are we to recognize the true from the fraudulent, if we are not to follow any thought that comes into our heads?

Evagrios, one of the authors of the *Philokalia*, describes the demonic and angelic elements of thought, and the discriminations we must make between them: 'We can infer from the object appearing in the mind which demon is close at hand, suggesting that object to us . . . All thoughts producing anger or desire in a way that is contrary to reason are caused by demons.'[17] The point to notice here is not the realistic, causal explanation of our stray thoughts (though it is not a wholly unreasonable one), but the signs that Evagrios gives of thoughts that should not be pursued. To be 'contrary to reason' is to be productive of hatred or lust—or despair or ennui or megalomania. Angelic thought, on the other hand, 'is concerned with the true nature of things, and with searching out their spiritual essences'.[18] If Evagrios were a technically exact philosopher, of course, it would have

---

[14] Plato, *Republic* 4. 432b.
[15] Plato, *Theaitetos* 149; cf. Aristophanes, *The Clouds* 137.
[16] See Plato, *Apologia* 40; Plutarch, *De Genio Socratis* 588E ff, 592B.
[17] Palmer *et al.* (1979), i. 39.
[18] Palmer *et al.* (1979) i. 42. Plutarch, *De Genio Socratis* 589B, notes that the daimon of intellect has no need of nouns and verbs to convey enlightenment.

occurred to him to wonder whether he was providing criteria or definitions: is truth what angelic thought uncovers, or is angelic thought what uncovers truth? His answer, fairly clearly, would have been the latter: angelic thoughts, those thoughts and chains of thought that serve as messengers of the Most High, are our route to what-is. He was undoubtedly a realist, not a constructivist.

Similarly St John, who urged his friends not to trust any and every spirit, but to test them, whether they are from God.[19] His criterion was whether they acknowledged that Jesus Christ was come 'in the flesh', or (equivalently?) whether they showed love. St Paul offered a similar test:

You know how, in the days when you were still of the nations, you were swept off to those dumb images, however you happened to be led. For this reason I must impress upon you that no one who says 'A curse on Jesus!' is speaking in the spirit of God. And no one can say 'Jesus is Lord!' unless in the holy spirit.[20]

Paul goes on to insist that there are many gifts, but one spirit, and that the best way of all is love. All God's people must contribute to the building-up of the community by whatever gifts they are given (the word of wisdom or the word of knowledge or gifts of prophecy or discrimination or 'ecstatic utterance' or the ability to interpret it). None of these gifts is worth anything without the love of God, displayed in the congregation of all faithful people.

What precisely John and Paul intended by their insistence on the centrality of Jesus is a topic that I cannot discuss here. For the present it is enough to suggest that what they had in mind was this: only if God's Word and Wisdom have been perfectly embodied in a human life that convicts and can convince its audience do we have any assurance that our lives and thinking can embody truth. Those who had seen the word of life made visible, what was eternally known to the Father made known to beings in the world, declared it to all

---

[19] 1 John 4: 1 f.
[20] Paul, I Corinthians 12: 2 f.

who would listen 'so that you and we together may share a common life'.[21] John wished it acknowledged that the Word of which we may have some faint intellectual grasp (that lights every man) was come in the flesh, embodied in the life and works and teachings of his master. Paul wished it acknowledged that the man Jesus was sovereign over all thoughts and spirits, that nothing was to be accepted that ran counter to the challenge and judgement He presented.

So what rule of evidence can be distilled from this unexpected source? One reply—perhaps the safest—would simply be to deny that any rule was being given. Certainly any attempt to set up a doctrinal formula that could be used to determine what was or what was not to be believed would run counter to Paul's own insistence that the Law is only the deliverance of an angel, a messenger as much under judgement as any other, or John's insistence that what came through Jesus was 'grace and truth', *hesedh we'emeth*, not the Law.[22] Followers of the Buddha are similarly unwilling to say what the truth of enlightenment rests in, though willing enough to outline the right way towards it, a way that involves the rejection of rage, lust, and despair. What we ought to believe, the thoughts we ought to cultivate, are those which do not work against enlightenment, against the love of God, but there is no simple rule that can be operated by those who are not enlightened, not in the spirit. Meno's problem seems still to be with us: those who know the truth do not need to seek it out; those who do not know would not recognize it if they saw it.[23] Those who are enlightened or in the spirit need no rules to tell them what to believe and do; those who are not cannot operate any such rules without falling into error. Were I to suggest that one ought to believe all and only those things that 'serve for edification' it would be difficult to avoid implications of a kind that I have already mocked. Even more subtle attempts may lead to disaster.

[21] 1 John 1: 1-4.
[22] John 1: 17; see Kuyper (1964).
[23] Plato, *Meno* 80d5 ff.

If the enterprise of rational thought is to be conducted at all we need to deny Meno's premiss: it is a law of practical reason that we are capable of recognizing and being convinced, convicted, of the truth. The question that faces us is how we are convinced of truth, and how we are convinced that our convictions are, sometimes, reliable. It is also a law of practical reason that nothing is believable that would make it impossible for us to understand each other. Those who think cannot think that they alone, as individuals or as groups, can think and discover truth. Thoughts that get in the way of understanding companionship are outlawed. Thoughts that deny the objectivity of existence are also outlawed: those who let themselves think of others, of the world, merely in 'practical' ways, as the instruments of their desire or rage, are living a private dream. To see things 'as they are' is to put aside the instrumentalist temptation of seeing them 'as we find them useful'.

Care is necessary here. One of the most damaging of modern errors is the creed of indifferentism, the notion that to 'see things as they are' it is necessary to put aside all emotional involvement, not to care what happens. The result, in practice, is that researchers exalt their own selves and purposes over the purposes and beings of the things they study. Objective research comes to mean the habit of treating living beings merely as material for our own purposes.[24] Such supposed objectivity is merely idiocy, in the precise etymological sense: it is a turning aside to private fantasy, a refusal to share the common life or accept that one is oneself as much material for others as they are for us. Sound objectivity, of the kind that I am here outlining, is entirely otherwise. One ought to acknowledge what is in the world, the compresence of other conscious creatures; one ought to allow them the same right to be as one claims oneself, the right to develop and unfold their natures. One ought not to believe or cultivate such passing thoughts or chains of thought as restrict one's vision and respect.

[24] Clark (1977a), pp. 145 ff.

Those who do the Father's will shall know the doctrine: the vision of things that unfolds for those who set themselves to see things whole, as those things choose to be, is the delicate web that Buddhists have called Indra's Net, a web of diamonds that each reflect all other jewels in the web.[25] Or in a different tradition: Philo's vision of cosmic democracy, in which all creatures get their turn.[26] Or the Book of Job: 'Yahweh describes himself as the wisdom that makes for the survival of the wild ass, the hamster, the eagle, the ostrich, of all living nature, and the wisdom that uproots mountains and annihilates angels.'[27] To receive this vision of things, of all things in the world and of the world itself, is not to be indifferent, but to be awestruck, even while we also acknowledge the evils of this mortal life. What we ought to believe is what enables us to see and understand and love our company. Nature, *natura naturans*, 'the force that through the green fuse drives the flower', is known in us as Logos.[28] The force that drives us through the sea of dreams, if we let it, is that same spirit that has spread the world so wide and summoned it to grow.

Less rhetorically, not less truly, we can describe the world of nature, *natura naturata*, as the embodiment over time (and in recalcitrant material) of patterns that strike home to us as beautiful, as what we have always half-known. All research programmes are more than the accumulation of external facts, more even than the invention of fruitful hypotheses: they involve coming to be a certain sort of creature, a certain sort of person. False objectivity is encouraged in researchers by requiring them to do things that they could not do if they retained any 'emotional involvement' in the object or victim of their enquiries. True objectivity, the angelic understanding and sympathetic penetration of things-as-they-are, also

---

[25] See Chang (1972), pp. 165 ff.
[26] Philo, *Quod Deus Immutabilis* 176.
[27] H. M. Kallen, 'The Book of Job as Greek Tragedy': Glatzer (1969), pp. 17 ff.; see Clark (1983c).
[28] *Stoicorum Veterum Fragmenta*, ed. J. von Arnim (Teubner, Leipzig), 1903–5, ii. 714: Long (1974), p. 148.

requires moral discipline, an insistence on allowing others to unfold themselves, an effort to live out of love and respectful prayer.

What does this require in practice, and how can such an approach avoid the problems that bedevil other epistemological policies, Clifford's or Chisholm's Rule? That we are to hold in view a certain ideal of openness and willingness to be instructed does not require that we always demand formal proof of a suggestion before 'taking it on board'. Nor does it require us always, whatever the dangers to decency, to seek out what would be believed by wholly disinterested observers: it is not right always to be disinterested. It does not require us always to adopt the pessimistic assumption that appearances are deceptive, that nothing can be taken for granted. This may seem like proper scientific rigour when it encourages investigators to repeat well-known experiments in case of error, and tragi-comedy when it is the manifestation of obsessive jealousy (for which signs of affection are symptoms of a guilty secret!), but such pessimism is always corrosive. Never to let any conclusion lie may seem proper scientific method, but in reality such a policy would mean the death of science and scholarship, since every experimental result would be merely historical as soon as the result was 'known'. Proper method does not, because it cannot, rest in questioning everything and in never being content with any testimony. It must rest instead in the effort to take account of what is offered us, to trust the community of which we are a part, even though we also know that it is not infallible.

Clifford's Rule, to accept nothing that is not formally demonstrable, must lapse. Chisholm's Rule, to accept what comes naturally until it is rebutted, must be amplified by some substantial conception of 'the natural'. The ideal I am describing offers that. Epistemological decency rests in devotion to the principle that all testimony is valid in its place, that what-things-are must be allowed to unfold to the attentive intellect, that we should not follow any and every thought but only those that have the flavour of the world of intellect.

These rulings cannot be expressed as formal rules without subverting them: we must rely instead upon the informal understandings of those who grow up as initiates and students of divine wisdom. What is really natural to believe, what needs no formal proof, is what is an expression of the underlying Nature that manifests itself, as in a glass darkly, both as the wide world and as the theory, *theoria*, the sight of it.

So why should we not believe, for example, the creed of British Israel? What is it that makes that something which honest reasoners should not accept? The doctrine is that the British and American peoples, all those descended from the 'Anglo-Saxon' races of the north-western fringes of Eurasia, are in reality the ten 'Lost Tribes' of Israel, guided by divine providence through exile in Scythia to a haven in the islands of the west. The House of Windsor are the direct descendants of the House of David, and 'the English-speaking nations' are the central thrust of God's action on Earth, despite their continual back-slidings. 'Liberalism' is one finger of the hand of Satan, encouraging Israel to forget its God-given role as the ruler of all nations and its divinely-commanded obedience to the rules of Victorian morality. This system is supported by what usually strike the outsider as entirely fanciful etymologies and alleged archaeological discoveries that fill in the gap between the fall of the Northern Kingdom and the arrival of iron-age Celts and Anglo-Saxons in the British Isles. The movement's journal usually contains articles of an extremely right-wing character, denouncing welfare-statism, permissive sexual morality, immigration and miscegenation, and advocating the return of capital punishment. There are sometimes also articles, as there are in the journals of more 'left-wing' eccentrics, that detail supposed failings of Darwinian theory and supposed evidence of long-lost civilizations that preceded the Flood.

The natural reaction of anyone brought up in the ways of scholarship to all this is clear. The evidence that is supposed to require the hypothesis of a movement of peoples from captivity in Assyria all the way across Europe, leaving no clear trace of their passage in the records of surrounding peoples, strikes outsiders as wholly inadequate. Such agreed facts as British Israelites can produce are susceptible of other explanations that have a higher initial plausibility and can be checked by their further implications. To a scholarly outsider the historical claims made by British Israel are farcical, and of the same kind as talk of flying saucers, or Robert Graves's Triple Goddess and her minions, or Illuminati. Such stories appeal to people for various reasons: they give those without the patience or the opportunity to enter into the world of orthodox scholarship a sense of being part of a more interesting history than the boring one they think they remember from their schooldays. They give those without any real political power the sense that life and history is on their side, the chance of day-dreams (regularly reinforced by their fellow-believers' rhetoric) about vengeance on their presently successful enemies. In short, there is no difficulty about showing that the creed of British Israel is absurd and unacceptable within the framework of decent scholarship.

The trouble is that a believer will be sure to dismiss these proofs. Within the framework set by naturalistic history it would be highly unlikely that any group of peoples should be held together as a homogeneous whole over a thousand years of wandering; highly unlikely that people of true Israelite descent would be sifted out of the swarming masses of an age of migrations; highly unlikely that they should then be converted to a version of their ancestral creed. Within the framework of liberal theology it is highly unlikely that the LORD should rest so much weight on racial descent and purity, that He should require us to kill those who, as we think, break His laws, that the returned Messiah should turn out to be Elizabeth Windsor's great-to-the-$n$th-uncle. But the believer will retort that the God of Abraham is one that leads peoples by the nose, that He promised Abraham to make his descendants as the stars of heaven, and David that his throne should not fail. The Jewish people are the tribe of Judah only; Ephraim and Manasseh are the (white) nations of the British Commonwealth

and of the USA. In them the ancient promises are to be fulfilled. Those who think otherwise are ill-informed, backsliders,
limbs of Satan, not to be trusted. The contradictions that are
likely to occur to outsiders can be managed by any resource-
ful believer. Why should the ten northern tribes have anything
to do with the House of David, which they rejected back in
Rehoboam's day? Why should we suppose that God's providence, that sifted Ephraim from the migrating hordes, has
now failed to sift contemporary immigrants: if Celts and
Anglo-Saxons are Israelites, why aren't Pakistanis or West
Indians or Vietnamese 'Boat People'? If, on the other hand,
it is vanishingly unlikely that these groups have a common
racial origin more recent than Mother Eve, and contemporary
migrations are a matter of historical accident, why were
things so different in the first millennium AD? These are
obvious questions, but true believers will regard them only as
puzzles, not as refutations. What their solutions are I do not
know: the question that concerns me is what fundamental
'rule of reason' such believers violate. Why is it wrong to
argue as they do, to take biblical prophecy as evidence for
historical fact?

The sort of reasonings that I have described are not, of
course, confined to British Israelites, nor even to currently
unorthodox sectarians. Some—not all—sociobiologists have
a very similar style, and 'argue' to rather similar ethical conclusions ('women are bound to want to stay at home while
men earn money; authority figures are needed for a peaceable
society; violence and race-hatred are endemic in the human
species and can't be cured').[29] Everything that human beings
do, with the strange exception of the literary efforts of right-
wing sociobiologists, is done—though we know it not—to
further the survival of our genes: just so the British Israelite
would hold that human history (with the strange exception
of twentieth-century migrations) is directed to the multiplica-
tion of Abraham's genes. Where British Israelites argue from

---

[29] e.g. Wilson (1975), Fox and Tiger (1972). Dawkins (1976) is not himself
guilty of these offences, but has unfortunately been employed to similar ends.

(their interpretation of) certain biblical prophecies that things must have happened so, even though there is no extraneous evidence unamenable to alternative explanation that they did, so right-wing sociobiologists argue from (their interpretation of) neo-Darwinian theory that human beings must have evolved as sexist, racist, and over-aggressive. What we know from other sources of human history can be forced into the Israelitish model, or the 'sociobiological', but it does not have to be.

One of the features that mark both schools of thought is the lack of any sympathetic understanding of the possible alternatives. Such fanatics, of course, if they are intelligent and ingenious enough, may well uncover facts of reality that the rest of us may at last be glad to acknowledge. We have no inductive grounds for insisting that refusal to be refuted is always and everywhere a bad thing—though 'uneasy pedagogues' are nervous about admitting that discoveries are often made by one who

> Trusting some map in his own head,
> so never reached the goal intended
> (his map, of course, was out) but blundered
> On a wonderful instead . . .
> Dare sound Authority confess
> that one can err his way to riches,
> win glory by mistake, his dear
> through sheer wrong-headedness?[30]

A society governed by the rules of reason, or rather by the spirit of tolerant and courageous inquiry, may license its loyal opposition. But a society governed by the spirit displayed in British Israelitish propaganda or right-wing sociobiology would be the enemy of intellect.

With the clues offered by examples such as these it is possible to discern, by contrast, the outlines of the proper use of intellect. We ought not to believe claims that make it impossible to recall the existence of alternative accounts. One secure truth is that it cannot be that there is one road only to

---

[30] Auden, 'The History of Science': (1966), p. 305.

so great a mystery, or if there is a sense in which there is One
Way, that royal road must be one with many resting-places,
many travellers. The Oneness of the Way, if it is one, cannot
rest in a narrow sectarianism: those who serve the decencies
of reason, who are ready to learn and to adjust their vision,
are citizens of a universal city. No matter the tradition in
which they first began, they can recognize their friends and
fellows. That is what is missing even in intelligent sectarians:
the sense of a community that transcends the limits of race
and ancestral creed and dogmatic formula.

So what ought we to believe? To this there is no general
answer, but we can catch glimpses of the nature of intellectual
virtue. To follow wisdom is to understand the existence of
alternatives, and to be ready to lay aside the maps we carry
in our head in the sure confidence that some map may at last
be drawn that serves us well. Truth, as I have said before, is
what the sane person sees, and sanity rests in willingness not
to be the sole source of enlightenment, to surrender one's
own wishes for the world, to think how things may seem to
others. The possibility of taking the world in many ways,
which is the root of relativism, is itself our clue to the right
intellectual attitude. It is those who can understand and
communicate who are our best embodiments of wisdom, and
we ought to believe what they do.

# Could Consciousness Evolve?

## I

'Consciousness', as Perry ((1904), p. 282) very reasonably complained, is a term so widely used, so ill-defined, and so much involved in matters of emotional and moral concern as to be very difficult to handle. When such terms as 'mind', 'self', and 'subjectivity' are added to the broth, it is easy to lose sight of the issues, and easy to indulge in aphorism:

> Could it be valid [sic] to suppose that the 'magic' of human consciousness somehow arises from the closing of a loop whereby the brain's high level—its symbol level—and its low level—its neurophysiological level—are somehow tied together in an exquisite closed loop of causality? Is the 'private I' just the eye of a self-referential typhoon?[1]

Once this question is stripped of its neo-Taoistic overtones, it amounts to this: could it be the case that the human organism's capacity to represent things to itself (or its doing so) influences events at the neurological level, and thereby (how?) enables it also to represent its own activity to itself, and could our sense of personal being simply be that reflexive model-making? To the first of these questions the answer may well be 'yes'—or so any reasonably 'holistic' science would suspect[2]—though there is some question whether the symbol level should so easily be identified with the whole cerebral field which partially determines the motions of the brain's parts. To the second the answer is unclear, for it is admittedly difficult to understand how any neurological event could give rise to such reflexive modelling, and doubly unclear how the holistic influence of the brain's symbol level could facilitate this. To the third question the answer is

---

[1] Hofstadter and Dennett (1981), p. 281.
[2] Sperry (1969, 1970).

probably 'no'. Why it is 'no' I shall be trying to explain during the course of this chapter, though the thought is not a new one: 'Suppose that a shock in consciousness and a molecular motion are the subjective and objective faces of the same thing; we continue utterly incapable of uniting the two.'[3] Confusion in this area is compounded by confusion about the relationship between the physical and the phenomenal. Scholars such as Tinbergen, who doubt our right to impute 'consciousness' to animals not of our own species, or to allow such consciousness any explanatory role, seem strangely credulous about the physical world.[4] That there are 'real bodies' to 'explain' the presence of phenomenal bodies is at least as questionable a doctrine as the equally compelling but logically unnecessary claim that there are 'real minds'.

Some physicists, of course, have attempted to come to terms with this general doubt by purporting to consider all material objects as mere constructs, so that 'the laws of nature deal with our knowledge of elementary particles'.[5] Idealistic pragmatism seems to be a popular position: 'the reality of the magnetic field in a vacuum consists of the use-fulness of the magnetic field concept everywhere'[6]—which amounts to a persuasive redefinition of 'reality' that I would rather resist. We therefore have the paradox that psychologists are busily 'accounting for' consciousness in terms of entities that physicists account for in terms of consciousness! As Uexkuell remarked, astronomy is a biological science, for it is because we have the sensory equipment that we do that we perceive stars as we do. And Ramsey: 'I don't really believe in astronomy, except as a complicated description of part of the course of human and possibly animal sensation.'[7] A paradox need not be a contradiction: maybe the world-as-it-is has

[3] Spencer (1870) s. 272; i. 625: cited by James (1890), i. 146.
[4] Tax and Callender (1960), pp. 185 f.
[5] Heisenberg (1958), p. 99.
[6] Wigner (1964), p. 251; see Eccles (1970), pp. 44 f.
[7] Ramsey (1931), p. 291; Uexkuell (1926), pp. 35 ff. Uexkuell adds that astronomers who forget this 'disintegrate the unity of the cosmic picture and substitute a dead abstraction for the living reciprocal action of intuition': see Clark (1975), pp. 193 ff.

chanced to produce beings whose modelling activity results in a mental 'copy' of that world (how should we know?). But it is hardly likely that the copy itself is adequate to the task of producing itself—unless we adopt a rather different attitude to the field of consciousness, and accept Rudolf Steiner's account of evolution.[8]

The confusion between phenomenal and physical object which makes the material seem less questionable, more 'objective' than the mental, seems widespread amongst behaviourists.[9] It also greatly facilitates the theoretical construction of 'higher mental processes' from apparently material beginnings: the emergence of a self-image within an already mental world is easy enough to imagine and even explain, and if that mental world is supposed to be identical with the material scholars can suppose that they have solved the problem. It has been suggested, perhaps unfairly, that physicalists of this stamp are effectively solipsistic, unable to conceive that the world is composed of any other furniture than is immediately theirs.[10] Once it is realized that the world of one's own consciousness (which includes the whole realm of nature as it is presented to oneself) is only one world among uncountably many fields of consciousness, it is no longer so easy to imagine that there is nothing in those fields but the material bodies which supposedly give rise to them (for we know that our own worlds do not exhaust the possibilities of being).

Further difficulties arise from the confusion of 'consciousness' and 'self-consciousness'. There is indeed something to be said for adopting James's neologism, 'sciousness', to mean a stream of thought which contains no intuitive or derived idea of the thinker itself, and reserving 'consciousness' for that mode of scious being which does include the idea of self.[11] In those terms Jaynes's baroque endeavour to prove that

---

[8] See Barfield (1963) for an accessible introduction to Steinerite cosmology.
[9] Henle (1977).
[10] Sprigge (1979), p. 142 (see also p. 116), after Findlay (1966), p. 186.
[11] James (1890), i. 304.

human beings have only recently emerged into consciousness after an era in which 'everyone was schizophrenic',[12] and controlled by hallucinated god-kings resident in the right hemisphere of the brain, can at least be understood, if not believed. It is not implausible to suppose that not all members of our species have always been aware of themselves as separate individuals, active agents whom different propositions might be entertained. Nor is it wholly implausible that self-consciousness begins with 'the introjected image of another'. But such awareness of one's self (even the mistaken belief in such a self) can only arise within a prior 'awareness' which we have no clear reason to deny to infants, hunter-gatherers, and servants of the King. Crook's own analysis distinguishes between 'subjective' focus on another object and 'objective' self-awareness (awareness of oneself as an object of one's own and others' attention).[13] Such awareness usually takes a past and not a present state of mind as its object: *pace* Descartes and his followers it does seem likely that even our thoughts are known to us only after they have happened—if we know them as objects.

An older terminology provides the distinction between Enjoyment and Contemplation: 'the mind enjoys itself and contemplates its objects'.[14] Not all self-knowledge is rightly treated as knowledge of an object that might be known by others. We also 'enjoy' our own being, prior to contemplating it, and this enjoyment (which is simply the same 'sciousness' within which self-consciousness can arise) is the object of our study when we study ourselves. Our ordinary mode of consciousness cannot be enjoyed without the contemplation of some object or other, whether this be merely intentional (like the three-eyed carpet seller of Shiraz) or seemingly identical with some object of the 'real, external world' (like the keyboard before me). Consciousness requires, it seems, an object. When we are most occupied in contemplation we have

---

[12] Jaynes (1976), p. 405; see Crook (1980), p. 31.
[13] Crook (1980), pp. 311 f., after Duval and Wickland (1972).
[14] Alexander (1920), i. 12 ff.

least attention to spare to consider our own occupation,[15] but it is very misleading to suggest that we would then be unconscious. Some students of these mysteries have suggested that there is a mode of consciousness that takes no object, not even its own past enjoyments: pure consciousness is enjoyment of its own enjoyment without further term. Whether this is truly possible, or whether it is a misdescription of unselfconscious enjoyment of some contemplated object (where the enjoyer makes no division between what she perceives and her own perception) is a question on which only the enlightened have much right to speak.

The dualism of contemplating subject and contemplated object arises within a self-reflexive consciousness: 'I can analyse my perceiving on the one hand and the object of my perceiving on the other with quite different results, and yet in the perception they are identical.'[16] Subject and object emerge from an undifferentiated consciousness. It is easy (given the regular confusion of physical and phenomenal realms) to suppose that one has passed beyond the quite different duality of Mind and Body. Both Minds (thinking things) and Bodies (extended things) are theoretical entities: proffered explanations for the regularity of our conscious experiences. Further investigation may reveal that one or other class is really superfluous, or really a subclass of the other, or really an irreducibly substantial part of the cosmos. This investigation is not assisted by reference to the apparently secondary nature of self-knowledge.

That minds are 'theoretical entities' (like electrons and billiard-tables) is not to say that consciousness or sciousness is merely theoretical. Physicalist commentators, seeking (for reasons that will become apparent) to eliminate consciousness from the real world, have sometimes appealed to James[17] as authority for their case. But when James asked 'Does Consciousness Exist?' it was not 'pure experience' that he was

[15] Crook (1980), pp. 322 f.
[16] Perry (1904).
[17] James (1976), pp. 3 ff.

querying, but the theory that there was an entity deserving of that title whose being lay in something other than the stream of thought. Berkeley had the same doubt: the being of subjects lies in '*percipere, velle* and *agere*', and there are for Berkeley no 'minds' outside these functions. If there were it could be that a mind could think only intermittently,[18] that it could be without thinking. Berkeley was no more a 'mentalist' than James, if it is mentalism to suppose that there is a special sort of soul-stuff made into individual packets that have the inessential property of 'thinking'. Such a doctrine would have no advantages over the theory—which I shall comment on below—that it was the body that sometimes thought, though thinking was no essential property of bodies. Both James and Berkeley were believers in the streams of thought, the multiple realms of 'pure experience'.

'Minds', or the 'having of a mind' may also reside in a capacity to acquire intellectual capacities,[19] to be able to come to do things which involve calculation and self-correction. It is not obvious that this requires consciousness at all. In our own experience calculations of a very complex sort are constantly being made (how fast is that car moving, and how far away is it, and how fast can I run?) which would never be completed in time if we had to attend to them, make them part of our conscious experience. Some of those calculations we have had to make consciously at some time; others are made, it seems, entirely behind our backs. We may of course suppose that there is some conscious being, some stream of thought, guardian angel, or right-brain golem, which performs the calculation. But it seems equally imaginable that the thing is done 'mechanically', that there are circuits in our brains —or whatever—which produce the right answer no more consciously than a home computer. Introspection, indeed, suggests that even those calculations which we suppose ourselves to be performing 'consciously' are not performed 'by

---

[18] Berkeley, *Philosophical Commentaries* A 580: (1948–56), i. 72.; *Principles*; s. 98: (1948–56), ii. 83.
[19] Kenny (1972), p. 46.

consciousness': answers simply emerge once we have phrased the questions adequately. The question whether computers 'think' can therefore be shrugged aside as one merely of semantics without affecting the far more intractable problem of whether we might eventually be constrained to agree that there was a stream of thought associated with some newly designed robot. 'Thinking' can mean both calculation and sciousness, which do not have any obvious connection with each other. It is for this reason that Griffin's remarks on the ability of bats to operate by sonar gives less ground for considering bats conscious than he supposes[20]—though I think that his data do give us reason to suppose that, if they are conscious, they are also minimally self-conscious (they locate themselves within a map of the world).[21]

'Minds' may also be considered as holistic systems: patterns of cerebral activity which lay constraints on the activity of neurons according to the normal rules for hierarchically organized entities. It has therefore seemed humane, to some, to emphasize a systems approach to animal behaviour.[22] Surely if we taught ourselves to see animals as whole organisms with 'high-level systems' or organization we should be more inclined to 'respect their integrity'? This may be so— recognition of such systems does play a part in increased carefulness, and even admiration—but the obvious response, that pocket calculators need no rights, gains force from considering Claude Bernard, whose recognition of 'system' was conjoined with a total refusal to consider the 'inner being' or 'consciousness' of the animals he vivisected.[23] That atoms, molecules, cells, organisms, and societies are holistic systems does not of itself show that there are scious streams associated with those entities. To claim, like Sperry, that a holistic interpretation of the mind easily accommodates consciousness is to move too fast: 'Pain as a subjective experience [is]

[20] Griffin (1976), pp. 13 ff.
[21] Clark (1981), p. 15.
[22] Boden (1980), p. 47.
[23] Bernard (1949), pp. 99 ff.; see also White (1971).

explained as a holistic property of a particular spatio-temporal pattern of cerebral excitation that as a dynamic functional entity directly determines the further course of brain activity.'[24] Perhaps it is, but what is gratuitously asserted may be as easily denied.

This confusion is linked with the final, most significant dispute: is consciousness, as the scious stream of thought, an illusion after all? The simple truth that consciousness is what marks the difference between being awake and being dreamlessly asleep can be cashed in two radically different ways: as the identification of consciousness simply with 'public' wakefulness, the appropriate avoidance of calamity and search for satisfaction; and as a device for drawing our attention to our own subjectivity, never logically equivalent to any public display of competence or calculation. The former identification has great advantages: it becomes relatively easy to see what creature is or is not conscious (i.e. awake and responsive). Even in this case there will be some hesitation about the boundary between mere reaction and response: an electric light-bulb which lights up when a switch is pressed is hardly 'alert'; a simple robot that responds to features of the environment when in the appropriate internal state may earn itself that accolade. But little hinges on the decision: to be alert, awake, conscious is to operate as a goal-seeking system within a changing environment. 'With the [magnetized iron] filings the path is fixed; whether it reaches the end depends on accidents. With the lover it is the end which is fixed, the path may be modified indefinitely.'[25] Subsequent research has strongly suggested that other systems than the human or animal may be interpreted teleonomically, not because they have conscious goals but because their behaviour or growth is indefinitely variable within large-scale programmes. Very often it is convenient to speak as if they had beliefs and desires, since it is knowledge of the preferred end-states and of the environmental parameters which best predicts the

---

[24] Sperry (1970); see Sperry (1969), Bindra (1970).
[25] James (1890) i. 7.

organism's behaviour. An 'intentional system', in Dennett's terminology,[26] is one that is easily or best understood in terms of beliefs and desires, and the question whether it 'really' has intentions is allowed to lapse: 'You can trick an apple tree into thinking it's spring by building a fire under its branches in the late fall'.[27] Chess-playing computers, chimpanzees, and amoebae are all intentional systems in this sense: all are functionally conscious (though maybe not of very much). Only when intentional explanations fail do we fall back on mechanical explanation: that the program has not been loaded properly, or that a microchip is loose. The computer's chess-moves can of course be described in non-intentional terms, but this would be a very unsuccessful way of predicting its moves. Animal-trainers have similarly found it unprofitable to avoid intentional description of their charges.[28]

## II

The functionalist approach has the great advantage that it avoids the problem posed by the supposed privacy of consciousness, that none of us has access to any other stream of thought than our own. At the same time it appears to provide us with a way in which we might learn the correct application of intentional terms. Post-Wittgensteinian philosophers tend to be especially sensitive about any suggestion that we could learn the meaning of the words we use solely by introspection, and therefore resist the claim that 'consciousness' means that condition of myself that only I can be acquainted with. The connection between my being conscious and the public evidence of my consciousness must, they suppose, be a logical one. From this it is only a short step to full-blown functionalism: the doctrine that being conscious is not an introspectible reality at all.

[26] Dennett (1978), p. 6.
[27] Dennett (1978), p. 272.
[28] Hebb (1946); Mathews (1978), p. 440.

But despite these advantages—which are perhaps not as secure as some suppose—the doctrine does leave us with some problems. Those who doubt that amoebas are conscious beings, for example, seem to be left without any way of saying so. When Jaynes remarks that despite the observer's 'passionate temptation' to attribute consciousness to protozoa, 'the explanation for their behaviour resides entirely in physical chemistry, not introspective psychology'[29] he seems to make sense: but if the functionalist interpretation of consciousness-attributing language is correct his words are without meaning. On the one hand, 'consciousness' does not name an entity or realm distinct from the physical: so that the supposed contrast between chemical causation and mental causation is unreal. On the other hand, intentional concepts are much more successful in predicting even an amoeba's motions than are physico-chemical concepts. The physical events which are coterminous with what was viewed as 'the amoeba's behaviour' may accord with ordinary laws of nature, but we are quite unable to follow all the chemical pathways of this one cell's growth and motion so as to be able to foretell what event will issue from those synergistic changes. Because we cannot do this, of course, we cannot in fact test the hypothesis that only physico-chemical processes are involved. Since we do not know by any calculation what would happen if they were, we cannot tell whether what does happen is the same, or if there is some other disturbing factor (as, it might be, a ghost in the amoeba). But even if there is no such other factor, we are still inclined to see the amoeba's motions as behaviour (for example, the efforts of a small amoeba to avoid being eaten by a larger, and trying out various stratagems to achieve this end),[30] and can use such descriptions to help predict what will happen next. If functionalists are correct that is all that is needed to make intentional language appropriate, without any suggestion of a real stream of consciousness or of the amoeba's grasp of its own

[29] Jaynes (1976), p. 5.
[30] Jennings (1906), pp. 17 ff.; see Washburn (1917), p. 47.

situation. Being conscious just consists in being the sort of thing that is usefully viewed in the intentional mode. Such intentional explanation does not compete with physico-chemical explanation, and is not refuted by the discovery of physico-chemical connections. Animals, to say nothing of apple-trees, are as conscious as we are, even if most of them lack self-consciousness (defined in a similarly functionalist manner).

The functionalist view of consciousness, then, has the drawback that the Cartesian view of animals is not merely mistaken in fact, but incoherent, though it might be possible to construct an analogue of Descartes's model by denying 'second-order intentions' to the non-human. It is also strongly counter-intuitive in its claim that we ourselves (that is, you and I) are conscious only in this functional sense: that we can be treated, even by ourselves, as intentional systems. Dennett sets himself to eliminate or discredit this intuition,[31] but his attempt to analyse 'inner consciousness' away includes so many overtly phenomenological terms (such as 'attention') as to seem a losing battle. 'Inner consciousness' in the sense of self-contemplation may usefully be understood as remembrance of things past, or the internalization of a significant other: James's 'pure experience' is not so easily eliminated.

That there will be some philosopher ready to defend any hypothesis, however ludicrous it seems to be, is no criticism of philosophers: that, after all, is what we are for. So it is not surprising that there are those who profess to find such talk, of 'inner consciousness', wholly opaque. For them, there is no problem (so they say). Now since the sciousness of which I am speaking is the sort of thing that can be experienced only by one who is scious, and cannot be identified with anything in the public realm, I am in no position to point their own stream of thought out to them. They can only have their attention drawn to it. The commonest way of doing so is by reminding ourselves of the reality of pain: to be 'in pain' cannot plausibly be identified with being disposed to squirm

[31] Dennett (1978), p. 154.

or shriek in response to physical damage, though this disposition is, in most normal cases, adequate evidence of such pain, and the notion of a pain which in no way inclined the sufferer to squirm or shriek or schriggle (whatever other manifestation its biology might dictate) is difficult to handle. In the interest of avoiding too familiar tracks through the philosophical wasteland, consider instead the experience of joy:

The corn was orient and immortal wheat, which never should be reaped, nor was ever sown. I thought it had stood from everlasting. The dust and stones of the street were as precious as gold: the gates were at first the end of the world. The green trees when I saw them first through one of the gates transported and ravished me, their sweetness and unusual beauty made my heart to leap, and almost mad with ecstasy, they were such strange and wonderful things. . . . All things abided eternally as they were in their proper places. Eternity was manifest in the Light of the Day, and something infinite behind everything appeared: which talked with my expectation and moved my desire.[32]

Traherne's experience may be wholly unfamiliar to some, but I would guess that most of us have on occasion been startled into that condition, and rested there until our habitual self-analysis or bad temper or greed lost us the vision. I guess this to be so: but I cannot know that it is so, for anyone but myself, unless they tell me. Not that their word is final proof: they may be lying or self-deceived or ignorant of what it is that Traherne is really saying. The vision is not wholly disconnected from public performance. But having such a vision is not identical with any public performance, and its quality can be known only to those who have experienced something like it. Nothing that can be experienced by one who has not experienced that vision in her own right (changes of brain-wave patterns, hormonal output, bursts of song or a tendency to tap-dance, a readier display of affection) can reveal the quality of the vision to the non-visionary. The visionary does not find that she has had such a vision by noticing the same features of her bodily output that the non-visionary could perceive. Nor does she, on the other hand,

---

[32] Traherne 3. 3: (1960), p. 110.

perceive something that no one else could perceive. Her descriptions are intelligible, to those who know. Clearly, more could be said about this particular example. My point here is merely that such experiences exist, that indeed all our experience has some affective tone, and that these tones are irreducibly subjective. They can exist only as modes of experience, and can be known only by those who experience them. There are features of our experience that can be known without acquaintance: those blind from birth may study the physics of light, or the etymology of colour-terms. They may even be helped to grasp certain affective analogues of visual experience—scarlet like the sound of a trumpet—and they may know enough about it to know, if they should be cured, what their new experience must be ('So this is what seeing is!'). But there is none the less a real difference between those who see and those who do not, as there is between those who know joy and those who inhabit what is in a sense the same world but without joy.

On the other hand, any realistic theory of conscious being must wrestle with the problem that the streams of thought associated with other entities than myself seem to be wholly inaccessible to me: what could count as evidence of another's conscious being, if that being does not consist in the complex responses she overtly makes? What can we imagine another's stream of thought to be? Tinbergen's hesitation is understandable. Even an earlier generation of animal psychologists were puzzled as to how to answer James's question, though they saw it as one both meaningful and fascinating:

We may, if we like, by our reasonings, unwind things back to that black and jointless continuity of space and moving clouds of swarming atoms which science calls the only real world. But all the while the world we feel and live in will be that which our ancestors and we, by slowly cumulating strokes of choice, have extricated out of this, like sculptors, by simply rejecting certain portions of the given stuff. Other sculptors, other statues from the same stone! Other minds, other worlds from the same monotonous and inexpressive chaos! My world is but one in a million alike embedded, alike real to those who may abstract them.

How different must be the worlds in the consciousness of ant, cuttlefish
or crab![33]

Those earlier psychologists were not naïve. They set themselves to consider 'what it is like to be a bat',[34] and realized
their limitations:

Anger, in our experience, is largely composed of sensations of quickened
heart-beat, or altered breathing, of muscular tension, of increased blood-
pressure in the head and face. The circulation of a wasp is fundamentally
different from that of any vertebrate. The wasp does not breathe
through lungs, it wears its skeleton on the outside, and it has the
muscles attached to the inside of the skeleton. What is anger like in the
wasp's consciousness? We can form no adequate idea of it.[35]

It seems to have been left to philosophers to add that anger
in us embodies a set of beliefs about having been wronged
and desires for revenge that may be difficult to attribute to a
wasp, though it may also be that philosophers are too intel-
lectualist about emotion.[36]

What is it like to be a wasp, a cuttlefish, a chimpanzee?
Can we imagine ourselves in them, and count upon the
predictions of their overt behaviour that we thereby make? If
we can, what does this suggest about their consciousness?
One recent suggestion[37] has been that 'consciousness' is an
adaptation of social organisms, ensuring that each is acquainted
with the inner causes of the other's behaviour? Our acquaintance with our own condition enables us to imagine what
others may do, without recourse to the painful accumulation
of behaviouristic information about their doings. This ingenious reversal of the more usual anti-Cartesian thought
(that it is by our acquaintance with what others do and
expect that we acquire the concepts to deal with our own
condition) is a bold attempt to answer R. W. Gerard's challenge 'Why is it adaptive for organisms to be aware of the

[33] James (1890) i. 288 f.
[34] Nagel (1974).
[35] Washburn (1917), p. 3.
[36] Fortenbaugh (1971); cf. Malcolm (1977).
[37] Humphrey (1980, 1981); see Crook (1983).

world and of themselves?', and James's: given that behaviour could be explained neuro-physiologically what could be the function of consciousness, and if it has none, how could it have evolved?[38] Dennett has argued similarly, though for somewhat different reasons, that it is a belief that other creatures have beliefs that marks off the crude behaviourism of dogs from the more sophisticated self-awareness of human beings.[39] It pays, in evolutionary terms, for social creatures to be conscious: for only conscious beings have an immediate acquaintance with the forces that govern the behaviour of other beings. By projecting this self-model into other beings (including ones that we do not seriously expect to be themselves aware) we are enabled to outguess the painstaking behaviourist who knows only what she has managed to record of their past behaviour. We can imagine what it would be like to be a wasp, an apple-tree, a quark: only when we are dealing with a creature with a similar self-modelling capacity can we realistically expect that she now really feels what we would. The feelings of other animals have no reality outside our projective faculty, unless the transformation into 'nature's psychologists' happened earlier than Humphrey supposes.

There is in fact evidence to suggest that non-human animals may attribute beliefs to others, that they can predict the behaviour of others in very much the same way as we do. Witness the young chimpanzee described by Goodall, who deliberately walks away from a luxury he has spotted, and surreptitiously returns only when the rest of his troup have thus been lured away. R. A. Mugford's experience of 'problem dogs' also suggests that they can manipulate human beings 'like good psychologists, and [are] very well aware of their own tomorrow'.[40] But this approach rings false at a different level. Firstly, Humphrey is not wholly clear whether he is explaining consciousness or self-consciousness. Secondly, it is not clear why a computer might not be programed to

---

[38] Tax and Callender (1960), p. 187; James (1890) i. 129.
[39] Dennett (1978), pp. 273 ff.
[40] Goodall (1971), p. 96; Mugford (1981), p. 43.

take account of its own programing, without our thereby being compelled to reckon the computer—or the embodied programme—conscious.

Consciousness or self-consciousness? If a creature is aware of anything at all there may well be some advantage to it in being aware also of its own being-in-the-world, so that it carries around with it a model of what other beings of a similar kind may be and do. But there seems to be no reason to insist that nothing is conscious which is not self-conscious, nothing 'scious' that is not 'conscious'. Even we are sometimes conscious without being self-conscious, and it requires more evidence than Humphrey offers to establish that un-self-conscious animals (or animals whose self-consciousness is minimal) are never joyful, miserable, hungry, or in pain. Their presumed lack of self-awareness implies only that they cannot make the distinction between themselves and their states that we sometimes remember. Accordingly, Humphrey's account may go some way toward explaining the emergence of self-awareness without adding anything to our knowledge of 'pure experience'. Why should it pay a creature, in evolutionary terms, to be aware, if the same motions can be brought about by unconscious processes—and in fact, if physicalism be correct, are brought about merely by these unconscious processes? And if there were no conscious beings, how should the beings there were get any 'advantage' from being self-conscious?

To this the reply must come that we are dealing with functional awareness, not the introspectible reality. Humphrey's effort is to pass from functional responsiveness (which is obviously adaptive) to the creation of an inner realm, mind as the map of nature. But this capacity to map the world, including that part of it which is the map-maker's own bodily nature, and to attribute similar natures to other beings in the world, is not limited to creatures we would ordinarily consider conscious. The chess-playing computer that can reconsider its own program, or anticipate its opponent's moves by reckoning what moves it would make itself and what reasonings would lead it to make them, may perhaps be conscious; there may perhaps be 'something it is like to be' that computer. But it is also possible to imagine that there is no 'stream of thought', that the steps of its 'calculation' are determined solely by the logic of its program (or meta-program), that not even an epiphenomenal consciousness troubles its circuits. It is in fact very difficult to suppose otherwise, while it is equally difficult to suppose that the dog, the chimpanzee, or one's human neighbour is like the computer in this. Accordingly, the self-mapping capacity to which Humphrey refers is not, of itself, an adequate explanation for the existence of subjective being, since there is reason to think that the same outward effect can be achieved by non-conscious mechanisms.

To this there seem to me to be four possible responses. The first, to deny the division: perhaps there is, after all, no more to being conscious than having the capacity to take account of one's own circuits. The second, to agree that there might be different ways of achieving the improved performance on which evolution relies, but that our ancestral genes just happened to devise the route of conscious calculation. We have no warrant to assume that extraterrestrial life-forms, even ones intelligent enough to build cities, travel in space, and communicate by giant lasers, will be strictly conscious beings: they may 'speak' in the first person, attach 'praise' and 'blame' to individuals, and 'try' to avoid damage to their circuitry, but yet have nothing like our own acquaintance with the world and with ourselves. In a real sense, they may have no souls. The third possible reply would be to claim that although consciousness is not the same property as complexity of neural response (for there are possible worlds in which they occur separately), yet it does arise as a matter of natural fact wherever there is an appropriate degree of complexity in the internal connections of bodily organisms: it is an emergent property, fixed in the evolutionary line (once it appears) by the advantages of such neural complexity. The fourth reply is to take conscious being seriously, and to deny that ordinary evolutionary forces can well explain it. This conclusion is the one to which I shall be arguing, but I do not claim that the other possible replies are not worth exploring. All have their merits, and a full exploration of the issues would range over the whole of the philosophical landscape.

## III

The second reply perhaps has few advantages. The strength of functionalism is that it ties consciousness to certain publicly demonstrable and evolutionarily advantageous facts, and thereby explains how there could come to be 'conscious' beings. The supposition that there might be other ways of producing just these results leaves us without adequate explanation of why this way has emerged, or any adequate reason to suppose that in fact it has. By this latter point, I mean that even our closest friends might in fact be automata, although they did the same things as ourselves. That this is a genuine, though unthinkable, possibility seems to me to be true (and the efforts of some philosophers to convince me that they were not introspectibly conscious almost persuades me that the possibility may after all be realized!). But Humphrey's case depends upon there being an evolutionary advantage, and a public distinction, between two sorts of possible being: the non-conscious, and the social calculator. If there is not always such a distinction he no longer has good reason to think that all and only 'social calculators' are conscious. The other point against the second reply, that we have no adequate theory to explain what it is that brought about just this mechanism of social calculation, or what physical difference would be associated with the different possible mechanisms, means that the second reply hangs between two possible positions, which would be better considered separately. On the one hand, perhaps consciousness is a genuinely causal factor: not the only possible way of bringing about evolutionary success for a social organism, but a real cause of that success where it occurs. On the other hand, perhaps it is merely epiphenomenal (as functionalists must be inclined to suppose), and the real causal work is done by neuro-physiology. Either neural complexity and its associated responses are enough on their own to secure evolutionary success, or they are not. If they are, then consciousness is superfluous, and unless it is linked by natural necessity to the existence of neural complexity (the third reply) there seems no good reason to expect it to survive in the evolutionary chain (any more than eyes in the fishes of underground lakes). There would be no evolutionary pressure to prevent its elimination. If neural complexity is not enough to ensure evolutionary success, then we need some theory to explain why this should be (as Humphrey's does not).

Accordingly, it is the other three replies which deserve attention: that consciousness is no more than complexity of neural response; that consciousness is linked to such complexity of neural response by natural necessity; that consciousness is entirely other. The first of these I have already disputed. The next needs further elaboration. Why have I suggested that the link must be supposed to be one of 'natural necessity'? Would it not be enough to suppose that there was simply a universal rule that neural complexity and consciousness occurred together? It has, after all, been usual to suppose that Hume demonstrated the merely 'accidental' nature of all causal regularities: nothing in the nature of what functions as a cause requires that the effect occur. Drawing a piece of white chalk across a blackboard might ignite the board, or release a flock of doves, as easily (so far as logical necessity is concerned) as inscribing a white line. Accordingly we cannot expect to find any intelligible connection between cause and effect. Hume drew the impeccable conclusion that our reliance on inductive inference was merely habitual[41]—a conclusion from which latter-day philosophers have shrunk—but the Pyrrhonian context within which Hume worked need not invalidate his arguments.

That the Humean analysis of causation is inadequate is an argument too vast to be attempted here. It is, at least,

[41] Hume (1888) i. 3. 14 ff.

inadequate to the needs of practising scientists, who seek some intelligible description of events that will rule out magic. Relations between supposed tool and supposed effect are merely magical when there is no intelligible reason why things should happen like that, when there is no way of describing the events in a common language. The effort of scientists in any field is to discover what description of events will reveal what has happened as an instance of some more general relationship. This will not, most probably, ever be such as to show that nothing else could logically have happened, that this is the only logically possible world. It should be such as to show that things could not have happened 'just otherwise' without there having to be other alterations in the scheme of things. The ideal characteristic of natural laws, as uncovered or postulated by working scientists, is that what seemed to be 'emergent' properties turn out to be describable as mere 'resultants'. The explosion that occurs when two lumps of uranium are appropriately conjoined looks to be emergent —for the whole is explosive when the parts, separately, were not—but the lumps were 'decaying' before they were joined, and an explosion is only a more rapid form of decay. There is a describable mathematical relationship between the properties of the parts and the properties of the whole: the formula which describes that relationship may not be (most probably is not) a mathematical or logical axiom, but it is one that is mathematically or logically connected with other formulae that describe other aspects of reality. The macroscopic properties of water, for example that it can be electrolytically decomposed into hydrogen and oxygen in the proportion $2:1$, are explicable by reference to the microscopic properties of hydrogen and oxygen atoms. Water is $H_2O$, and there could not be any stable stuff having the same macroscopic properties (or all but the one named property) which was $H_6O$, without there being quite radical readjustments elsewhere in the system of physical reality.[42] In other words, genuinely emergent properties seem to be incompatible with

[42] Swinburne (1979), pp. 171 ff.

the scientific programme of understanding reality in terms of convertible and interconnected mathematical formulae. It is very difficult to find any plausible examples of genuine emergence—except when we consider the relationship between physical and phenomenal properties. The taste of sodium chloride seems to be something that bears no mathematical relationship to the other properties, the 'physical' properties, of salt and of the human nervous system. This is not to say, as my own earlier efforts to express this argument seem to have suggested to some of my auditors, that I would expect there to be some necessary truth, knowable *a priori*, describing the connection between neural and phenomenal happenings: the point is, that if the relationship between neural and phenomenal events is to be of the same order as relationships between, say, electrical, magnetic, and gravitational forces, there must be some formula of general applicability, delineating what quantity of phenomenal affect is to be found with what quantity of, say, electro-cerebral activity, and such as to be logically and mathematically linked with other formulae, describing such things as the relationship between the age of the universe and the number of electrons in the universe.

And that, of course, is the difficulty. Maynard Smith very properly pointed out in discussion that we do not have any intelligible account even of how an acorn grows into an oak: as I remarked earlier, we have little chance of following through all the biochemical pathways and calculating their synergetic effect to see whether they are enough to produce even the non-mental properties of an oak, or a chimpanzee, or a human child. But though we cannot trace the whole story, there seems nothing especially offensive in the notion that there are relationships of the kind that I have described in this process. It seems quite possible that, given the physical properties of carbon, nitrogen, oxygen, and the rest, amino-acids and biological organisms will have the properties that they do. They could not have had wholly different properties —been impervious to temperatures in excess of 500 °C, or capable of growing to any size without concomitant adaptations of bodily shape (for example, to avoid the problem posed by the ratio of volume to surface area)—without the universe as a whole having to have radically different properties. We can understand why elephant-sized mice would have to have baggy skin and proportionately larger ears (or some analogous structure) by considering that they would need to increase their heat-flow efficiency if they were not to boil to death.

But nothing of this kind seems even an intelligible possibility when we turn to the relationship between physical and phenomenal properties. What sort of formula could it be that described such a relationship in general terms and in such a way that there were logical and mathematical links with other formulae describing other features of the universe? Does it even make sense to talk about 'a quantity of phenomenal affect'? How can a phenomenon, an event in a stream of thought which is knowable only by subjective means, stand in any mathematically describable relationship with properties of shape or size or speed or electrical charge? Apparently different things can be shown, surprisingly, to be modifications of some underlying reality (so that electricity and magnetism turn out to be describable by the same formulae, with variables—for example, speed relative to observer—given appropriately different values). But what could the underlying reality be that can be manifested both as sodium chloride in a non-subjective world and as the manifold tastes of salt in the indefinitely many streams of thought? What mathematical transformation is imaginable that would change a mental event into an electromagnetic one, and vice versa? Could we imagine that the 'mental' was an additional dimension, rather as some cosmologists have considered time, and postulate some formula that would equate units of mentality with units of physical energy? Does not this hypothesis obviously substitute some other, 'objective' reality for the subjective stream that we seek to explain? What could a 'unit of mentality' imaginably be? What other formulae would have to be different if the relationship between physical and phenomenal properties were different, and why?

My questions do not demonstrate that no such formula will ever be devised. But the balance of probabilities does seem to me against it: we lack not merely knowledge of what that formula would be, but even of what it would be like. If we ever discovered it we should surely have to make very radical adjustments in our understanding of other properties of the physical universe. What we could not do, and continue with the scientific programme, is dismiss the matter as merely magical. If consciousness is a property of complex neural networks then we have to admit both that we have no idea at all what other properties of those networks, and of the universe as a whole, have to be as they are if there is to be consciousness, and also that there are such linked properties. If the wholes are conscious then the parts have properties that, within a well-worked-out system, entail the property of being conscious. In short, as Nagel very convincingly argues, consciousness can only be the property of physical wholes if the parts of those wholes have psychic or mentalistic properties themselves.[43]

Such panpsychism, as Nagel says, is simply one more in the list of 'mutually incompatible and hopelessly unacceptable solutions to the mind–body problem'. If it were true, we should have some hopes of an explanation for the evolution of consciousness from 'mind-dust'.[44] Conscious beings evolve because the parts of which they are made are themselves already 'conscious', though in some mode of which we have now no understanding. We could come to understand why there are just the forms of consciousness that there are (and not certain logically imaginable others—no consciousness embracing a whole life-span, or wholly dedicated to the unending transformation of geometrical shapes, for example) by considering what other features of the universe would have to be different if these were to exist. No other mechanism for social calculation would evolve since any neural or silicon-chip

[43] Nagel (1979), pp. 181 ff.    [44] James (1890) i. 57.

mechanism capable of the craft would automatically be conscious in addition to its other properties.

Unfortunately there are three massive drawbacks to the scheme Nagel proposes. First, it is difficult to see what such mind-dust could be. What are these properties that all elementary particles possess that combine to produce our consciousness? Is consciousness the sort of thing that can have parts at all? If it were, then one might be on the way towards detecting 'units of consciousness' that might enter into mathematically describable relationships with the units of other forces (though I doubt it), but there seems to be good reason to dismiss the claim. Nagel himself suspects that 'a chain of explanatory inference from the mental states of whole animals to the proto-mental properties of dead matter . . . is a kind of breakdown we cannot envision, perhaps is unintelligible.'[45] What is it like to be an elementary particle that has the additional property of forming what it is like to be a mongoose when appropriately conjoined with indefinitely many other 'somethings it is like to be'? Water can be electrolytically decomposed: what decomposes a consciousness? One can conceive that 'a consciousness' comes to have fewer and less organized contents: but is that to say that the stream of thought, the bare fact of experience, is decomposed into lesser streams? Our own experience of being conscious, at any rate, is of a unitary kind: the thing of which I am conscious may be multiple, but my being conscious does not seem likely to be the sort of thing that is composed of anything.

The second objection is that, just as we have no grasp of what these 'proto-mental' properties might be, we also have no grasp of what combinations of mind-dust are needed to produce a higher mind. If twelve men each think one word of a twelve-word sentence, 'nowhere will there be a consciousness of the whole sentence'.[46] When do mind-molecules make a mind-cell? We are easily convinced that there is something about neural complexity that is necessary for consciousness,

[45] Nagel (1979), p. 194.        [46] James (1890) i. 160.

but what grounds this conviction? Why should not anything at all be conscious if all things are made of the same proto-conscious particles? Not all combinations of molecules make a crystalline solid, and we can go some way to seeing why. But what sort of reason could there be to prevent any combination of mind-particles making a mind?

These objections, to a believer, may be no more than interesting problems that we cannot as yet solve. The third objection, so it seems to me, is conclusive. Panpsychism rejects a magical emergence of properties at the price of admitting an equally baffling conjunction. If there is no possibility even in principle of devising a formula which will equate physical and mentalistic properties in such a way that necessary connections are recognized between our mode of consciousness and the state of the physical universe, then there is also no answer to the question 'Why do particles with physical properties $a$, $b$, and $c$ also have mental or proto-mental properties?' This conjunction of properties of a radically different kind at the elementary level is as brute an unintelligibility as the supposed emergence of mentalistic properties from the sheerly physical. Maybe—as one might suppose in Humean moods—the universe does rest upon a brute contingency; maybe it even rests upon the panpsychist contingency rather than the emergentist contingency. But the former has no advantage over the latter, and poses additional problems.

Of the three usable responses to the problem of consciousness's evolution that I have considered, the theory of emergence seems to be the most immediately attractive, but conflicts with fundamental demands for scientific intelligibility. Before we have understood how something happens we need to have devised a system in which any other happening would necessitate radical changes elsewhere in the universe. But we have no grasp of any theory which makes such a necessary connection between mental and non-mental happenings, nor any understanding of what the proto-mental properties of Nagal's panpsychism might be. Accordingly, we cannot understand consciousness as merely the necessary concomitant of the neural and behavioural complexity that breeds evolutionary success. 'Functional consciousness', the responsiveness of organisms, can be provided with an evolutionary explanation. Real consciousness, of the kind that functionalists profess not to understand, has no evolutionary explanation. Since there is no evolutionary pressure to maintain its existence it ought not to exist, and cannot be assumed to exist unless we have direct experience of it, or unless we can provide some theory of things which makes its presence understandable. In the absence of such a theory, we seem doomed either to a counter-intuitive functionalism, or a despairing solipsism (if these doctrines are genuinely distinct).

Functionalism is tied to such bizarre conclusions (for example, that a room containing a monolingual English-speaker who responds to Chinese ideograms in accordance with a set of algorithms so as to conduct what is, from the outside, an orderly conversation, really understands Chinese —the room understands Chinese, that is, not the individual man)[47] that it would require a lot of argument before I consented to it even as an account of other creatures' consciousness. In grasping my own consciousness I acquire the capacity to attribute a similar stream of thought to other loci of perception: what I am, others may be, though their own being is something of which I can at present have only a theoretical knowledge. I believe them to be conscious partly because I believe this to be the sort of universe in which it can be expected that there will be conscious beings. In brief: I suggest that since real consciousness cannot intelligibly be supposed to have evolved and since it is none the less a reality we should conclude that it had no need to evolve. It was here already.

---

[47] Searle (1980).

## IV

As I pointed out earlier, many physicists will readily agree that 'the material world', considered as something other than the set of phenomenal realities which are the contents of our consciousness, is a theoretical construct, designed to explain why we make the observations that we do. But if it comes to be seen that no material event can strictly explain our observations (what is it about sodium chloride and our neurons that explains, or renders necessary within the context of physical theory, the brute taste(s) of salt?), we must begin to ask ourselves why we take the material world seriously as the true cause of our experience. The known reality of our lives is the lived reality, the world present to me, and to uncounted others. It seems at first that we must posit a material world if we are not to lapse into solipsism, but this turns out to be an error. That there is a single world, the set of all consciousnesses and their contents, is one fact. That these worlds, or many of them, are so related to each other as to allow each world to be mapped into the others (so your world is reflected into mine as your body and its actions), is another. That there are occult realities which explain or render these conjunctions intelligible, is a third. That those realities are best understood as pure objects, devoid of their own subjective existence, is a fourth, and strictly indemonstrable, claim.

Some of our problems are occasioned simply by confusion over the term 'objective'. An objective world is one that exists independently of our will and perception. An object-world is one composed of objects and not subjects, describable solely in terms involving no subjective element (if that is possible). An objective explanation is one that reveals objective causality, not one that involves no mention of subjects. Subjects, whose being lies in '*percipere*, *velle* and *agere*', are as much a part of the objective world as objects are. If the emergence of subjectivity cannot be explained in terms of pure objects and their relations, perhaps we should consider instead whether objects might not be explained in terms of subjects and their relations; better still, perhaps we should take seriously the discovery that nothing can be described without subjective elements. If that is so, the whole problem of consciousness's 'emergence' from a non-mental world of pure objects can be allowed to lapse. There never was such a purely non-mental world, as all attempts to describe it must reveal.

Once upon a time the only ideas present to any mortal consciousness were those of pain and pleasure, contiguity and distance, and direction. The tick, to use Uexkuell's example, has no need for any grasp of spatial order and her imagined place in it: she has only to sit on a grass-stalk, for up to eighteen years, until the scent of butyric acid (what we call butyric acid) impels her to land on a passing mammal, suck blood, drop to earth, and lay her eggs.[48] These are not her ideas, of course, but ours: it does not seem necessary to suppose that she has any sense of time elapsed, or conception of the class of mammals. If McGonigle is correct, even animals with whom we can more readily identify may not have quite the grasp of objects with a continuing identity that we do— though I suspect that his experiments only uncover the usual practicality of animal intelligence.[49] Most animals are too busy to be concerned with those properties of creation that are not usually relevant to their concerns: we cannot always be sure whether a creature has not noticed some feature that we see, or has little interest in it. But suppose that phenomenal objects, of the kind with which we are acquainted, only came into existence with the appearance of a distinctively human consciousness: how in that case can we locate this latter appearance within a world of objects, spatio-temporally locatable, which purports to have existed before human consciousness? Explaining, or pretending to explain, human evolution by reference to mere constructs of the human imagination is hardly less ridiculous than explaining astronomical observations by reference to the stellar constellations of Scorpio or the Great Bear. As Barfield, drawing upon

[48] Uexkuell (1957).        [49] McGonigle (1982).

Steiner's arguments, has proposed in ingenious parody of of Socrates' speech:

An externally real second earth . . . could be no more than a kind of spectre, which the inventive mind or brain of man has capriciously interposed between itself, the constructor, and the world of nature which it confidently tells us is its construct. And if the spectre does not and cannot exist even now, but is a mere figment of man's bemused imagination, I pray you by Zeus and all the other gods, my gifted friend, to explain to me how it was contrived to exist millions of years ago, before there was ever such a thing as a brain or a mind or an imagination to produce for it even the pretence of existing.[50]

To explain evolution we must have recourse to such entities as do not depend for their existence on the outcome of that process. Whether it is possible even to begin to construct a theory of what such entities would be like in the absence of any conscious theorizer seems uncertain. But even if we can, it will do us no good when it comes to the question of the explanation of consciousness itself, for the reasons that I have been exploring. To explain 'the evolution of consciousness' in another sense, its progressive development and differentiation, may be a better bet: but if we attempt that effort we cannot rely on levels of consciousness that did not previously exist. The pre-human or pre-mammalian world was not, on this account, a realm of causally related material objects, but the ancestral Dreamtime: 'Perhaps the consciousness of animals is more shadowy than ours and perhaps their perceptions are always dreamlike'.[51] But if, as Wigner also supposes, James's black and jointless continuity of space (the imagined realm of physics) is a theoretical construct only, and the world of experience the primary reality,[52] it can only be from within that Dreamtime that the rise of human consciousness can be understood. The processes that lead from the relatively undifferentiated, episodic, uncritical forms of conscious being to our own happy state would have been those described in myth. The psychoanalytical interpretation

---

[50] Barfield (1963), pp. 85 ff.     [51] Wigner (1964), p. 261.
[52] See Eccles (1970), pp. 44 ff.

of mythology would be correct: but the mythology would also give a cosmic history.

This approach to our problem can be lent a little more plausibility by considering again our capacity for 'getting under the skin' of the most unlikely objects. Empathizing with other creatures, whether they be wasps or trees or quarks, is indeed one of the most significant of our exploratory techniques.[53] We so readily interpret things in an 'intentional' way that there is perhaps some reason to ask ourselves if we may not be right so to do. If we are led to explain the emergence of our present consciousness and its objects by the processes of the Dreamtime, we should perhaps note that we do have some access to those processes. When a scientist imagines what 'she would do if she were' a pi-meson, a protein molecule, or the like, maybe she is remembering what that mode of consciousness was and is like. The mathematical equations, the material models that we use are symbols or mementos of what earlier ages would have recognized as gods or angels. The 'objectivist' methodology that is usually considered essential to modern science, that depends upon denying any real place to intentionality in the interpretation of events, should not be allowed to dominate our ontology, nor dictate what methods should be used for ever after. There is more to be said for an animistic ontology and methodology than has been allowed. Even if we accept Morgan's Canon, that 'simpler' explanations be preferred (the misbehaving dog cowers from unformulated unease, not moral guilt), as a working programme, it does not follow that all explanation in terms of consciousness and its contents should be eschewed. It is simply a proposal not to attribute a greater degree of differentiation of consciousness than we need.[54]

But though this sort of animism has a better prospect than physicalism of answering James's plea for 'an evolutionary account of how a lot of originally chaotic pure experiences

[53] Humphrey (1976).
[54] Washburn (1917), pp. 25 ff; see Griffin (1976).

became differentiated into an orderly inner and outer world'[55] (note that this is not, as sometimes supposed, to be an account of how consciousness developed from purely non-conscious entities), it shares one assumption with Morgan and with naïve physicalism that deserves to be queried: namely, that we must suppose that simple and undifferentiated scious being came first. This is sometimes used to infer that other forms of life, being 'lower' forms, are bound to have 'lower' forms of consciousness. But wasps, of course, are not ancestral forms of human beings: they are quite distinct products of evolutionary change, and it is not clear that we have any good reason to expect them to possess simplified versions of our own consciousness. Even Uexkuell's tick may not really have the etiolated consciousness we suppose: it may merely be that the degree of overlap between her consciousness and ours is fairly small—we do not sense those objects that occupy her attention. Even if the spectre of a 'mindless' universe is dismissed we are left with a serious question, whether we have any good grounds for supposing that forms of consciousness will turn out to be mutually comprehensible. What is there in my consciousness that will enable me to put on or empathize with other human beings, other mammals, or more alien forms? Both Morgan and the animist I have so far described seem to assume that evolutionary change is orthogenetic. Why should it be? We grow from the same root, maybe, but why should the shoots be similar?

One traditional answer has been that human consciousness is a true reflection of that mode of conscious being from which all things take their beginning, and within which they dwell. If so, then we can reasonably expect that all other forms of consciousness will find a replica in us, and that if there are living beings elsewhere in the universe they have some chance of being recognizably anthropomorphic. This anthropomorphism will be only partial, residing in the fact that both the aliens and ourselves are 'theomorphic'. Without this assumption it seems vanishingly unlikely that the hopes

[55] James (1976), p. 18.

of science-fantasists will be fulfilled. Even if the theistic postulate were true, of course, there might be no other 'hnau'[56] than ourselves: but there is better reason to expect them on the theistic than the physicalist hypothesis, or the merely animistic. Briefly, if we find friends 'up there', that will be confirmation of theism!

This hypothesis is Berkeley's. Berkeley is so frequently misrepresented that it is necessary to insist that his non-physicalism requires the real recalcitrance of things, both 'spirits' and 'ideas', subjects and objects: *esse* is not merely *percipi*, but *percipi aut percipere*. Subjects are the streams, fields, realms of consciousness that together with their contents make up the furniture of the universe. The contents or objects of those fields are presented to us by that infinite, free spirit whom Berkeley names as God. Putting it differently, we can suppose ourselves to have more or less of the contents of God's realm made known to us as we make our choices. Encountering new items in the world is like traversing the imaginary space of a computer adventure game—with the caveat that the computer is unlikely to contain that space in any realistically subjective sense. Berkeley himself was ambivalent as to whether, for example, the moon's other face (as we should be permitted to see it were we suitably placed) is now and always present to God (so that we may really perceive the selfsame objects), or whether instead He merely has a permanent intention to impress certain ideas on each of us (perhaps in accordance with an archetypical idea of the moon that our ideas can only copy). My preference here is for the former model, for it is this which returns the pre-human realm to its realistic status. Our theories of it, at their best, concern what really was present to God and His angels, even though none of it was manifested to a mortal perception. Other aspects of God's 'fantasy game' are equally occult to us: with new perceptions new worlds open up, promising us 'a happiness large as our desires, and those desires not stinted to the new objects we at present receive from some

[56] A term coined by Lewis (1938) to mean such creatures as are rational animals.

dull inlets of perception, but proportionate to what our faculties shall be when God has given the finishing stroke to our nature and made us fit inhabitants for heaven.'[57] Consciousness did not evolve out of the absolutely non-conscious, nor has it merely been developed out of earlier, more primitive, less differentiated forms. Such development there may well have been amongst the spirits who roam God's fantasy, but they are on the way home, and their theories about what was there, before they came to be what they now are, are not wholly misleading.

It is worth adding that Berkeleian theism, which is to say merely traditional theism grown conscious of its own implications, evades the charge brought by Mackie against Swinburne's similar argument,[58] that it involves as magical a connection to found matter upon mind as mind upon matter. Mackie acknowledged that consciousness was real, and really distinct from merely neurological or behavioural facts, but insisted that 'the mind–body gap must be bridged somewhere and somehow'. If the way in which material event produces mental event is unintelligible, so also would be the way in which mental events produced material. It is, indeed, the very same unintelligible connection. But, as Mackie also recognized, the problem does not arise for Berkeleians: the connection between my imagining an orange and there being an orange is contingent, and the orange's coming into being on my imagining would be as magical an event as my imagining's coming into being when some neuron fires. But the connection between imagining and image is not magical: my imagining an orange and there being an imagined orange are not accidentally connected. What I can do for myself, God does for all. If I explain the existence of the phenomenal world by referring to God's action, the claim is not that God formed a plan that, by natural and unintelligible necessity, became reality (that doctrine has no advantage over

---

[57] Berkeley, *Sermon on Immortality*: (1948–56) vii. 12; *Essay on the Future State*: ibid., p. 184.
[58] Mackie (1982), pp. 119 ff.

materialism, at this point). The claim is rather that God's imagining, which is essentially linked to there being images, is the framework within which we live. There is indeed a difference between image and imaginer, so that Berkeley was not, *pace* Mackie, a monist, but the link between act and object is not magical.


V


From this theoretical perspective, and very briefly, it is possible to return to those problems about evidence which have impelled investigators to take up functionalist accounts of consciousness. Such accounts as these have the great advantage that they allow us to ignore the gap between evidence and reality: if the public operations of consciousness are one thing and consciousness itself another, as I believe them to be, it is always logically possible for one to exist without the other. In that case our reason for believing that the operations were indeed *evidence* of real consciousness would, on the usual view of empiricists, have to be empirical: but by hypothesis the reality of another's consciousness cannot be directly discovered, and we therefore have no empirical proof that consciousness and the supposed operations of consciousness are conjoined. We seem bound to lapse into agnosticism, though it is doubtful that a genuine scepticism could be long maintained without social backing. Those who genuinely doubt the existence of other human minds end up in asylums; those who genuinely doubt the real existence of animal minds are confirmed in their doubts by the approval of their scientific peers and the needs of laboratories.

   In this difficulty, which is paralleled in many other areas of scientific and ethical enquiry, it is understandable that some enquirers should decide either that they are only interested in the public event, or else that a correct understanding of the supposedly private worlds of consciousness would reveal that they were nothing more than the public events, that evidential claims define the meaning of the supposed truth for which they are the evidence. Such anti-realism is displayed in claims about historical truth, and mathematical, and ethical: to be 'true' in these areas is simply to be confirmed by the common sense of scholars on the basis of appropriate evidence. To be conscious just is to be awake (without any sense of what it is like to *be* awake). To be historically or mathematically true just is to be what current data can confirm (without any sense that what they confirm is truth). To be ethically true just is to be deduced from general statements about human nature or where happiness resides (these claims as well must be reduced in meaning to the evidence which has hitherto supported them).

All these claims, however, display the same fallacious reasoning. Moore's objection to the 'naturalistic fallacy', so called, rests squarely on the realization that no proposition can be evidence for its own truth.[59] That celibacy is bad for people cannot at once be our reason for believing that celibacy ought to be eschewed and the very same fact (if it is one) as that. That the records are rationally consistent only with the hypothesis that Hitler was the leader of Nazi Germany, not of Switzerland, cannot be the same proposition as the latter if is to be our reason for holding the latter. Just as Moore demonstrated that it is logically an open question whether loyalty, courage, and good temper are genuinely good (though it is an ethical truism that they are), so also is it a logical possibility (the supposition is not unintelligible) that our friends are 'intelligent' but 'unconscious' beings, objects and not subjects, though this is a claim that no sane person would make, or that the world was made five minutes ago, complete with compelling memories of times that never were. The truisms of morality, the guiding presuppositions of science and scholarship, are all synthetic truths, not analytic ones. Since they are the guiding truths of their disciplines they cannot be demonstrated from the axioms of logic, nor

[59] Clark (1980, 1984).

learnt from experience. We bring them to our study of the world and our place in it. Some thinkers have been inclined to end with this blank fact: that we make demands upon the world and have not yet been radically disappointed. In essence this existential commitment to realism hardly differs from the more radical-sounding constructivism, that 'facts' are only what we determine to rely upon, and 'objective truths' only those propositions that our current rules license us to propose. As I have repeatedly emphasized: if realism is to be secure we must advance some account of what sort of universe this is if creatures of our kind are to have such ready access to empirically and logically indemonstrable truth. We cannot believe it to be a brute fact that we get things right, for brute facts are precisely ones that we have no right to expect: it must be supposed to stem from the nature of things, that we do. If we are 'offspring' of a single consciousness whose workings are such as we, its offspring, reckon rational then such inbuilt metaphysical principles are to be expected. Otherwise I doubt that they are. My provisional conclusion is therefore that our choice lies between a theistic realism and atheistic constructivism. If we adopt the latter view, then consciousness is at once the very context of all our endeavours (such that all apparently realistic claims must be interpreted as shorthand for our projections and commitments) and also itself the unintelligible product of a mindless universe. Modern atheism hovers uneasily between metaphysical materialism and sceptical constructivism. Neither, so it seems to me, offers any good account of consciousness.

So where do we stand? In the absence of that direct access to the contents and subjectivity of other consciousness that God, the ground of our consciousness, must have, our natural conviction that we are confronted by another focus, locus of awareness must be accepted as good reason to believe that we are right until we are proved wrong. The cosmos is composed of such realms of consciousness, and the abstract map we make of it can only be a way of symbolizing to ourselves what dreams may come. I (this realm of conscious being) could have been, maybe I have been, 'a boy, a girl, a bush and a bird and a dumb fish in the sea'.[60] The creatures whose form is mapped into my own consciousness also map me in theirs. 'Even the trodden worm contrasts his own suffering with the whole remaining universe, though he have no clear conception either of himself or of what the universe may be. He is for me a mere part of the world; for him it is I who am the mere part.'[61] Jaynes replies that the worm's agony is only ours, not the worm's: 'Its writhing is a mechanical release phenomenon, the motor nerves in the tail end firing in volleys at being disconnected from their normal inhibition by the cephalic ganglia.'[62] But the fact that there is such electrical activity (that our observations are rationalized by supposing that there is) does not prove the absence of consciousness on any reasonable theory. On the theory that I advocate our conviction that the worm, or rather the attendant realm of conscious being, is troubled rests upon our natural response to the symbol it presents, a response that we can trust, however carefully, because we can believe ourselves to be the offspring of the Primal Consciousness.

Chuang Tzu and Hui Tzu were taking a leisurely walk along the dam of the Hao River. Chuang Tzu said, 'The white fish are swimming at ease. This is the happiness of fish.'
'You are not fish', said Hui Tzu. 'How do you know its happiness?'
'You are not I', said Chuang Tzu. 'How do you know that I do not know the happiness of the fish?'
Hui Tzu said, 'Of course I do not know, since I am not you. But you are not the fish, and it is perfectly clear that you do not know the happiness of the fish.'
'Let us get to the bottom of the matter', said Chuang Tzu. 'When you asked how I knew the happiness of the fish, you already knew that I knew the happiness of the fish, but asked how. I knew it along the river.'[63]

[60] Empedocles 31 B 117: Diels and Krantz (1952).
[61] James (1890) i. 284.
[62] Jaynes (1976), p. 6.
[63] Chuang Tzu: Chan (1963), p. 210.

# 8

# Animal Rights and
# the Peaceable Kingdom

## I

That all human beings have 'rights', and that any government which disregards them is at fault, are propositions very widely accepted in the civilized community. Quite what these rights may be, or whether they are to be understood as easily defeasible, or what may rightly or expediently be done to compel governments to acknowledge them are matters of debate. Even the vocabulary of 'rights' is not always used to the same effect. Do people have rights in a strong or a weak sense? Do those rights, that is, impose positive or merely negative duties on others? Am I required to help others to obtain those advantages to which they have a right, or only forbidden to deprive them of those advantages? Do their rights constitute a reason for us to act or refrain from acting, or is it rather the case that talk of rights is merely a way of saying how (for other reasons) we ought to act?

My own suspicion is that talk of rights must be conceived either as legal metaphor for the ways in which we ought to act, or as a relic of some more ancient system in which this apparent metaphor was realistic. Creatures have rights, maybe, as being protected by a celestial lawgiver, the god of hospitality or the god of oxen. The god will avenge any wrong done his creatures. Leaving this aside for the moment, we may agree that if talk of rights is to have any serious content it must at least require that the individual 'right-holders' are not to be treated merely as means to some generally desired conclusion. If my supposed rights can rightly be overridden as soon as there is the slightest general advantage in so doing, then I have no rights. To say that I have rights is at least to say that I ought not to be compelled to serve a supposed general good. My own view of what should be done should be allowed a considerable weight, at least about those matters which are of vital concern to me. This opinion can be made compatible with a generally utilitarian approach to ethical decision: things are done better, and the general happiness more effectively preserved, if individuals are permitted to make their own decisions about matters 'within their territory'. Some libertarian thinkers carry this to extremes, insisting merely on a maximal liberty compatible with an equal liberty for all, and forbidding all legislation except that which forbids direct harm to, or coercion of, others.[1] A more widely acceptable conclusion would be that individuals ought to live their own lives, and be assisted to do so. Individuals ought not to injure or unlawfully coerce others, but ought also to assist others—and may lawfully be compelled to assist others—to be responsible members of the community. In brief: we ought always so to act as to respect humanity in ourselves and others.

This general concern for human beings as such, their right to live their own lives with such assistance as others ought to provide, has many historical roots. That it is not self-evidently correct should be obvious: not all cultures have paid even lip-service to such a view of human beings. Perhaps only those with civil status were rights-bearers, and all others to be treated as mere means to the general advantage (whether or not their own presumed pleasures were relevant to the calculation): Untouchables, and slaves, and women, and strangers have all found themselves in this uncomfortable position. Perhaps those things which were held to be of 'vital concern' to the individual were not always those that liberal society would now consider such. Perhaps no one at all was to make her own decisions, but live entirely by the ancestral pattern: so that all personal decision was heresy or rebellion. The liberal view that all human beings just as such are equal members of 'the kingdom of ends' is far from obvious.

[1] See Rothbard (1982).

One root of the doctrine, and historically perhaps the most important, is the claim that all human beings are intended to be the companions of God. Because they are capable of acknowledging God's reality and entering into rational relations with God every one of them is valued by God as a unique potential companion. All are to be accorded respect; none are to be made merely to serve another's vision, for all have their own contribution to make to the divine polity; all are valued by God as they are (or as they are meant to be). The liberal humanist, abandoning God, prefers to say that all human beings are to be valued merely as members of that ideal community, to which each may make a unique contribution, or as avatars of the Goddess Reason, who may bestow a different partial truth upon each rational soul. With this background it is easy to see why infants, imbeciles, lunatics, and the senile are still owed the same respect: their uniqueness, their equal standing in the eyes of God or the Goddess Reason rests not upon their empirically discoverable natures but on the metaphysical thesis that really they are all rational souls. As liberal humanists grow less confident of this claim in its turn, so their assurance that all human beings have equal rights is muted. Lunatics and the senile are assigned rights because we rational right-holders might find ourselves in that position; infants and imbeciles are accorded rights out of irrational sentiment.[2] Only rational beings really have rights, because only they can be conceived as members of a rational community to which they may make a contribution. It seems likely that some yet more hierarchical concept of right will eventually be espoused, and society return to the older view that only those with the right civil status can really make their own decisions for themselves or expect others to support their efforts.

The view that all and only human beings 'have souls', have real natures that are to be fitted into God's kingdom, has been backed up by the view that 'animals' do not. Animals have been held to be mere mechanisms,[3] or at best concerned

---

[2] Frey (1980), pp. 30 ff.
[3] e.g. Malebranche: see Rosenfield (1968), pp. 43, 70.

only with immediate gratifications. In the latter case they 'have souls', but only in the sense that they are alive and sentient: they lack rational soul, and therefore supreme value. Accordingly, they have no rights, can make no rational contribution to the kingdom of ends, and can only be of service by serving the ends of the true subjects of that realm. This claim too, like the corresponding belief that even imbeciles are really human souls, rested not on observation but on metaphysical theory. Animals were not observed to be insentient, but required to be. Nor were they observed to be concerned only with immediate gratification, all of a kind, and incapable of any 'personal' response to God. What observations could warrant any such conclusion?[4]

That this is not the only possible attitude to take towards animals is also clear. The records of the saints are full of cases where particular animals were welcomed into as-it-were personal relationships.[5] The main strand of the biblical tradition has been that animals also live at God's hand, and are destined to membership in His kingdom when 'the wolf shall live with the sheep, and the leopard lie down with the kid'.[6] God's reply to Job can be paraphrased, as I mentioned before, as the flat declaration that human beings cannot expect any special treatment, and that all creatures are allowed their time and their liberty within the bounds that God has sent.[7] But despite these themes it has seemed plausible that only human beings could seriously be admitted as citizens of the kingdom: both because only human beings can recognize obligations of law and mutual respect, and because there seems no naturalistically imaginable condition of mutual peace in the non-human realm. We can at least imagine that people, while remaining people, should live at peace: but can the lion eat straw like the ox, unless he ceases to be a lion?

To deal with this problem it is necessary to examine the

[4] Clark (1982*a*, 1983*a*).
[5] Waddell (1934).
[6] Isaiah 11: 6 f.: also 65: 25 f., Hosea 2: 18; see Primatt (1831).
[7] Glatzer (1969), especially pp. 62 f., 73 f., 83 f., 177.

metaphysical presuppositions of humanism a little more closely. To say that all human beings, whatever their appearance, have a certain nature is to rely upon a form of essentialist typology which is no longer widely approved of in biological circles. On the older view, to be a given sort of creature was to have one-and-the-same nature as all others of that sort, a nature not shared with creatures of a different sort. Certainly that nature might be more or less accurately embodied in phenomenal reality. But what creatures empirically were was to be explained only by reference to what metaphysically they were. All phenomenal circles have a common essence, imperfectly embodied. All human beings likewise were held to have a common nature, which would at last be physically realized. The problem with this view always was that difference and variety were defects. Perfect people would be identical —but in that case it was difficult to see why individual idiosyncrasy should be respected. The more emphasis was placed on each individual's unique nature, the less sense there was in speaking of the common nature. One reply could be that human beings shared a generic nature, but had particular natures as well: but this ran the risk of emptying the generic nature of all content. Another reply might be that really identical people would act and behave in different ways in different circumstances. So how we should all behave is how anyone should behave in the appropriate setting. Individuals may then be understood as applications of the universal nature, universal law to particular occasions, and be valued as such. In so far as we do not do what anyone whose nature is identically human should do in our present circumstances, we do wrong.

Correspondingly, all animal types are monotypic: there is one way of being a dog (that may result in different behaviour in different settings) and to be a dog is to embody more or less defectively the essential idea of Dog. Modern biologists generally reject this claim, usually labelling it (inaccurately) 'Aristotelian'.[8] Aristotle's own view, in fact, was not so

[8] Mayr (1968), pp. 65 ff.; Hull (1964-5, 1965-6).

Platonic,[9] but later taxonomists drew on Aristotle, as well as on the rigid classifications of Leviticus, to construct a world of perfect types, such that there were absolute divisions between kinds. Although a creature might be a very defective dog, it still was a dog by virtue of its empirical character's being explained by (and judged against) the Ideal Type. To know what a dog was it was necessary to conceive a perfect dog, one that would perfectly embody the Type, one that would be what a dog ought to be.

This account of biological nature is still not wholly implausible. It has certainly not been disproved by any empirical investigation. If we chose to do so we might still maintain that all present species are of this kind, and even that they were created so. The fossil record is compatible with, and even seems to require, the relatively rapid emergence of new kinds, without the infinitesimal variations of Darwin's own theory. Such 'quantum evolution', so called, might be taken to suggest the existence of metaphysical types that are being intruded upon or mirrored in the world. There is, for that matter, no conclusive demonstration that evolution has occurred at all. The evidence, as I pointed out in chapter two, is compatible even with the special creation of this world and all the kinds there are.[10] But neither typology nor 'creation science' is now well thought of, and it seems better to see what follows from the presently dominant theory before dismissing it in favour of these relatively unexplored alternatives.

On the current view a species is a set of interbreeding populations. There is not, and could not be, a perfect specimen of a kind such that all other members of that kind must be its exact images or else defective specimens.[11] There is no common nature of a specifiable kind at all. This is not to say that no form of essentialist analysis is compatible with current theory: it remains clear that individuals do have

---

[9] Balme (1980).
[10] Gosse (1857), p. 345: 'the great plan of Nature: a grand array of organic essences . . . the whole constituting a beautiful and perfect unity, a harmonious scheme, worthy of the infinite mind that conceived it'.
[11] Sober (1980).

essences, i.e. have properties which they could not lose without ceasing to be the very individuals they are. It is also true that there is an essence of species-membership: to be a dog essentially is to be a member of a particular mammalian genealogy. But dogs are not to be regarded as more or less defective specimens of Dog, and it is not impossible (as it was on the older view) that an individual be a member of more species than one, as a hybrid or as being amongst the first of a new species. Each species is an individual genealogical unit: on the older view a species might vanish from the earth and reappear; on the current theory no such reappearance is possible, however similar the supposed revenant.[12]

This is not to say there are no such things as species. Creatures are not, as it were, scattered randomly over conceptual space. They cluster in genealogically related groups whose members do bear a family resemblance to each other. It is sometimes important to know which species a given individual really belongs to. But there is, none the less, nothing like the metaphysical division between humans and non-humans that the older typology required. There could be creatures, there have doubtless been creatures, that are genealogically related and morphologically similar to both human beings and apes. There could be, and doubtless there will be, hybrids that breed 'true': a Shanghai researcher, Que Yongxiang, is reported to expect a human–chimpanzee cross, which would (he supposed) be a suitable experimental subject.[13] Individuals do not have the character they do because an Ideal Type has been more or less well stamped upon them (such that to impose two such Types would generate a mere monster, a freak, or perhaps an example of the higher Type that both those specific Types belonged to).[14] They have their characters because the particular genotypes

[12] Hull (1978); Ghiselin (1974).
[13] David Bonavia: *The Times*, 11 Dec. 1980.
[14] See Rorty (1973), p. 412: 'the mule is a heap that walks like a substance' —a most un-Aristotelian thought!

they have inherited by Mendelian laws, with whatever chance variation, have produced under their circumstances the phenotypes they have. No individual is, biologically, a better example of its kind than another. A mongol child is not an imperfectly embodied Human, but a genotypic variation within the boundaries of the human population that does not seem to be capable of separate, sustained existence—there is no subpopulation of mongols. Even those offspring of human parents who seem genetically incapable of human speech and action are not defective embodiments of an Ideal Essence: they are simply what they are.

So on modern theory we can no longer take it for granted that all human beings have, or would have if circumstances allowed, a distinctive rational capacity. We no longer have the metaphysical assurance that imbeciles are really rational souls and chimpanzees are not. Nor do we have any metaphysical assurance that the human species is a clearly distinct group of creatures. It has no more (and no less) reality than a race or clan or family, save only that the barriers against out-breeding are more successful. Even this factor is perhaps of less moment than it was. Genetic material does get trans-ferred between species, not only by hybridization but by viral infection. Genetic engineering promises, or threatens, that characteristics of one genetic line (e.g. the capacity to fix nitrogen) could be inserted in another. We can no longer think of ourselves just as humans, any more than just as Britons or academics. We are the individuals we are, bred through millions of years, and carrying in us the possibility for further evolutionary change. Our descendants, if we have any, will one day not be of our species, will not be what we call human.

Again: it has been part of the older synthesis that it was for the sake of humankind that all the world was made. Liberal theologians have preferred the 'Ireneaean' form of theodicy, suggesting that the perils and changes of this mortal life, the evolutionary ages when humankind was not, were necessary for the production of free moral agents like ourselves, that in us the world finds its being:[15] a view which I rejected in chapter four. Farrer, it is true, added that God would not wholly have missed His aim if humankind never had developed, since animal and plant life also is of value. But even he seems to have believed that human beings could be expected to develop, unless some massive catastrophe had struck down the mammals as it struck down dinosaurs.[16] It is axiomatic in humanism and in liberal Christianity that God is more like us than He is like animals, that it is our rational capacity that makes us the image of God in the world, that it is chiefly for us that the world is made.

Once again, it is not possible wholly to disprove this view. But empirical study and current evolutionary theory do not support it. There does not now seem any good reason to expect that, if life has developed on some other world, it will have produced creatures like ourselves in being linguistic, rational, individualistic, and socially concerned. The invention of grammar and mathematics is not one that must be made. That it has been made only once in four thousand million years, and that neither apes nor cetaceans have (on the present evidence) managed it, is good reason to think that it is a very much less obvious discovery than, say, eyes or wings or social order. There is now no single crown to the 'tree of evolution': we are a remarkably successful breed, but so have other limbs of that tree been. We have no more assurance in empirical history of our own continuance than of any other kind's. So how can we any longer pretend to believe that the Creator is concerned only or even chiefly with the production of such agents as ourselves? He could have produced them far more often: as it is, Haldane's judgement is more plausible. Asked what we could infer about the Creator from terrestrial life, he replied, 'He has an inordinate fondness for beetles'.

It is also no longer possible to take it for granted that

[15] Hick (1968), ch. 15, s. 5.
[16] See Farrer (1966), pp. 69 ff., 98 f.; he also supposes (p. 153) the existence of e.g. a 'fundamental dogginess' that 'tends to prevail, and bring the individual [dogs] out true to type'.

human beings could survive by themselves. So strange a belief is this that I must devote some time to suggesting that it tends to be a liberal assumption that we might, that there might be nothing in the world but people and unliving things. Only on some such assumption does it make much sense to imagine human survival away from the earth of which we are a part, either by astronautics or by resurrection. To speak as if human beings could be resurrected bodily, yet there be no other living creatures born again, is nonsensical. It takes a universe to give me bodily life, from the algae on the sea shore to the stars of heaven. I would not survive as the bodily being I am without the support of the whole terrestrial biosphere and the cosmic environment on which it feeds, any more than I could be resurrected bodily without my liver. It is perhaps a half-recognition of this fact that has led liberal Christianity to abandon 'too physical' an interpretation of the resurrection—so that only the idea, the phantom of the Lord was raised. It only seemed that he was bodily—for if He had been, He would have raised the world with Him. He could of course, like Lazarus, have been raised into an existing world that went on unchanged; if he ascended and carried a body into the courts of heaven, he must also carry a physical world, the multi-millionfold creation (which is not to say a material world). To raise a body is to raise an indefinitely large biosphere.[17]

So the world is not what liberals have thought. How then shall God-fearing intellectuals contemplate it, and what can be said about the rights of all the creatures with whom we share God's world? That God aims only at us, and that only we are destined for His companionship seems no longer sound. What shall we say instead?

## II

The older humanism held that all and only human beings (unless perhaps there were angels) were to be respected as

[17] Galloway (1951), p. 47; Clark (1977a), p. 113.

being embodiments of Reason, or as capable of entering into intellectual relationships with other humans, though this capability was not always physically realizable. The more biblical view, perhaps, is that humans are to be honoured as the creation of God, beings who rest upon His providence and can call out to Him for vengeance. The blood, which is the life, is God's alone, and it is an offence against God to use His creation as if it were entirely ours. The creation story of Genesis decrees that humankind was made in the LORD'S image—but it is not said that all creation was directed to that goal. On the contrary, each stage of the creation is declared good, and in the folk-fable setting of the second creation-story it is not humankind alone that speaks. It is not implied that humans are like God in being rational, nor in being uniquely capable of contemplating and obeying His divinity, but that God made Himself a viceroy, not chosen for any special skill or capability, but as one on whom the Lord's Spirit rested. The biblical view of the animal creation includes the notion that their mouths are closed to speech— but they can be opened. Animals may serve as types of God and His saving action as well as humans. God's care reaches out to them, and they are to be included in the coming kingdom. If humans are allowed to use them it is on terms— 'thou shalt not muzzle the ox that treadeth out the corn'; if humans are allowed to hunt them, it must not be to their utter destruction; if humans use the land to grow their crops, they must not forget the wild beasts who share that land.[18]

The command to love the Israelite neighbour, and the stranger in Israelite territory, 'for he is a man like yourself', was to be one of the roots of that gradual extension of love, or lip-service, to all humankind. It does not rest on a rationalist appreciation of the essence, of humanity, but on the recognition of another subject of the LORD against whom we should not hold grudges.[19] What mattered was to

[18] Deuteronomy 25: 4; 22: 6; Leviticus 25: 6 f.; 26: 34 f.
[19] Leviticus 19: 18, 33 f.

build up a community to serve the LORD, and that service was to recognize our utter dependence and to make no idols. The powers of the nations, whose service ended always in bloodshed and idolatry, were to be seen against the backcloth of God's creation. God was not the idol of a larger nation, the self-image of human arrogance, but the One Incomprehensible of whom we must think only that He is not less than us, but who is no more like us than He is like anything that He has made.

The image of God's community was reinforced by Stoic meditation on the kingdom of the wise, that might be found in any nation or race. It has come to seem easy to suppose that all humans might some day live in peace—though they never have—and the duty of one who perceives that ideal is to treat all humans with an equal consideration. Any of them could, in principle, appeal to human courts established on this principle. Non-humans have been relegated. But if we look at the world with a biblical perspective, and acknowledge that the blood of all victims is poured out to God, that all creatures live in dependence on His grace, that not a sparrow falls to the ground without His knowledge and His care, we may remember another possibility.

In the present dispensation universal peace among humans, in which all just demands are met and no one's interests are injured, is a distant prospect, but it may be held that it is at least conceivable. No human being should depend for his or her livelihood on the oppression of his or her fellows. Some do, but they need not. It is open to us to seek out relationships that enable all of us to gain, governed by feelings of mutual respect and willingness to forgo the specious advantages of free-riding. Such a restoration may be more difficult than liberals perceive: what is to be done about the innocent descendants of brigands who now occupy land that the heirs of the aboriginals may justly claim? But we do have some inadequate grasp of what a just settlement between such feuding parties might be like. It is open to us also to modify our attitudes and behaviour toward the non-human, but it seems difficult to conceive of building up a community spirit between, say, tigers and North Indian farmers. By staying out of the tigers' way the farmers may avoid being injured. By helping those farmers not to have to cultivate land that is the tigers' prerogative other human beings may help to preserve the peace. But the tigers are unlikely to be encouraged to live at peace with humans, or understand the mutual advantages that humans and tigers could acquire. Something like such a social bargain has of course been concluded in the past: humans and dogs adopted each other long ago, though humans have so redrawn the bargain as to win the game.[20] But not all animals are open to such domestication or casual companionship.

Nor, of course, are tigers and deer likely to remain literally at peace. Even if human beings restrict their own depredations with a view to maintaining an uneasy truce, even if human saints demonstrate in their lives and actions that the wildest of wild beasts may grow to love a human companion, still predators must catch and eat their prey. There is no imaginable peace in the animal world, no justice that leaves all claims to life and liberty and the pursuit of happiness fully satisfied. 'One law for the lion and the ox is oppression.'[21]

The barb directed by Ritchie against believers in animal rights, that we ought then to defend the worm against the blackbird, the deer against the wild dog, I have sought to answer elsewhere,[22] by insisting that in most cases this cannot be our job. My concern here is with a slightly different problem: could there be a peaceable kingdom? And could we live by the rules of that kingdom, as we could (perhaps) by the rules of Kant's kingdom (though we don't)?

The first approach to the problem is to ask what rules of mutual relationship could now be maintained. The second to ask what sort of world it would have to be if some ideal rules

[20] Downs (1960); Ingold (1974), pp. 524 ff.
[21] Blake, *Marriage of Heaven and Hell* 24: Keynes (1966), p. 158.
[22] Ritchie (1916), p. 109; see Clark (1979, 1983c).

obtained. Our attitude to the first question will depend on our prior attitude to creation. If God, the source and epitome of value, maintains and approves of this world (apart from human sin) then the pattern of behaviour manifested in that world has to be understood as admirable. The same conclusion follows from a pantheistic declaration that the world itself is God (once again, with the possible exception of human sin). What is 'natural' would then be the blueprint for what is good, though it might not follow that human beings ought not to alter the existing pattern. Maybe God approves (or is) the transformations initiated by humankind, as well as those initiated by alligators. But it is more likely that those who take this attitude to creation suppose that Nature (apart from human action) is what ought to be admired or preserved.[23] To ask what rules of mutual relationship can now be maintained is therefore to ask what rules ought to be maintained: there is no gap between the ideal and the natural (as opposed to the artificial).

Those who reject the notion that the world as it now is can honestly be regarded as ideal, preferring to suppose that God is at war with a darkness more widespread than mere human folly, still have to ask the same question. It will not be enough to say what God would have the world to be, if this is beyond our power to bring about (even with the aid of prayer). We must also ask what can be done. The same or a similar problem faces humanists: granted that human rights ought to be preserved and protected, we must still deal with a world of nation-states in which no existing government either does or should have the power to enforce those rights. We have to reckon not only with the rules of a humanist utopia, but with the realities of power. Conversely, we must not only reckon with those realities, but hold the vision of the world that should be in our hearts.

So what rules can now be maintained? What rules would be maintained if humankind did not 'interfere'? Popular ecomysticism makes much of the supposed 'balance of

[23] See Clark (1983c), pp. 187 ff.

Nature', in which prey and predator work together to maintain roughly the same pattern. 'Upsetting the balance of nature', by acting so as to benefit one or the other, is held to lead to too-rapid expansion of the favoured kind, together with unpredictable effects on the surrounding environment. Some writers have a more or less rational suspicion that negative feedback mechanisms will sooner or later call a halt to the expansion. Lovelock, for example, has detected such loops in the biosphere as will maintain the ozone layer against depletion, or the level of oxygen in the atmosphere.[24] At a more local level it seems likely that although a new balance will be achieved eventually it will not much resemble the old: forests can be transformed to deserts. Once one balance has been lost it may prove impossibly difficult to restore it. There is no good reason to think that only humans ever upset things. Cosmic accident and evolutionary variation within particular genetic lines may lead to a collapse from whose degenerating spiral some new balance may at last be formed. The unchanging hills are an illusion: all things flow. The 'balance of Nature' rests in this, that local ecospheres, and the terrestrial biosphere, are such as to maintain the conditions for their own continuance against minor accidents. Established ecospheres are those that have not eliminated themselves, but rather (by the mutual interaction of innumerable organisms) made the environment for those organisms more hospitable. The biosphere is the complex of such mutually supportive ecosystems. They are not stable in the sense that they are immune to outside interference or to evolutionary change, but only in that one generation succeeds another without marked difference. 'Climax communities' are those relatively rich communities of organisms, that maintain an environment congenial to just those organisms, and a range of kinds sufficient to leave something living if disaster strikes, from which after many successive stages a new climax may be reached. Some such communities display an alternation of kinds, so that first one and then

24 Lovelock (1974), pp. 31 ff., 76 f.

another is dominant in the area, each making life easier for the other's growth. Failure to remember that such shifts are not irreversible sometimes makes us think that, for example, elephants are destroying the plant life of an area for ever, whereas their depredations are part of a continuing cycle. Attempts to interfere may not always be in the interests of the organisms and their heirs.[25]

Talk of the 'balance', or insistence that we do not interfere with it, often leads, paradoxically, to massive interference on our part with a view to maintaining what we take to be that balance. A better solution might seem to be that we do not change our techniques of land use too radically or too often. Conservation is, inevitably, conservative: established patterns in which different organisms have each their niche, 'paying the price of their mutual injustice',[26] are likely to be less obnoxious than the shifting patterns initiated by widespread 'improvements'. All kinds do alter, and all alter their surroundings, but they do so slowly and allow other lines to change their ways. Very rapid change gives a selective advantage to opportunistic species, equipped to take rapid advantage of novelty: many of these are sufficiently versatile and fertile as to constitute grave dangers for our own opportunistic expansion.

The rules of such a conservative approach to the world will be ones that rebuke *hubris*, emphasize limits, remind us not to take too much nor to demand too much protection against other kinds: the rules, in fact, of Deuteronomy and Jubilee. In such a world the wild dogs will continue to hunt down zebra, and display in their behaviour the most touching loyalty to and affection for their own kind. Wild dogs, despite their many natural virtues, would doubtless hunt the world bare, if they could, and so perish or turn to cannibalism. Unfortunately for us, we can, and must therefore be restrained not by brute impotence, but by respect for the other kinds with whom we live, and by fear of the judgement.

In such a world of finite, though infinitely reusable

---

[25] See Ehrenfeld (1972), pp. 148 f.
[26] Anaximander 12 A 1: Diels and Krantz (1952).

resources, can conservatives retain the humanistic passion to preserve and multiply the human form? Obviously not. What grounds could there be to hold all 'human' life sacred, and no other, whether by 'human' is meant what is capable of reasoned discourse, of merely what is born into the spatio-temporally locatable line known as humankind? If we are creatures like any other, who carry a particular form of life down the years, and must live within limits, claiming only that liberty which is compatible with an equal liberty for all —that is, the liberty to live for a season and to die—we should be very hesitant about devoting our resources to preserving and multiplying specifically human life. That world is the best that we can manage that allows a place and time for all, and no one must outstay her welcome.[27]

In developing this conservative response I have spoken of kinds, or forms of life, almost as if it were these kinds that ought to be respected, rather than individual creatures. A particular zebra has no general right not to be eaten by wild dogs: we cannot say that the wild dogs ought to be prevented from killing and eating her. Has zebrakind a right not to be eliminated? Those typologists who believe that zebras are the earthly and imperfect copies of a singular Form may claim, implicitly, that this Form has a right to earthly continuance. Perhaps they may even claim that it will continue, since 'the soul of sweet delight can never be destroyed'.[28] New creatures will one day manifest that likeness—as species after species has arisen to act out the drama of life at sea (sharks, fishes, icthyosaurs, cetaceans, penguins, seals, and manatees) or life in society (ants, ter-mites, bees, jackdaws, wolves, people). The True Zebra will return, though none call it so. In the absence of such meta-physical entities what can be said for the notion that kinds as such have 'rights', that 'they' ought not to be eliminated, or have a claim upon the support of those that can help

---

[27] See King-Farlow (1978), pp. 265 ff.
[28] Blake, *Marriage of Heaven and Hell* 9: Keynes (1966), p. 152; see Lessing (1982), pp. 62 ff.

them? A pure individualism can have no answer here: if individuals are all that matter then it does not matter if there are no more individuals of any given kind, unless this makes some painful difference to surviving individuals of another kind. A better understanding of what it is to be suggests that individuals (so called) exist as elements or nodes or slices through a wider whole. I could not exist without the world of which I am a part. My normal conviction (as a member of Western society) that I am that being which was born and will die and is separate in some real and important sense from all its contemporaries is perhaps a delusion. The being I am, or the being that mysteriously has this point-consciousness, is a segment of a spatio-temporal, and an intellectual, whole. It is those wholes which are the chief bearers of value: the understanding of the world through rational discourse; the world itself which is to be understood. It is, accordingly, not the individual zebra (human), nor yet zebrakind (humankind), that has 'rights' in any ultimate sense. It is the world itself, and the joyful understanding of the world, that ought to be admired, preserved, and cultivated.[29]

And is that all? It is perhaps the best that we can achieve, but perhaps it leaves something out, and that the answer to my second question: what ought the world to be? To which a third can now be added: what is this point-consciousness I am, that seems somehow not to be strictly identical with the very being (born thousands of millions of years ago, and stretching to the boundaries of space ) in which I find myself? On the one hand, the world could not be without the mutual exchange, the parody of love, that is predation. On the other, I could not be without the world, without the culture in which I speak, without the neighbours in whom I find my personhood. But it has seemed none the less that there is something more to Being than being the world that is, and more to Me than the very being I was born.[30] Are these questions linked?

[29] Clark (1975) pp. 189 ff., (1983c), pp. 193 ff.
[30] See Madell (1982).

### III

On the conservative view, zebras as such have no rights against wild dogs, although there perhaps ought to be zebras (or something like them), and an evil is done if the dogs take over all the world. Gandalf to Fangorn: 'You have not plotted to cover all the world with your trees and choke all other living things.'[31] Correspondingly zebras as such have no rights against people (nor people against tigers), though people are perhaps capable of a more sympathetic response to a zebra's plight than dogs may be. Conservatives, accordingly, stop short of advocating an ideal vegetarianism, though they may well (and rightly) boycott the denatured products of present-day farming practice, that treats the world and our fellow creatures merely as material, rather than as the companions of a more respectful day. If individuals do not matter all that much, then their deaths do not matter all that much either. Liberal tenderness about inflicting or allowing death (whether of farm animals or of moribund humans) is, on this view, the product of a superstitious regard for individual existence in the world.

But there is an alternative route to ideal vegetarianism, to which Barth bears unwilling witness.[32] To live without offering direct harm to God's creation is to anticipate the Kingdom, to live as far as possible by the laws that will obtain when God shall have made all things new. My discovery of the point-consciousness I am lies in realizing an obligation, a vocation, that transcends the being that I am associated with. In order to avoid confusion, it might be better to adopt Plato's locution: my Being resides in the point-consciousness that is aware of itself in becoming aware of obligation and world-transcendent destiny. The individual, or the world-segment, that is labelled 'Stephen' is not identically me, but only *has* me.[33] Stephen has a soul,

---

[31] Tolkien (1966) ii. 192.
[32] Barth (1961) iii. 4, p. 355.
[33] As a particular qualified by a universal is not identical with but only possesses, reflects, or copies the Form—which is not to say that the essential I is

but I am one. It is of some relevance that the older typology let (for example) the Dog stand to individual dogs as I stand to Stephen, not merely as Human stands to Stephen. Humans are peculiar in being individual Forms, while it is the Species-Form that adequately explains non-human creatures. With the collapse of typological explanation as a respectable scientific theory comes the realization that other animals than us may have such individual souls (as Plato, of course, already believed), even if they are not so far awake to their own being.

In recognizing myself as a transcendent soul, only contingently connected with Stephen (though it is of course true that I am known to myself only under the guise of some particular being), I recognize the ideal existence of a world beyond the world in which all things are done as they ought to be, the empirical beings perfectly united with their souls. Description of such a realm verges on the mythological. The Being that has or is had by the wolf lies down with the Being that has or is had by the lamb. Not that wolf-as-such lies down with lamb-as-such, for this could not be (save by occasional dispensation) and the creatures be what they are. But the I of the wolf and the I of the lamb do dwell together.

In waking up to this world-transcending discovery, that the Self is no part of the world,[34] we may reach further than the conservative. Once again, animals as such have no rights (any more than humans). But each creature is the outward sign of an equal soul, and to be respected as such. One who sees a friend looking out of the eyes of a beaten dog[35] can no longer think only of the ever-changing 'balance of nature'. To beat or imprison or kill is to close the eyes of one's own soul, to refuse to recognize our friends and equals through the windows of the world. It has long been understood that

an abstract universal, but only that it is like universals in being non-identical with the very being that is commonly said to 'be' it. See Eccles (1970), pp. 80 ff. for a discussion of the puzzling question: why am I identified with this particular genetic knot?

[34] Clark (1983b), p. 227; Wittgenstein (1961), s. 5. 632.
[35] Pythagoras, according to Xenophanes 21 B 7 Diels–Krantz.

to keep a fellow human as a slave is to refuse to be 'human', to insist on being that lesser thing, a master, a mere element in a social nexus. In refusing to play our part as elements in the biological nexus of prey and predator we remember ourselves as friends and equals from beyond the world.

Is this a memory that all of us could retrieve? On the face of it, it is not. The world rests upon predation and exchange, even if our human world should do so far less than it does, and should be restrained within bounds. It seems plausible that we should bow down in the house of Rimmon, serve the powers that be, remembering always our dependence and interrelatedness. Those who are called and compelled to bear witness to a wholly other way of being, to a realm where none compete for space or for resources, must surely be few in number—till the world is changed. Must not their life be agonized? There can, for them, be no thought that they have done all their duty: whomever they help they know that others go unhelped, and that 'one law for the lion and the ox is oppression'. A partial answer, in the tradition, has been that where a saint's eyes are opened other creatures too remember themselves and cease to rely on predation. 'The calf and the young lion shall grow up together, and a little child shall lead them.'[36] Isaiah doubtless meant no more than that the creatures would be so tame, by the Lord's contrivance, that they could be led as easily as cattle. Later tradition has made of that 'little child' a prophecy of the Lord Himself: a little child, one new-born to God's kingdom, will find in her remembrance of that day a joy that swallows up despair, and lead all creatures that she encounters into peace, into a reflection of the world beyond the world.

Those who believe that other creatures than the human 'have rights', that there is a way of justice in which all obtain their due, can adopt at least these two stances. According to the first, we ought to act by the principles of conservative justice, allowing the world to continue and acknowledging the limits that are placed on us. *Hubris* and cruelty and

[36] Isaiah 11:6.

*pleonexia* (i.e. always wanting to have more) are sins, are the very essence of sin. Such a conservative may refuse to participate in the careless practices of our corrupt and superstitious age, but will not hold it right always to refrain from killing fellow creatures, in such honesty and regard as possible.

The more radical view reminds us that each of us is more than the creature, or the world, with which we at first identify ourselves. Our life is to live out the implications of that higher vision, offering the promise of a world from which this realm is a temporary aberration. The radical's refusal to rely upon oppression, her recognition that the powers-that-be are not the ultimate recourse, makes sense within a radically transcendent metaphysic. Those who are called to it, to live out their own memory of being friends and equals in the world beyond, are as it were the waking beings in a world of sleep-walkers. Because they exist, even the conservative is reminded of the real value of the lives she deals with under the law of earthly justice. Catholic Christianity has been loath (with good reason) to admit that there may be two ways, the more and the less perfect. Other traditions (with good reason) have insisted that there are. Most of us must live under the authority of the powers that be, having not been granted the miraculous foretaste of the Kingdom that some saints have known. We must still pay the penalty for our mutual injustice, and cannot yet expect the miraculous birth to which St. Paul refers.[37] But if we are not to lapse into pantheistic idolatry we must bear that other life in mind. We are the children both of earth and heaven, and all living creatures are the same.

[37] Paul, Romans 8: 19 ff.

# 9

# The One and the Many

I

Attentive readers will by now have begun to suspect the existence of unresolved tensions in the thesis I am expounding. On the one hand, it is necessary to suppose that the source of universal order is also the source of our fundamental principles; that Consciousness is something quite distinct from Intelligence or cerebration, and had no need to evolve, as having been 'there' already; that scholarship rests upon a fundamentally optimistic trust that our hopes and ideals are appropriate. On the other hand, we have no good reason to believe that the LORD is more like 'us' than He is like other creatures; 'our' capacities are to be understood as those of placental mammals, not wholly alien to the world around us; and scholarship rests upon a readiness not to be ruled entirely by our favourite theories.

> This discord in the pact of things,
> this endless war twixt truth and truth,
> that singly hold, yet give the lie
> to her who seeks to yoke them both—
> do the gods know the reason why?
> Or is truth one without a flaw,
> and all things to each other turn,
> but the soul, sunken in desire,
> no longer can the links discern,
> in glimmering of her smothered fire?[1]

Boethius' hope was that we might one day add the truths we have forgotten to the truths we half remember, and so see that there is no inconsistency between truth and truth. Until that high moment, it must be admitted, we must often accept

[1] Boethius: Waddell (1952), p. 59.

antagonistic theses, each of which seems true and good-to-be-believed, but whose conjunction poses a riddle we cannot yet resolve. Some riddles we have seen: we know already how a thing may fall for ever and yet be stationary above the earth (in geosynchronous orbit), how solid glass may flow, and light be both particles and waves. Other riddles seem more difficult: how can it be that we are both physical creatures, indistinguishably part of the whole sidereal universe, and transcendent beings, individual selves that can separate themselves in thought from the very beings they physically 'are'? How can it be that the world is at once the awe-inspiringly beautiful object of high contemplation, and the cess-pit of the heavens, the shambolic muddle that we, or our less fortunate colleagues, must endure?

Intellectual virtue, like ethical virtue, rests in a mean,[2] about the acceptance of opposing claims and the pursuit of consistency. Those who pursue absolute consistency by refusing to entertain all propositions that conflict with their ruling hypothesis are bigots; those who devise merely *ad hoc* solutions to apparent contradictions, never admitting that one or other thesis must by now have been refuted, are fanatics; those who are content to contradict themselves, and do not seek the answer to any riddles, are buffoons; those who believe nothing, but make no effort to imagine order, are merely bores. Intellectual virtue rests in yoking these twin passions, to 'save the phenomena' and to save consistency. The good intellectual does not expect her system to be perfectly consistent, but does not despair of finding that reality of which she has such partial views. The good intellectual holds fast to the law of non-contradiction, as the condition of all rational discourse, but does not take it for granted that she can infallibly detect a contradiction.

We have now no complete and perfect theory about the

---

[2] See Clark (1975), pp. 84 ff: Aristotle himself did not apply the doctrine of the mean to intellectual virtue. I should add that I intend no insult to any bigots, fanatics, buffoons, or bores that may be reading this!

world, no single perspective from which (uniquely) all other perspectives can be understood. That, paradoxically, can be the key to an informal understanding of the universe. What is real are the manifold perspectives, Uexkuell's 'countless multitudes of iridescent worlds'[3] and what is true and honourable is our acknowledgement that each of us is but one jewel in the net. That God is, in some sense, neutral between Job and Satan, and 'gives to all His creatures His boundary so that each may become fully itself',[4] is the beginning of wisdom. But it must at once be added that, in some other sense, God—the supreme value—cannot be neutral between Good and Evil. We are apparently required to believe both that every perspective is as good as every other, and that some perspectives are indubitably better. How can we resolve this riddle?

How can I expound any solution without presenting one more partial truth? How can we expound what we believe if we simultaneously announce that the opposite opinion may be as true as ours? To this one traditional response has been that the One Truth is indeed incomprehensible, that even the angels cannot grasp the One:

The angels, despite their proximity to the throne of His liberality, the great extent of their burning love for Him, their glorification of the majesty of His might, and their proximity to the unseen of His kingdom, are capable of knowing only what He has taught them of His affair, although they are of the Sacred Kingdom in terms of rank. It is because they possess knowledge of Him only as He created them that they say 'Glory be to Thee! We know not save what Thou hast taught us!'[5]

Those who are 'firm-rooted' in the truth acknowledge that the One Truth is more than they can ever comprehend, that their small partial truths are given them. To say anything at all of the One Truth is to limit it, to turn it into something we can handle. At the same time, it has been traditional to think that the One has set its own images in the world, that

---

[3] Uexkuell (1926), pp. 71 f.
[4] Buber (1949), p. 195: Glatzer (1969), p. 63.
[5] Chittick (1980), pp. 31 f.

the One Truth has so created us as to find some model of the One, that is willed for us. Although no positive description that we could give is strictly true of the One Truth, yet there are some things that we should think of it, although they are not true, or not the only and comprehensible truth.

It is by the balance of negative and analogical imagination that theologians have worked. On the one hand, even our best endeavours can only depict God as He has chosen to appear for us; on the other, if He has so chosen, what God-fearer could reject the gift? We cannot conceive what it is to be God, or what it is to be those qualities that God must be. If we say of Him that He is all-loving or omniscient or almighty, it is not because we can conceive what it is like to be these things, or because we know exactly what follows from the possession of such attributes. All that we can rightly mean by such claims is that He is not subject to mortal limitations: in Him there is no shadow of turning—but what it is that the shadows do not hide is more than we can say. Similarly the Buddha:

The extinction of greed, the extinction of anger, the extinction of delusion: this indeed is called Nibbana . . . There is an Unborn, Un-originated, Uncreated, Unformed. If there were not this Unborn, this Un-originated, this Uncreated, this Unformed, escape from the world of the born, the originated, the created, the formed would not be possible.[6]

Of the Unborn by which the enlightened find themselves illumined Gautama said, could say, nothing, except that it was to be found in the extinction of greed, anger, and ignorance. If we have images of it, these derive from mamma-lian parental care, or dominance relationships, or sexual fantasy.[7] We may be right to think of God like that, but this is not because these thoughts are true of God.

The negative way has had a poor press amongst Western philosophers since Hume pilloried Demea in his *Dialogues*. How does an incomprehensible deity differ from no deity at all, or from incomprehensible material substance? If we

---

[6] Anguttar–Nikaya 3. 53, Udana 8. 3: Goddard (1970), p. 32.
[7] Clark (1982a), pp. 94 ff.

cannot understand what God, having the nature that He does, would do, how is God an explanation of anything? We only explain the truth of $p$ by adducing an hypothetical truth $q$ if (1) $p$ is more likely to be true if $q$ is true, and (2) $p$ & $q$ together are not less likely to be true than $p$ alone. But if we cannot tell what is more or less likely to follow if it is true that 'God exists', because we cannot conceive what it is for God to exist, what it is that we suppose exists, then such an hypothesis can have no content. Maybe God's existence does explain the world's, but not to us. What would be at stake between a purely apophatic theist and a generous atheist?

Berkeley, as so often, had observed the crux, and accepted that there are many ways of using language. Statements of a positive nature about God, or the One Truth, were not judged to be correct because they were accurate, but because they evoked the proper sentiments, of awe and love, and the proper actions.[8] Similarly James:

It is more than probable that to the end of time our power of moral and volitional response to the nature of things will be the deepest organ of communication therewith that we shall ever possess. In every being that is real there is something external to, and sacred from, the grasp of every other. God's being is sacred from ours. To co-operate with His creation by the best and rightest response seems all He wants of us. In such co-operation with His purposes, not in any chimerical speculative conquest of Him, not in any theoretic drinking of Him up, must lie the real meaning of our destiny.[9]

The difference between Demea and the mere agnostic is that Demea supposes, as the agnostic does not, that there is a way of responding to the First Cause, the One Truth, the Incomprehensible Beginning. He follows the road that is signalled by the flood of 'religious feeling' whose force Hume's Philo also acknowledges.[10] Whatever it is that God is, it is worshipful; it is worshipful precisely in that it cannot be adequately

---

[8] Berkeley, *Alciphron* 7. 5 ff: (1948–56) iii. 291 ff; see also ibid. 301: 'Faith is not an indolent perception but an operative persuasion of mind.'

[9] James (1897), p. 141.

[10] Hume, *Dialogues* Part 12: (1976), p. 245; see Cupitt (1971), pp. 69 ff.

characterized in its own nature. It is not an explanatory hypothesis in the same sense as ether or phlogiston or Planck's constant—a being that, in conjunction with other beings and in accordance with laws not of its own making, may be supposed to bring about the experiences we have. To treat it is as such is to adopt the attitude of one who is detached from the scene, no part of the movement of the Spirit to its source. Genuine religion rests in awe and in obedience, not exposition.

That there is a truth here can hardly be denied. Although I have offered good reasons, as I suppose, for thinking that the explicability of the universe—what Einstein called its one incomprehensible feature, that it is not incomprehensible —is explicable, and expectable, on the theistic hypothesis alone, I do not wish to make this a mere hypothesis. That the universe can be understood is one thing, and well explained by the supposition that the universe and the human mind have a common intellectual source; that the Source is wholly comprehensible is another, and unlikely thesis.

So the One Truth is not one that we can formulate in words: to try and do so is to formulate some lesser truth or half-truth, and maybe to mislead the innocent. Instead the religious intellect must learn to rest in the response of the Spirit, to let in the life of which we, and all things phenomenal, are the partial images. We cannot know God as an object or imaginary object external to our lives; to know God, in the only way open to anyone, is to recognize the godly response in us; to know God is to know a little of what God knows, and the route to this knowledge is through love.

In this I follow Platonic precedent. The perceptible world is the image of the intelligible, the hint given to the sleepy soul. The Logos, which is the totality of the divine Ideas, is immanent in the perceptible world, and is awakened in us as Eros:[11] to love is to be wise, or as wise as we can be. The technical vocabulary in which later Platonists cloaked their

[11] Plutarch, *De Iside* s. 373, *Dialogue on Love*: s. 746 ff. Dillon (1977), p. 206.

thought has many subtleties which more expert mystagogues than I may recognize as making sense of their experience. My concern here is to expound a little of the metaphysical theism that has been developed to cope with the paradoxes of apophatic and analogical theology. Any image that we have in our hearts of the One Truth is only an image. Of God Himself we can say nothing, even that He exists, without at once denying what would usually be implied by the attribution of such a property to a created being. The proper religious response to life is awe and obedience, not the projection of our fancies about God into the Void. But if that is the proper response it is inevitable that some images will be appropriate, some not. If we declare that 'God is not anything that we can name or conceive', it is not to propose an image of inscrutable and untouchable power. To be inscrutable, dispassionate, impassible, changeless, and without particular nature is, for creatures, to be something less than human, less than mammalian. What is meant in saying that God is these things to deny that any image is His equal, not that He is what we would tend to think of Him if He were an arbitrary and irrational tyrant (which is what inscrutability and lack of limitation means to us). Blake[12] was right to offer the image of a reptile for such a god—not that actual reptiles (non-amphibious vertebrates that are neither birds nor mammals) are like that, but that the character of dispassionate egoism is what we associate with the breed. We need such images as evoke in us the awe and obedience and love that is the only route to knowledge of the One. What we know in experiencing that awe is part of what He knows; the life with which we know it is the divine life immanent in us.

Orthodox believers may recognize my reconstruction of Trinitarian doctrine, not as this is expounded simply in the Christian churches, but as the common sense of late Platonic, Alexandrian and medieval Jewish, Eastern Christian and Islamic thought. There is the One beyond all categories.

[12] Blake, *Europe* 10. 16: Keynes (1966), p. 241.

There is the Logos, the pattern that the One eternally begets through which the phenomenal world retains its being. There is the movement of the Spirit through which the Logos is experienced, and which partakes both of the One and of its Word.[13] That Spirit, I should emphasize, is not to be understood as less than rational: very often it is known as Nous, the intellectual grasp of what cannot be demonstratively proved. Some of those moved by the Spirit look chiefly toward the Logos, the intelligible pattern by which the worlds were made; others look toward the One, finding no words to say of it, but being a sign for others—being indeed the Logos for those others. Both routes are to be approved.

Philo, the Alexandrian Jew and Platonist whose study is a necessary prolegomenon to any understanding of the Christian Fathers, distinguished between the children of the Logos and the children of the One. Perfection, for him as for most mystics, required that we rise 'above the intermediary world of Logos, Sophia, Angel and Anthropos to the presence of God himself'.[14] It was St. John's conviction that the only-begotten Son (which is to say the Logos) was our only link with the Father, but that to 'know' the Logos embodied in the man Jesus was to participate in that same life, to be filled by the same Spirit—and so, in the end, to be directed to the Father.[15] To 'know' the Logos in Jesus was a greater gift than to 'know' it in the Torah and in tradition or even in Moses (as Philo proposed), for the knowledge involved was of the participatory kind.

The true knowledge of God lies in the doing of His commandments, or the letting-through-us of divine enlightenment. The metaphysical system to which I have drawn attention is itself no more (and no less) than a useful image. To say that the Divine is 'made up' of One and Logos and the Life, that it is Being, Mind, and Joy, is itself a gesture at the level of the Logos. The One Truth is not known by

[13] Porphyry, *Vit. Pythag*: Dillon (1977), p. 347.
[14] Philo, *Confusion of Tongues* 147: Dey (1975), pp. 31, 44.
[15] John 1: 1–14; 14: 9–21.

scholasticism; nor is the Logos (as it is immanent in our best intellectual endeavours) the sort of thing that it is easy to characterize; nor can the Life be lived in any other way than through the living of it. But these truisms should not distract us from philosophy: there is an error committed both by naïve believers and by certain modern theologians.

## II

The error is the one of supposing that the religious life, the life of the Spirit, requires no intellectual effort. Amongst the naïve believers this issues in the claim that religion is a matter of pious emotion, that there is no scope for argument or for coherent exposition. Glossolalia becomes the only permitted speech about the Unborn and Indestructible. Amongst the 'moderns' it results in an insistence that 'God' does not name an objective reality that is met with in many different aspects (which is perhaps the main criterion of a real thing, that it crops up in more guises than one), but simply the internal object of religious and ethical devotion. God, as a being even of the most oddly metaphysical kind, should be abandoned in the name of religion. Neither position is an entirely foolish one, and though I have already made my disagreement clear I would wish to agree with much that has been said by such thinkers against the literalistic nonsense of too many philosophers. As I have hinted before, some atheists seem to find it necessary to believe that theists, to be 'real' theists, must believe in the existence of Nobodaddy or Ialdobaoth: an individual person of vast power and unknown policies who unpredictably interferes with what would otherwise be expected to go on.

There might be such beings. Science fiction is full of them. There might even be events that called for such an explanation, or that were (at least) susceptible of such an explanation. It is not wholly unreasonable to explain astronomical events (quasars? supernovas? dark patches in the sky?) by reference to interstellar civilizations with the power to use the energy of whole stellar systems, though I know of no events that absolutely require such an hypothesis. If there were such a 'Galactic Empire' it might even have an interest in terrestrial affairs, and good reason not to be too open about its involvement here. It might even have sent messengers to us, whose garbled words of hope live on in sacred texts and proverbial wisdom. Such an 'empire' might even be of a kind that deserved our loyalty and admiration, so that we rightly felt something like religious awe for it—though this, I suspect, would rest in part on our perception of the heroic courage it displayed, or the sheer unexpectedness of its achievements. Finally (to complete the analogy) such an 'Empire' might turn out to be something more than a confederation of individual beings: maybe it speaks with one voice, as being of one mind and spirit. Maybe it embodies almost all that we have ever thought about the perfect life.

Such a story, of course, may serve religious purposes as well as earlier stories about angelic hierarchies in the heavens (they are indeed the same stories, in a different mode).[16] It is not too difficult to be convinced (if once one wishes to be convinced) that there is likely to be life elsewhere than here, that it has had time enough to grow towards a temporal perfection, that there are signs and stories in our human history that suggest that maybe we have been visited. Equally, it is not too difficult to convince oneself of the opposite: that 'life' or living matter is a fluke, that any extraterrestrial parallel is likely to be quite unlike us, that there is no reason (except that provided by analogical theism, as I expounded it before) to expect such aliens to have achieved any humanly conceived perfection, that the episodes and artefacts dredged up by pamphleteers have simpler explanations than Galactic visitors, that any empire that permits the shambles of our history is lacking in benevolence or power.

A supposed theism that had the same structure as my fantasy would deserve obloquy, especially if its supporters then began to force their fantasy on others, or to proclaim

16 See Lessing (1979), especially pp. 35, 195 ff, 357 ff.

that they alone knew what the Empire wanted us to do, or
that enemies of the Empire must be enemies of all decent
life. Such an endeavour, surely, would be recognized as
egoism? Or else (which is the same thing) as an action of the
angelic powers, in open rebellion against the One, the Great
First Light. The Galactic Empires of science fiction are
oppressive and narrow-minded as often as they are embodiments of decency.

What is it about such fantasies that speaks to our condition, and why are they beside the genuinely religious point?
If earlier ages found it possible to believe in angelic hierarchies, associated with the planets and fixed stars, why
should it not be proper for this age to suspect the existence
of Galactic Empires and the like? To believe in them would
transform our every perception of the sky at night, would
make the universe at once more homely and more frighten-
ing in a way that does evoke much the same feelings as more
ancient mythologies. One difference between the two sorts
of mythology is that angels were conceived as standing
wholly outside 'nature' (in the sense of what grows from
small beginnings by innate principles): angels were created
as they were. The Galactic Imperials, on the other hand, have
come to be by ages of evolutionary and historical change.
But this distinction is not absolute. On the one hand, some
have held that angels were our elder siblings, that we too
would grow to their maturity (for good or ill), or even if
there were a great gulf fixed between the mortal and
immortal folk, yet angels (or gods) were creatures that began
and grew; on the other, it is possible to conceive that the
Imperials are of another kind than ourselves, that they are,
for example, crystalline or electro-magnetic life-forms, not
individual and maturing beings. Even angels were part of
'nature' in the other and wider sense: the system of inter-
relations and dependencies that might not have been, that
rests for its existence on the creative act of the One.

This points to the first reason why belief in Galactic
Empires, or in angels, or in gods is not to the theistic point.

Any such story might conceivably be true, but they might all be false. Whether there are Imperials, or angels, or the gods of Greek, Egyptian, or Scandanavian mythology depends on factors not in their control. No being that is of a kind that comes into existence, or that could exist only in some possible worlds, can be responsible for its own existence. The rules under which it exists, whether it exists for a time or even for all the time there is (in some particular possible world), are such as to constrain its being and its powers. A contingent being, one that exists if and only if something else is the case, is not what theists are talking about. That being than which nothing more perfect can be conceived is not one whose existence and character is dependent on something else beyond its own control. A perfect being, if it exists at all, must exist 'of necessity'. If it does not, then this cannot be because of some failure in an external causal chain—as if 'God' would have existed if the Big Bang had gone slightly differently, or if a different range of amino-acids had formed in interstellar dust. If the most perfect being does not exist it can only be because there is some flaw in the very concept, because it simply does not make sense (if not-$p$ then not-$q$). Conversely, if it does make sense to speak of God (the One, the most perfect being), then God does exist (if not not-$q$, then not not-$p$: i.e. $p$). This argument, of Anselm's,[17] is, I believe, entirely valid, though it is open to determined atheists to deny that talk of God makes sense. What is not possible is to admit that such talk makes sense and yet deny that God, so understood, exists. The One towards whom theists look is not identical with any contingent being, and mythologies that identify the One with angelic hierarchies, Galactic Empires, or Universe Incorporated (the eleven-dimensional mega-beings who constructed our particular cosmic bubble as a commercial venture: it has an Arts Council Design award . . .) are mistaking the case.

For the same reason, my own exposition of the

---

[17] Anselm, *Proslogion* ch. 3: Hick and McGill (1967), p. 6 f.

epistemological argument for theism would be misleading if the conclusion were merely that the world is constructed according to a blueprint of which we have at least fragmentary memories—that might well be true in a world made by Universe Incorporated. The problem would then be how the mega-beings knew their environment, and so unendingly. What is needed is an explanation that explains itself, that could not be otherwise, and therefore needs no additional hypothesis. That is provided, if at all, by nothing but the One. To deny the One is to deny the possibility of explanation, to say that all things happen 'just as chance would have it', and so at last to give up rational discourse.

But there is one more point to be made before abandoning Galactic Empires. Attentive readers will have recognized that my own exposition takes more seriously than most recent theological discourse the ancient claim that this world is full of demons. As believers in Galactic Empires suspect that events in human history or in the heavens are really to be understood as acts of the Imperials, so I am ready to suppose that all mundane events are the outward and visible sign of demonic activity. My reason is that the processes of scientific investigation appear to involve something like a communing with what lies behind appearances. To investigate is to imagine oneself into the subject. More generally, to think at all (for most of us, most of the time) is not an act of ours: thinking is rather the passing of thoughts through our attention. What control we have is a matter of direction and rejection, not of creation. Evagrios suggested that we could learn to recognize what demons were besieging us, by the characteristic images that came floating into our minds:[18] the faces or bodies or voices of those who have irritated or aroused or embarrassed us, snippets of conversation or outmoded theories. The art of thought, very often, is to know what not to think, what path not to follow, what theories to forbid ourselves to use. Demon-possession is what follows when we have abandoned the right way.

[18] Evagrios: Palmer *et al.* (1979), p. 38.

That this is how the world is is a hypothesis, though by no means an arbitrary one. The world 'might not' have been like this, though I am not sure what it could have been like instead and still been intelligible to its inmates. If this is how the world is, then James[19] was wrong in one crucial respect in claiming that 'in every being that is real there is something external to, and sacred from, the grasp of every other': wrong, or at any rate misleading. On the view of things that I have been expounding individuals are not to be regarded as entirely atomic or monadic beings. James would indeed have agreed in other contexts. As long as we regard our friends or our universe merely 'from outside' we do not understand them. If all we can do is record what is made known to us through the senses we never know, can hardly even conceive what it is for them to be what they presently are. To know them is to share experience with them, to live with their life. On the materialistic hypothesis this can be no more than self-delusion. Lovers may imagine that sexual congress is a true coition, but 'in reality' they only experience their own delights, even if some of these depend on their belief that their partner is delighted (in his or her own way) as well. However accurate the medium of communication (and how accurate it is is something we can never know) individual souls are sacred. On the hypothesis I am exploring, this is not entirely true. The life I live may be one that others live as well: the self-same life, not one of the same kind. The thoughts I think, that move through the consciousness I am, are ones that others have as well. One demon may possess a nation, so that all its members find great difficulty in remembering what other lives there are. 'Obsession' and 'inspiration' are words born out of such an understanding. Those who 'fall in love' are fallen into the world-view of what was once a deity. Such demons are not all amenable to reason, though they may themselves devise what sound like reasons to their victims. Peter Dickinson, in the person of a Jewish doctor, tells the story of Saul, possessed by a 'Rational

[19] James (1897), p. 141.

Demon', Rakah, who finds and creates reasons for what we should call Saul's paranoid distrust of David.[20] In calling his condition 'paranoia', of course, we explain nothing, and in hoping eventually to find some chemical correlate of the condition we betray our misunderstanding of what could be an explanation. No events of a material kind strictly explain subjective conditions, for reasons that I discussed in an earlier chapter. Whatever drugs we find to ward off Rakah will play the same role as the Jewish doctor's herbs and charms. What really matters is angelic help, where 'angels' are understood as those powers of the world that still owe allegiance to the one straight way.

Participatory knowledge, the process of living with the same life as those we would know, enables us to know from within what we could not otherwise know at all. Two points need to be made. The first, that Reality as I am sketching it is something that cannot be known merely externally. What makes most stories of Galactic Empires irrelevant to religious concerns is that the Imperials are conceived as merely external beings, 'out there' in the world. But it is the central thesis of theistic and semi-theistic doctrines that the principles and powers of the world are not merely 'out there', but here within. The false conclusion has sometimes been drawn that they should be regarded merely as 'psychological constructions' (a topic to which I shall return). The point is rather that we, as we normally conceive ourselves to be, are the psychological constructions. Jung saw this truth, though he does not seem entirely to have understood it. In 1958 he dreamt of lens-shaped UFOs that turned to magic lanterns pointing at him: 'Still half in the dream, the thought passed through my head: We always think that the UFOs are projections of ours. Now it turns out that we are their projections. I am projected by the magic lantern as C. G. Jung. But who manipulates the apparatus?'[21] If imaginative cosmography is to be true to the religious life it must allow

---

[20] Dickinson (1980), pp. 117 ff.
[21] Jung (1967), p. 355; see Clark (1983*b*), pp. 219 ff.

that the stories are to be understood from within. If the Imperials are not only to be found through the senses as objects, but also experienced from within as the powers that make our lives, then they may be an approximation to the truth. But it is probably better not to think that we should find them 'out there': that distracts attention from the real centre.

The second serious point is this. If enjoyment as well as contemplation is a mode of knowledge, and the powers of the world are to be known by inward means, by sharing in their life, the way is open for a mode of divine knowledge that reveals a truth in the popular error that religion is a matter merely of emotion. We cannot know the One as an object, cannot articulate any truth about it and be sure what follows. What we know is, at best, the best that we can conceive, the pattern set in things and in our hearts. We know that the best of all things must exist, but what that Best may be is beyond our grasp. We 'know' by participating in the one straight way, by turning from the distractions of the demon-world. To love is to be wise. Those who find the centre in themselves that is also the centre of all other life, the source from which all things get such strength as they have, are the ones who are the voice of the divine. To that extent it is correct to say that religion is not a matter of external judgements, descriptions of how the world is. True piety is to live by the Spirit. But it does not follow that we can have nothing at all to say about what the universe must be if such a life is to be possible, and appropriate. If we were truly nothing but placental mammals on a ball of grubby rock, in a universe that falls 'as chance would have it', with no powers but those that served to spread genetic material, piety would be as insignificant as hunger or sexual desire or scholarship.

### III

The One is incomprehensible, not to be grasped by intellectual means. Piety resides in going along the one straight way,

---

[22] Clark (1977a), p. 145 ff.

holding to the intention of thankfulness and love: holding also, perhaps, to the sense of being forgiven. Although popular religiosity often revolves around the notion that we are being, or might deservedly be, punished, there is good reason to suspect that this belief is one of those demon-inspired thoughts that we should doubt. Love and thankfulness, which are the keys to happiness, are hardly possible for those who are convinced of their own guilt, or are waiting for some punishment. Religious ritual acknowledges that fear and guiltiness only to dissolve it. It is unfortunate that, for whatever causes, we have confused 'forgiveness' with 'being let off with a warning', and God the Forgiver with a lax magistrate. 'Knowing ourselves forgiven' is an experience or life that other traditions than the Christian know, though other words are used: the realization of Nirvana, for example, that cannot be achieved by one's own effort to act or to believe.

But if all this is so, if there are no unequivocally and uniquely true statements about God (as if God were one being amongst many), and if what counts is religious piety, the realization of forgiveness, the walking of the one straight way, is there not something to be said, after all, for those who have slipped from orthodoxy into 'Christian atheism' and its equivalents? Obviously there is. If my account of the universe is correct, after all, then even those who do not consciously acknowledge its truth will find that its procedures work even for them. We do not need to assent to theism in order to be able to do mathematics, even if I am right to believe that we would have no good reason, if there was no God, to expect our mathematical science to apply to the world. It is not a condition of mathematical success, or even of earthly happiness, that we believe that there is a God, even though it is a condition of these things that there is One. Atheists, accordingly, for as long as they manage to evade the doom of nonsense, can find out some of the psychological procedures that help to guide us through the demon-world. Atheists can even employ religious rituals, as long as they don't think too carefully about what they are doing. But of course such 'Christian atheists' will wish to claim that atheism is a genuine implication of true piety.

One supposed argument for the inescapability of atheism is that 'the scientific world-picture' leaves no room for any rational belief that our moralities, art, and religions are endorsed by the universe at large. If this were true we should have to add that it also left no room for the scientific enterprise itself. Fortunately, the argument is as inane as one which first describes the world without mentioning the colour of anything, and thence concludes that the world is colourless.[22] The whole notion of a 'scientific world-picture' that somehow excludes any belief in the One, the Logos, and the Life is devoid of substance. The only world in which it would not be right and reasonable to believe in the Logos, the intelligible pattern that is accessible to intellectual endeavour and by which the world hangs together, would be a world where nothing could rightly or reasonably be believed. Theists have not agreed either that there could be no such world, or that there could not. That this is such a world is certainly not something forced on us by a 'scientific world-view'. Nor is the claim that there are no cosmic powers with which we can communicate.

Another argument for pious atheism rests on the observation that some religious traditions deny the importance of gods, or of a god. Buddhists, notoriously, do not worship gods, though they may propitiate them, and revere the Buddhas. But, as I have pointed out before, we need to be sure that we understand each other before drawing rash conclusions. Gautama trusted in the Unborn and Indestructible. His followers pursue the Buddha-nature. 'Gods', as Buddhists understand the term, are more like angels than like God. God, as Christians understand the term, is more like Buddha-nature than like Brahma. Buddhists are not atheists, if by this is meant that they deny the possibility of spiritual insight, spiritual aid. Their path is a path

[22] Clark (1977*a*), p. 145 ff.

backwards to the Joy that is before the temporal beginning. If they are more likely to reckon this world a mere mistake than orthodox Christians, that too is an opinion not unknown in the West. Maybe the sheer unmeaningness of mundane existence is one route to enlightenment, even if the enlightened characteristically discover that the mundane turns out to be the temple of the Presence.

One further important argument for the non-factual nature of religion is roughly this. Whatever can be stated as a fact, whether in the field of history of of physics, can intelligibly be regarded either as good or as bad, as worshipful or as loathly. No mere 'fact' implies a 'value'. It may be admitted that Francis gave his inheritance away—but was that filial impiety or Christian vocation? It may be that the Star of Bethlehem was a supernova—but was that a providential act of God or a cosmic accident? Cupitt concludes from this that no 'factual' claim, however grand it may seem or however metaphysical its language, can be of the essence of religion, any more than of morality. Just as Universe Incorporated or the Galactic Empire would have, of themselves, no necessary religious value, so even the God of the Philosophers is irrelevant: 'interest in any extra-religious existence of God . . . would be a frivolous distraction,[23] and God 'exists' only as the projected ideal of religious ritual and experience.

The charm of this argument is that it seems to prove that genuinely religious persons are committed to precisely the conclusion that irreligious moderns have reached; that 'God' is the name we give our own ideals, projected on to emptiness, that the universe apart from us is empty. Plotinus had the answer to this heresy: 'If He is absent from the Universe, He is absent from yourselves, and you can have nothing to tell about Him or the powers that come from Him'.[24] If the universe is really to be regarded as a cosmic accident, devoid of value, then all values 'we' invent are

[23] Cupitt (1980), p. 9.
[24] Plotinus, *Enneads* ii. 9. 16: (1969), p. 148.

equally contingent, equally absurd. If the universe is not founded on anything remotely like the values we 'project' then nothing that we do or value is more than a pastime.

Fortunately the indifferentist creed, even in this latest manifestation, has little to commend it to those who still retain any aspiration to conduct their lives and arguments by the rules of reason. The claim is as follows: (1) all facts are 'mere facts'; (2) any mere fact can intelligibly be the object of love or fear or hatred or indifference; (3) the object of religious worship is one which it would be unintelligible not to worship, once it is known; therefore (4) the object of religious worship is not a mere fact, and hence (5) not a fact at all. Religious conclusions can never be derived from merely factual premisses: so religion is a matter of our attitude to life, the universe, and everything, not a report on its nature. Accordingly, whether 'God' exists or not is a matter of indifference to the religious quest.

This argument does conceal some insights, but it is necessary to explore its stages before drawing the even stronger conclusion, which Cupitt seems to desire, that the religious attitude positively requires the non-existence of God. This latter conclusion, obviously, negates the weaker conclusion: if it does not matter, from the point of view of religion, what 'the facts' are, how can it matter if 'the facts' include the existence of traditionally conceived deity?

What of the first premiss, that all facts are mere facts? This is to say that nothing is true that has, by itself, logical implications about what should be done. Any truth can intelligibly be conjoined with hypotheses concerning what should be done about that or any other truth. As it stands this is mere assertion, amounting to the denial that statements about our obligations can be genuinely true. For this claim no argument is usually advanced beyond the truism that such supposed truths would be unlike other truths that did not carry moral implications. It is, moreover, rather difficult to maintain the case: to call something true is, amongst other things, to say that it ought, *ceteris paribus*, to be believed. Despite the puzzles I have raised about epistemic obligation in earlier chapters, it seems very difficult to imagine what it would be like to make no such connection between truth and the obligation to believe. That something is true is, at the very least, one reason (even if not a final reason) for believing it. If this is so, every truth carries at least one moral implication; and so no facts are 'mere facts'.

None the less, there is a certain strength to the first premiss. It may well be helpful to insist that facts have implications only in the context of other truths. That, indeed, is hardly surprising. That Jehane is married to Zechariah only implies that Zechariah is married to Jehane if there is a suppressed premiss about the commutivity of marriage, a premiss that might (in a sense) be false. Truths are tied together in the web even of factual inference by implicit rules that we do not always trouble to mention. No conclusion can ever be strictly drawn from one premiss on its own, even the most impeccably logical. If we are to draw 'ethical conclusions' we shall need ethical premisses whose denial can be understood. This is the partial truth that the second premiss seeks to state, that we know what it would be to regard any fact at all with enthusiasm or with abhorrence.

But though we know what it would be to do so, and though the principles behind such disparate attitudes could probably be stated, it is clear that in many cases we would deny that the principles 'made sense', or that we could 'understand' those who took some radically opposing view. If someone agrees that Zechariah is cruel, miserly, cowardly, and self-deceived, but adds that for that very reason he is to be admired and imitated, I may 'understand' what is said, but firmly deny that I understand the speaker. The thesis that such persons are very much not to be admired is indeed a synthetic one, but that does not mean that I can easily grasp what anyone who denies is on about.[25] 'Mere facts', that of themselves have no implications about what our attitudes must, logically, be, may still be facts to which

[25] Clark (1980), pp. 238 ff.

there is only one humanly intelligible response. Aliens who did not recognize that some imaginable responses were wholly inappropriate must misapprehend the situation— though this is, emphatically, not to say that it is never right to offer an unusual response, one that observers may at first find difficult to comprehend. The genuinely religious heart may, as I have already indicated, sometimes respond to life in para- doxical ways, and must always suspect that 'God's response' (as it were) is deeply opposed to our most usual, and worldly, ways.

So what of the third premiss, that the object of religious awe cannot intelligibly not be worshipped? To this the initial response of anyone acquainted with the history of human- kind must be one of baffled laughter. Is it not part of the doctrine of any religion that 'we have erred and strayed like lost sheep'? Some believers have even supposed that there might be, or there were, creatures whose response to the One would always be one of rejection and despairing hatred. That is what Hell has been supposed to be: the discovery that one hates the very root of one's being, that one cannot be at ease with that by which alone one lives and which cannot or will not let one cease to be. It may be that such a doctrine as this is one of which we should be wary: all too easily it becomes instead the claim that God, conceived in the image of our own worst selves, will punish us unendingly for disobeying arbitrary laws that He simultaneously makes it difficult for us to know and almost impossible for us to obey.

> What meaneth Nature by these diverse laws?
> Passion and Reason self-division cause:
> Is it the mark or majesty of Power
> to make offences that it may forgive?
> Nature herself doth her own self deflower,
> to hate those errors she herself doth give . . .
> If Nature did not take delight in blood,
> she would have made more easy ways to good.[26]

That God is the very Devil. It is also clear enough, at an intellectual level, that the serious attempt to deny and vilify

[26] Fulke Greville, 'Mustapha': Gardner (1972), p. 118.

the One Creator can only result in nonsense. To say that God, the One God, is a lying spirit, is to say that nothing that I say or think can ever be trusted—for my powers derive from His.[27] But though there is something unintelligible about an obdurate rejection of the One, it is not difficult to understand the act, nor is it quite a contradiction in itself to say that the One is not to be revered. It is, of course, false. If the One is not to be revered, then nothing is or can be.

Accordingly, the supposed argument for the independence of religion fails. Misotheism, the hatred of God, can be understood or not understood in much the same way as any depressive state. Those who are not in it can hardly grasp what the victim is on about. Any attempt to state the supposed reasons for what the victim believes runs into absurdity. Those outside the influence of the victim's personal demon cannot see why anyone should think that the supposed evidence that depressives (paranoiacs, cultists, atheists . . .) adduce is even remotely relevant to the conclusions they purport to draw from it. Those who have once noticed the shadow of the One upon the world, who have had their attention drawn momentarily aside from mundane matters, who gave glimpsed the Unborn and Indestructible of which even the best that they conceive is far too small, 'must' respond by worship. They 'must' do so, for not to do is absurd: but it is not logically or naturally inevitable that they should. Successfully to defy the One would be self-destruction, if it were possible at all. Self-deceived and rationally hopeless defiance is entirely possible—so there is no need to claim that the proper object of religious adoration cannot be a fact, even if it were true that we could, in some sense, adopt any attitude we pleased to facts.

Underlying this last argument is another, and perhaps the most significant. If the One, the Logos, and the Life are real then we have obligations that are not the product of our own legislation. If some versions of liberalism are correct (which Cupitt, for example, thinks that none but the 'spiritually

[27] Clark (1977*b*), pp. 255 ff; (1982*b*), p. 342.

vulgar and immature'[28] would reject) we can have no obligations but those 'we' as individuals, autonomously decree for
ourselves. Accordingly, 'theological realism can only be true
for [sc. be supposed to be true by] a heteronomous consciousness such as no normal person ought now to have'.[29] It ought
to follow, of course, that 'normal persons' no longer acknowledge any obligation to argue coherently or respect 'liberal
values'. Nor should they be persuaded that they have an
obligation to be 'autonomous', unless they so choose. Cupitt,
unfortunately, has swallowed the incoherent *mélange* of
voluntarist indifferentism that I have rebuked in earlier
chapters.

But is there a truth here? To give absolute obedience
to any external being is to forget that we, as individuals, are
equally the channels of divine existence. The canon of
individual autonomy, so far from being in opposition to
theological realism, is its child. It is because God speaks in
each of us that no one of us should claim despotic power.
And for the self-same reason none of us should think that
we are licensed to determine just what obligations we have
without regard to the honest thought of others. There is a
story of a monk recently initiated into and having partly
experienced the truth of the teachings of some Hindu sect:
walking down the road he heard a royal elephant rushing
towards him, with the rider shouting 'Make way!' Reminding himself that he was God (that the One was to be found
within), he decided that it was not for him to stand aside.
The elephant, as she reached him, grasped him round the
waist and tossed him aside. Staggering back to his master,
he complained that he had thought that, since he was God,
nothing could hurt him. To which his master replied: 'Why
did you not obey the voice of God telling you to make way?'

---

[28] Cupitt (1980), pp. 10, 43; (1982), pp. 12, 88.
[29] Cupitt (1980), p. 12. Cupitt's confusion is intelligible (even pardonable) as
a maddened reaction against those believers who spare themselves the pain of
intellectual enquiry by granting uncritical obedience to what they call the Church's
or the Bible's teachings, and demanding the same from others.

## IV

The puzzle remains. On the one hand, nothing that we can say even about the world of our mundane experience is ever likely to be simultaneously accurate and readily intelligible. On the other hand, we must accept that the world may rightly be understood by means of the categories we are equipped to discover. On the one hand, James was probably right to think that our 'moral and volitional responses' are our best route to recognition of the divinity that shapes our ends. On the other, it is a refusal of the talents given us to refrain from intellectual examination of the world and its signposts to the One. On the one hand, we can expect riddles and obscurities in any reasonable story about God and the World. On the other it is an exasperating failure of nerve and theological responsibility to fall back too soon upon such anodyne phrases as 'Life is a great mystery, and we are not meant to understand too much'. On the contrary, we are meant to understand as much as we possibly can; but 'understanding' does not necessarily mean transforming the subject into matter for disinterested contemplation. Cognition is not incompatible with piety. To understand, to have in mind, the Logos is to experience terror, shame, obedient love. To follow the straight way through the passions that beset us is to understand.

Most of us do not much want to be buddhas, or saints, or wise. Or if we do, this is only one desire amongst unnumbered jostling fantasies. The one straight track through this demon-ridden world is walked only by those who can draw upon the underlying pattern that is represented to us in the figure of angels or bodhisattvas or the Holy Spirit or envoys of the Galatic Empire. If we manage, momentarily, to do so, it is to catch sight of what each of us is meant to be, an experiment in living, one of the names of God.

The story I have been telling is an ancient one. Deity is best understood as the One beyond all human categories that eternally expounds its nature in the Logos, to contemplate which is to be filled with the Life from which all seemingly individual lives take their beginning. The Logos is reflected in the universe as the several powers that govern phenomena, powers that may fall away from obedience and are owed none by us. The best that we can conceive of Deity is that it is the beginning and the end of all things, that it is being and consciousness and joy. Not to conceive this is to lie down with demons, to be lost among the ungoverned waves of thought.

The six worlds of Buddhist cosmology (gods, titans, humans, animals, the hells, and hungry ghosts) represent, amongst other things, the modes of consciousness. In each world, as they are pictured, is the tiny figure of the Buddha. Similarly:

> if I climb up to heaven, thou art there;
> if I make by bed in Sheol, again I find thee;
> if I take my flight to the frontiers of the morning
> or dwell at the limit of the western sea,
> even there thy hand will meet me
> and thy right hand will hold me fast.[30]

It is the mark of what is real that it can be found in many ways and places. Truly, 'not by one path only can one reach so great a mystery'.[31] What is most real can be found everywhere, and so risks never being found at all. In theology, everything that is true will at the last prove obvious. 'As the heart of the Tathagata [the Buddha-nature] is not born and does not perish it mirrors itself in all things, as the moon on water.'[32]

---

[30] Psalm 139. 8 f.
[31] Symmachus, *Relatio* 3. 10: (1883), p. 282.
[32] *Ghanavyuha Sutra*: Hocking (1936), p. 120.

# 10

# Conclusions

The attempt to explore and face the possibilities which is philosophical endeavour is, all too often, a matter of fighting one's way through fog. There are occasional patches of clearer weather, and the 'featureless faces' to which John Wisdom refers can sometimes be seen in greater detail. But it remains true that much of the intelligible universe is quite unintelligible to us. There are those who prefer to stay in the well-lighted places, driving the fog back step by anxious step. Others, of whom I am—obviously—one, prefer to strike out across country, trusting that we can at least make a rough map of the territory, that there will be moments of clarity. We are prepared to tolerate dissonance, to accept that there are riddles we have not yet solved, and that the light of common day may not reveal all truth. Our sketch-maps are not intended to be definitive doctrinal statements, and if others assume that we whole-heartedly believe the tales we tell, and never believe the opposite, they are likely to feel disappointed. Poets and philosophers do not 'believe'—or 'disbelieve'—all that they say.[1] We are as prone as anyone else to fall in love with our own creations, and interpret critical comment as a reflection on our integrity or virtue, but it is almost as exasperating (ungracious as this seems) to receive uncritical praise, as if one were wholly to be identified with the thesis one has offered. The exasperation is, of course, partly because such uncritical approval some-times amounts to no more than self-recognition. One is praised for having said, so the speaker supposes, what the speaker already thinks. Those who criticize must at least spend some effort in discovering what one actually has said, though it may be admitted that 'must' here means only that

[1] Kamber (1977), p. 344.

they should, not that they always do: we are all inclined to assume that we already know what 'people of that kind' say, whatever kind it is.

Accordingly, if I were asked whether I 'really believe' that there are gods and demons, that the point-consciousness I identically am is only contingently associated with the segment of physical and social nature that I attend upon, and that the material universe is an awe-inspiring image of the Inimitable, I am inclined to ask, in return, why it matters to anyone whether I do or not. What matters, surely, is not what I am inclined to answer on any particular occasion, nor even what my motives and personal character may be, but what force the arguments may have.

Sir James Johnston happened to say that he paid no regard to the arguments of counsel at the bar of the House of Commons, because they were paid for speaking. JOHNSON: 'Nay, sir, argument is argument. You cannot help paying regard to their arguments, if they are good. If it were testimony, you might disregard it, if you knew it were purchased. There is a beautiful image in Bacon upon this subject: testimony is like an arrow shot from a long bow; the force of it depends on the strength of the hand that draws it. Argument is like an arrow shot from a cross-bow, which has equal force though shot by a child.'[2]

To this it should be added that no argument known to me is ineluctable, no arrow absolutely lethal. Anyone determined enough to evade the point can do so, at some cost. Nor do I see that such behaviour is always reprehensible. Those who stubbornly refuse to listen to 'reason' when 'reason' runs counter to their fiercest feelings are often spared erroneous conclusions. But it is still as well to seek reasons and not to trust entirely to 'gut response' and social prejudice. Philosophers have a duty to explore the landscape of the mind, to map the possibilities for those who follow after. We try things out.

What I have sought to do in this exploration is to state the principles upon which I, as a philosopher, rely. Philosophers and poets do not wholly 'believe' their systems, but I think

[2] Boswell (1953), p. 1283: 30 May 1784.

it is fair to say that we (or at any rate I) believe that intellectual endeavour can clarify issues, can dispel at least some of the fog: that there is an intelligible universe. My argument has been that this one presupposition of our craft generates other beliefs, or at least makes it impossible intelligently to believe much of what passes now for common sense. To suppose that the universe is 'just as chance would have it', that our capacities and fundamental categories are generated solely by the selfish gene, that there are no absolute values, that human beings are the only value in a universe devoid of value, that 'God' is the name of something like the Loch Ness Monster, and the like are the doctrines of insanity. Really to think through what such doctrines imply is to fall into the void, to abandon intelligence. Or rather, it would be if we then consented.

To explore the possibilities, even those upon the edge of madness, is the task of the philosopher, as it is the task of the shaman to face individual or collective neurosis, with a view to resolving the discord or exorcizing the discordant.[3] If my account of the metaphysical system that best makes sense of this endeavour is correct then shamans are not so far wrong in their own images of things. In saying this I in no way impugn the efforts of those who, not realizing the strength of shamanistic, neo-Platonic theory, have sought out the material connections that govern our lives in this world of change and chance. As I said in my first chapter, if a friend reveals that she really does doubt that the world is intelligible or suspects that she is the only conscious being in the world, one's immediate reaction (even as a philosopher who has explored these possibilities) is to wonder about her diet, her recent history, whether she has flu. It may well be that the images of desperation that afflict us are better driven off by giving up sugar, coffee, or meat, taking enough exercise, and reviewing our occupations. These are, in essence, the traditional devices of the healer, and nothing that I have said implies that these are not to

³ Glass (1974), pp. 190 ff.

be employed.[4] Some foodstuffs, some activities are rightly associated with assorted devils, because a devil is experienced by us precisely as a shift of mood that may be symbolized and practically controlled (not 'caused') by outward signs.

For this same reason nothing that I have said should be taken to imply that the so-called 'talking cures' are necessarily better suited to the treatment of 'neurosis' or 'psychosis' than are cures involving drugs (preferably herbal or homeopathic). That these rationalizations and distorted principles (distorted by the standards of metaphysical sanity) should be taken seriously, thought through, is one thing. That the best hope of a cure comes solely through philosophy, still less what passes for philosophy in some consulting rooms, is quite another. Letting oneself sink into the world-view of a devil is something that only the strong and well-defended should attempt, if that is their calling. I do not believe that it is wise to encourage those already tempted by despair and self-hatred to go on about the wrongs that they imagine have been done to them, or the failures of their parents, or the irrational beginnings of all thought, or 'the existential abyss'. The devil cannot endure to be mocked—it can quite well endure the concentrated attention of psychotherapist and patient.

We experience devils as a shift of mood, or as an obsession. In such moments even the external world seems filled with its peculiar character: in moods of anger, for example, the light is more glaring, and other creatures are (it seems) infected by irritability and indignation. The world we then perceive is one antagonistic to us, and other people are in fact more likely to quarrel, at least with us. It does some good to remind oneself that they may not in fact be in as bad a mood as oneself. It does no good at all to start pretending that they have no mood, no consciousness at all, and that the one true outlook on the world is one that holds back from all identification, all participation. If one person is in a foul temper the likelihood is strong that others are

[4] I should emphasize that this is not to blame anyone for their own afflictions.

as well. Being in any mood, in fact, can realistically be understood as participating in a mode of the world's existence that
can be (and often is) a shared one. This sharing is represented
on a chemical plane, it may be, by the passage of phero-
mones, or by the shared presence of lead in the atmosphere,
sugar in the bloodstream. To pass out of the mood it is
necessary to find another mode, to remember our identity
as members of another unity.

Each person everywhere sees itself, thinks of itself, as a unique and
extraordinary individual, and never suspects to what an extent it is
a tiny unit that can exist only as part of a whole . . . But what is the
mechanism, the machinery, that creates a group, a whole, and then
develops a dissident member—develops thoughts that are different
from those of the whole? . . . If he or she is not expelled, or does not
expel herself, but remains, contemplating her position, then a certain
train of thought is inevitable. She has been part of a group mind,
thinking the same thoughts as her peers. But now her mind holds other
ideas. Of what whole is she now the part? Of what invisible whole?[5]

The effort to rediscover equanimity when 'in a bad temper',
and the effort to uncover truth when at the mercy of social
prejudice, are very similar. Both seem to involve a putting
of oneself at the disposal of the universe. Grandiloquently:
'to follow God's way is to surrender to a reality which exists
prior to man's effort to bear witness to it'.[6] Those who speak
from that unity speak truth; those who live from it dispel
the pollution of greed, anger, and ignorance. The devils run
from them.

To find oneself a member of an invisible, wider unity, and
to realize oneself as (perhaps immortal) Nous, are two ways,
I suspect, of expressing the same insight. MacIntyre urges
that 'Catholic Christianity' differs from Platonism in holding
that 'the soul' is no separable substance, but rather the one
person considered as a member of earthly and heavenly
communities.[7] On his terms, which he equates with the

[5] Lessing (1981), pp. 272–5; see Clark (1983c).
[6] Rubinoff (1974), p. 95.
[7] MacIntyre (1981), p. 161; see Clark (1984).

dominant view of 'pre-modern' humanity, there is no I apart from my existence as a member of this family, household, clan, tribe, city, nation, kingdom, heavenly city. He is probably right to emphasize what I have called this age's single greatest philosophical discovery, that there is no *I* without a *We*. But the point-consciousness, Nous, in which this Stephen participates, was something that 'came from outside' even for Aristotle[8] (whom MacIntyre identifies as a good Catholic on this issue). And not even Plato thought that immortal souls were solitary substances, or that eternal life was without company. Awakening to our true natures that we had before our birth is a return to comradeship, and to a purer air. In the divine parade we were (we are) the followers of different gods, each contemplating our distinctive view of Eternal Truth, in obedience to Zeus, who orders and organizes all the lesser powers.[9]

Devils, of course, are only fallen angels. That there are moods which are diabolical none but the most foolhardy would deny. Even if we have never lived out our anger, greed, and ignorance to the bitter end (never betrayed or killed or stolen from our fellows—the groups of which we are unconscious units—in ways that external lawmakers would forbid), yet we know what it is like to be self-righteously indignant, greedy, arrogantly lustful, ignorantly contemptuous. These moods, and their associated worlds, are recognizably—at any rate to those momentarily escaped from them—such as to enclose us in our particularities, so that nothing lives in us but a complaint. Being thankful for things as they are, praying for one's supposed enemies as they are, rejoicing in the sense of being a unit in a wider and a happier whole—these are ways in which we can escape despair. I should add that these techniques, obviously enough, may be corrupted into sentimentalism and conceit, marked by the arrogant conviction that one is better able than one's

[8] Aristotle, *De Generatione Animalium* 2. 736b27 f; cf. Clark (1975), p. 182 for a different, equally plausible interpretation of Aristotle's theory of Nous.
[9] Plato, *Phaidros* 246d6 ff.

fellows to know how they are really feeling. This is all too easily transformed into indignation that they do not agree.

Evil moods and their associated worlds perhaps turn out, when understood, to be elements themselves of wider and happier wholes. Even devils were once merely angels (messengers), and may perhaps be brought into communion in the end—though this is a dangerous thought for creatures all too ready to mistake their anger for righteous anger, their greed for love, their willing ignorance for determined faith. Angels too are known as moods, and ways of the world's working. But perhaps the most evocative account of what I mean is given by Otto in his account of the Homeric gods. Hermes, for example:

The marvellous and mysterious which is peculiar to night may also appear by day as a sudden darkening or an enigmatic smile. This mystery of night seen by day, this magic darkness in the bright sunlight is the realm of Hermes, whom, in later ages, magic with good reason revered as its master. In popular feeling this makes itself felt in the remarkable silence that may intervene in the midst of the liveliest conversation; it was said, at such times, that Hermes had entered the room . . . The strange moment might signify bad luck or a friendly offer, some wonderful and happy coincidence.[10]

Christian commentators found such godlings dangerous, with good reason. Hellenizers, with good reason, thought that it was fear and unthankfulness that painted Hermes black. The gods can be sinister. The moods they are (or that they engender) may conflict: witness Euripides' insistence, in his *Hippolytos*, that Artemis and Aphrodite are set at odds when someone seeks to honour only one. Polytheism is the recognition that there are more ways, more common moods than one, and that we need to acknowledge their power. As Armstrong testifies:

Even if we retain any sense of a divine presence in the world, we have to admit that it manifests itself in innumerably various, apparently clashing and conflicting, often inscrutably odd and horrifying ways.

---

[10] Otto (1954), p. 118.

Divine unity, not divine plurality, requires an effort of reflection and faith to attain it; and when attained, it does not necessarily exclude plurality.[11]

Faith in the Divine Unity amounts to faith in the intelligibility of things, that there is a single pattern, the Logos, which contains all that is durable in the several powers. That faith was represented for Hellenes, especially the neo-Platonists, in the figure of Zeus, on whom all powers depend. But though it is right to have such a faith—or else to abandon all hope of ever talking sense—the Logos is not now evident to us. Rational polytheists deplore the tendency of monotheists to imagine unity too soon, a unity sustained by simply ignoring all those aspects, modes, and moods of Reality that do not fit the monotheists' story. You will remember James's quotation from M. I. Smith, insisting that what the distressed experience is Reality: 'it gives us an absolute phase of the universe', not something to be ignored or explained away.[12] Rational monotheists, in their turn, deplore the polytheists' tendency to speak as if it were satisfactory enough to have many different 'levels' of explanation, many different and incommensurable world-views, many ways of being what one should be. The rational philosopher will not deny either story.

Wishing to be a rational philosopher, I conclude that every mode and mood of our being, of the world's being, should be acknowledged as a fact, and as something to be 'welcomed' (though some of them require divine assistance if we are even to endure them)—on conditions. Being 'in a foul temper', the potentially homicidal presence of that demon whom the Greeks called Ares (though this is not to propose that there is an individual demon of that name), will (we may be confident) turn out to be an image of a truly righteous anger. It would be an error both to surrender to that power, and to hope it will be cast out for ever—even if, for our purposes, we must suppose it chained. Being in

[11] Armstrong (1981), p. 184.
[12] M. I. Smith: James (1907), p. 30.

that condition of indifferentist despair to which too many
moderns, were it not for the blessing of more immediate
worries, would surrender, is a revelation also.

> This too is an experience of the soul
> the dismembered world that once was the whole god
> whose broken fragments now lie dead.
> This passing of reality itself is real.[13]

What is to be found everywhere is actually found nowhere.
If the Divine Presence were not, seemingly, withdrawn, how
should we remember it? It is in its seeming absence from the
outer world that we are reminded of its presence within. It is
in the spectacle of a world devoid of humane significance
that we look out over the edge of what might be, and understand that all our cosier dreams may turn out to be less than
accurate.

The universe will, in the end, prove to have made sense,
and it will prove to be a sense already evident to that 'invisible
whole'. But the sense it proves to make will, doubtless, not
be the one that we now cosily imagine. If the story I have
told is not too inaccurate then the following theses, in some
form, can be regarded as the proper way to walk.

Consciousness (the Nous I am, the Nous you are) is the
myriadfold offspring of the One, that which stands above and
beyond all categories. Consciousness exists as that which
enjoys itself and contemplates its object, and our recall to the
Consciousness of which our mortal being is the image lies in
contemplating (as we can) what It does: the intelligible
world. That world, for us, is something not yet evident,
something to be glimpsed beyond and through the moods
and modes of our mundane existence. We hold on to that
faint vision only by relying on the presence in us of the
divine life. That is what, if tradition is correct, we shall
wake up to recognize upon our earthly death.[14]

The royal road is the road of right reason, which is only

[13] K. Raine, 'Isis Wanderer' in *The Pythoness* 1948: Raine (1981), p. 21. See
Barfield (1963), p. 179.
[14] Clark (1983b), p. 227.

to be followed with profound assistance: that is why the Anointed of God is called the Logos, because he makes us 'logical'.[15] In half-remembering our identity as creatures of the Most High, sharers in the divine life, we can no longer pride ourselves upon our human ancestry, or our cleverness. As I wrote in an earlier work, 'we'—which is all of sentient creation—are on our way home.[16]

We must recognize distractions, demonic errors, even as we also recognize that these too are real, not things that will for ever be forgotten. The image of things most popular in this age amongst the educated, half-educated, masses is one that cannot itself be coherently believed, but that serves as a reminder that the truth lies deeper in. We live, as it were, upon the outskirts of the (good) Empire, deep in the fog of chance and of despair: but there is a way to Heaven even from the gates of hell, a door to enlightenment even amongst hungry ghosts.

[15] Origen, *Commentary on John* i. 37: Wiles (1960), p. 93 f.
[16] Clark (1977a), pp. 31 f.

# Bibliography

Alexander, S. (1920), *Space, Time and Deity* (Macmillan, London).
Almeder, R. (1975), 'Fallibilism and the ultimate irreversible opinion' in N. Rescher (ed.), *Studies in Epistemology* (Blackwell, Oxford), pp. 32 ff.
Armstrong, A. H. (1981), 'Some advantages of polytheism', *Dionysius* 5, pp. 181 ff.
Auden, W. H. (1966), *Collected Shorter Poems 1926-56* (Faber, London).
Bacon, F. (1855), *The Novum Organum*, tr. G. W. Kitchin (Oxford University Press, Oxford).
Balme, D. (1980), 'Aristotle's Biology was not Essentialist', *Archiv für Geschichte der Philosophie* 62, pp. 1 ff.
Barfield, O. (1963), *Worlds Apart* (Faber, London).
Barth, K. (1961), *Church Dogmatics*, ed. G. W. Bromley and T. W. Torrence (T. & T. Clark, Edinburgh).
Berkeley, G. (1948-56), *Complete Works*, ed. A. A. Luce and T. E. Jessop (Thomas Nelson & Son, Edinburgh).
Bernard, C. (1949), *Introduction to the Study of Experimental Medicine*, tr. H. C. Greene (Dover, New York).
Beveridge, W. E. B. (1953), *The Art of Scientific Investigation* (Heinemann, London).
Bindra, D. (1970), 'The problem of subjective experience', *Psychological Review* 77, pp. 581 ff.
Black, J. (1970), *The Dominion of Man* (Edinburgh University Press, Edinburgh).
Boden, M. (1980), 'The case for a cognitive biology', *Proc. Aristotelian Society*, Supp. Vol. 54, pp. 25 ff.
Boswell, J. (1963), *Life of Johnson* (Clarendon Press, Oxford).
Brown, P. (1971), *The World of Late Antiquity* (Thames & Hudson, London).
Buber, M. (1949), *The Prophetic Faith*, tr. C. Witton-Davies (Macmillan, New York).
Chan, W. T. (1963), (ed.), *A Sourcebook in Chinese Philosophy* (Princeton University Press, Princeton, New Jersey).
Chang, G. C. C. (1972), *The Buddhist Teaching of Totality* (Allen & Unwin, London).
Chisholm, R. M. (1957), *Perceiving* (Cornell University Press, Ithaca, New York).

Chittick, W. C. (1980), (ed.), *A Shi'ite Anthology* (Muhammadi Trust, London).

Chroust, A.-H. (1978), 'Inspiration in Ancient Greece' in E. D. O'Connor (ed.), *Charismatic Renewal* (SPCK, London: first published 1975), pp. 37 ff.

Clark, S. R. L. (1975), *Aristotle's Man* (Clarendon Press, Oxford). Paperback edition published in 1983.

— (1977*a*), *The Moral Status of Animals* (Clarendon Press, Oxford). Paperback edition published in 1984.

— (1977*b*) 'God, good and evil', *Proc. Aristotelian Society* 77, pp. 247 ff.

— (1979) 'The Rights of Wild Things', *Inquiry* 22, pp. 171 ff.

— (1980) 'The lack of a gap between facts and values', *Proc. Aristotelian Society* Supp. Vol. 54, pp. 255 ff.

— (1981), 'Awareness and self-awareness' in Woodgush *et al.* (1981), pp. 11 ff.

— (1982*a*), *The Nature of the Beast* (Oxford University Press, Oxford).

— (1982*b*), 'God's Law and Morality', *Philosophical Quarterly* 32, pp. 339 ff.

— (1983*a*) 'Humans, animals and "animal behaviour" ' in H. B. Miller and W. H. Williams (eds.), *Ethics and Animals* (Humana Press, Clifton, New Jersey), pp. 169 ff.

— (1983*b*), 'Waking Up: a neglected model for the afterlife', *Inquiry* 26, pp. 209 ff.

— (1983*c*), 'Gaia and the forms of life' in R. Elliot and A. Gair (eds.), *Environmental Philosophy* (University of Queensland Press, St. Lucia), pp. 182 ff.

— (1984), 'Morals, Moore and MacIntyre', *Inquiry* 26.

Clifford, W. K. (1901), *Lectures and Essays*, ed. L. Stephen and F. Pollock (Macmillan, London).

Collier, A. (1977), *R. D. Laing* (Harvester, Hassocks).

Crook, J. H. (1980), *The Evolution of Human Consciousness* (Clarendon Press, Oxford).

— (1983), 'On attributing consciousness to animals', *Nature* 303.5912, pp. 11 ff.

Cupitt, D. (1971), *Christ and the Hiddenness of God* (Lutterworth Press, London).

— (1980), *Taking Leave of God* (SCM Press, London).

— (1982), *The World to Come* (SCM Press, London).

Dawkins, R. (1976), *The Selfish Gene* (Oxford University Press, Oxford).

De Bary, W. T. (1969), (ed.), *The Buddhist Tradition* (Vintage Press, New York).

218     BIBLIOGRAPHY

Dennett, J. C. (1978), *Brainstorms* (Harvester, Hassocks).
Dey, L. K. K. (1975), *The Intermediary World and Patterns of Perfection in Philo and Hebrews* (Scholars Press, Missoula, Montana).
Dickinson, P. (1980), *City of God* (Gollancz, London).
Diels, H. and Krantz, W. (1952), (eds.), *Die Fragmente der Vorsokratiker* (Weidmannshe Verlagsbuchhandlung, Zurich/Berlin).
Dillon, J. (1977), *The Middle Platonists* (Duckworth, London).
Dixon, D. (1981), *Life after Man* (Harrow House, Edinburgh).
Dodds, E. R. (1965), *Pagan and Christian in an Age of Anxiety* (Cambridge University Press, Cambridge).
Dostoevsky, F. M. (1962), *Letters to Family and Friends*, tr. E. C. Mayne (Chatto & Windus, London).
Douglas, M. (1973), *Natural Symbols* (Penguin, Harmondsworth).
Downs, J. F. (1960), 'Domestication', *Kroeber Anthropological Society Papers* 22, pp. 18 ff.
Duval, S. & Wickland, R. A. (1972), *A Theory of Objective Self Awareness* (Academic Press, New York).
Eccles, J. C. (1970), *Facing Reality* (Springer-Verlag, Berlin/Heidelberg).
Ehrenfeld, D. W. (1972), *Conserving Life on Earth* (Oxford University Press, New York).
Farrer, A. (1966), *Love Almighty and Ills Unlimited* (Fontana, London). First published in 1962.
Fawcett, D. (1921), *Divine Imagining* (Macmillan, London).
Feuer, L. S. (1983), 'Noumenalism and Einstein's argument for the existence of God', *Inquiry* 26, pp. 25 ff.
Feyerabend, P. (1975), *Against Method* (NLB, London).
— (1981), *Philosophical Papers* (Cambridge University Press, Cambridge).
Findlay, J. N. (1966), *The Discipline of the Cave* (Allen & Unwin, London).
— (1974), *Plato: the Written and Unwritten Doctrines* (Routledge & Kegan Paul, London).
Forder, H. G. (1927), *The Foundations of Euclidean Geometry* (Cambridge University Press, Cambridge).
Fortenbaugh, W. W. (1971), 'Aristotle: animals, emotion and moral virtue', *Arethusa* 4, pp. 171 ff.
Fox, R. & Tiger, L. (1972), *The Imperial Animal* (Secker & Warburg, London).
Frey, R. (1980), *Interests and Rights: the Case against Animals* (Clarendon Press, Oxford).
Galloway, A. D. (1951), *The Cosmic Christ* (Nisbet & Co., London).
Gardner, H. (1972), (ed.), *New Oxford Book of English Verse* (Clarendon Press, Oxford).

Ghiselin, M. (1974), 'A radical solution to the species problem', *Systematic Zoology* 23, pp. 536 ff.

Glass, J. M. (1974), 'The philosopher and the shaman', *Political Theory* 2, pp. 181 ff.

Glatzer, N. N. (1969), (ed.), *The Dimensions of Job* (Schocken Books, New York).

Goddard, D. (1970), *A Buddhist Bible* (Beacon Press, Boston, Massachusetts).

Goodall, J. von Lawick (1971), *In the Shadow of Man* (Collins, London).

Gosse, P. (1857), *Omphalos: an attempt to untie the geological knot* (J. van Voorst, London).

Graham, F. (1970), *Since Silent Spring* (Pan Books, London).

Griffin, D. R. (1976), *The Question of Animal Awareness* (Rockefeller University Press, New York).

Hardin, G. (1969), (ed.), *Population, Evolution and Population Control* (Freeman & Co, San Francisco).

Harris, M. (1975), *Cows, Pigs, Wars and Witches* (Hutchinson, London).

Hebb, D. O. (1946), 'Emotion in man and animal', *Psychological Review* 53, pp. 95 ff.

Heidegger, M. (1949), *Existence and Being*, tr. W. Brock (Vision Press, London).

Heisenberg, W. (1958), 'The representation of nature in contemporary physics', *Daedalus* 87.3, pp. 95 ff.

Henle, M. (1977), 'The phenomenal and the physical object' in J. M. Nicholas, (ed.), *Images, Perception and Knowledge* (Reidel, Dordrecht), pp. 187 ff.

Hick, J. (1966), *Evil and the God of Love* (Macmillan, London).

Hick, J. & McGill, A. (1967), (eds.), *The Many-Faced Argument* (Macmillan, London).

Hocking, W. E. (1936), 'Chu Hsi's Theory of Knowledge', *Harvard Journal of Asiatic Studies* 1, pp. 109 ff.

Hofstadter, D. R. and Dennett, D. C. (1981), (eds.), *The Mind's I* (Harvester, Brighton).

Hollis, M. (1973), (ed.), *The Light of Reason* (Collins-Fontana, London).

Hull, D. J. (1964-5), (1965-6), 'The effects of essentialism on taxonomy', *British Journal of the Philosophy of Science* 15, pp. 314 ff; 16, pp. 1 ff.

— (1978), 'A matter of individuality', *Philosophy of Science* 45, pp. 335 ff.

Hume, D. (1888), *Treatise of Human Nature* ed. L. A. Selby-Bigge (Clarendon Press, Oxford). First published in 1739-40.

— (1962), *Enquiries*, ed. L. A. Selby-Bigge (Clarendon Press, Oxford). Second edition of reprint of 1777 edition.

— (1976), *Natural History of Religion* and *Dialogues concerning*

*Natural Religion*, eds. A. W. Colver and J. V. Price (Clarendon Press, Oxford). First published in 1777.

Humphrey, N. K. (1976), 'The social function of intellect', in P. P. G. Bateson and R. A. Hinde (eds.), *Growing Points in Ethology* (Cambridge University Press, Cambridge), pp. 383 ff.

— (1980), 'Nature's psychologists' in *Consciousness and the Physical World*, eds. B. D. Josephson and V. S. Ramachandran (Pergamon Press, Oxford), pp. 57 ff.

— (1981), 'Having feelings and showing feelings' in Woodgush *et al.* (1981), pp. 37 ff.

Inge, W. R. (1926), *The Platonic Tradition in English Religious Thought* (Longmans, Green, and Co., London).

Ingold, T. (1974), 'On reindeer and men', *Man* 9, pp. 523 ff.

Jaki, S. L. (1974), *Science and Creation* (Scottish Academic Press, Edinburgh).

James, W. (1890), *The Principles of Psychology* (Macmillan, London).

— (1897), *The Will to Believe* (Longmans, Green, and Co., New York).

— (1907), *Pragmatism* (Longmans, Green, and Co., New York).

— (1964), *The Moral Philosophy of William James*, ed. J. K. Roth (Thomas Y. Crowell, New York).

— (1976), *Essays in Radical Empiricism*, ed. F. Bowers (Harvard University Press, Boston).

Jarvis, E. A. (1975), *The Conception of God in the Later Royce* (Nijhoff, The Hague).

Jaynes, J. (1976), *The Origin of Consciousness in the Breakdown of the Bicameral Mind* (Houghton Mifflin, Boston).

Jennings, H. S. (1906), *The Behaviour of Lower Organisms* (Columbia University Biological Series 10, New York).

Jeremias, J. (1971), *New Testament Theology* ed. J. Bowden, (SCM Press, London).

Johnson, S. (1950), *Prose and Poetry* ed. M. Wilson (Hart-Davis, London).

Jones, B. E. (1970), (ed.), *Earnest Enquirers after Truth: a Gifford Anthology (1888-1968)* (Allen and Unwin, London).

Jung, C. G. (1967), *Memories, Dreams, Reflections,* ed. A. Jaffe, tr. R. and C. Winston (Collins-Fontana, London).

Kamber, R. (1977), 'Liars, poets and philosophers', *British Journal of Aesthetics* 17, pp. 335 ff.

Kant, I. (1949), *Critique of Practical Reason and Other Writings*, ed. L. W. Beck (University of Chicago Press, Chicago).

Kenny, A. (1972), 'The origin of the soul' in *The Development of Mind* (Gifford lectures 1972-3 by Kenny *et al.*), (Edinburgh University Press, Edinburgh), pp. 46 ff.

Keynes, G. (1966), *Complete Works of William Blake* (Clarendon Press, Oxford).

King-Farlow, J. (1978), *Self-Knowledge and Social Relations* (Science-History Publications, New York).

Kipling, R. (1927), *Collected Verse: Inclusive Edition* (Hodder & Stoughton, London).

Knight, E. (1959), *The Objective Society* (Routledge & Kegan Paul, London).

Koyre, A. (1968), *Metaphysics and Measurement* (Chapman & Hall, London).

Kuyper, L. J. (1964), 'Grace and Truth', *Interpretation* 18, pp. 3 ff.

Lakatos, I. (1976), *Proofs and Refutations*, eds. J. Worrall and E. Zohar (Cambridge University Press, Cambridge).

Lehrer, K. (1970-1), 'Why not scepticism?', *Philosophical Forum* 2, pp. 283 ff.

Leopold, A. (1949), *Sand County Almanac* (Oxford University Press, New York).

Lessing, D. (1979), (1981), (1982), *Canopus in Argos* I: *Shikasta;* III: *The Sirian Experiments*; IV: *The Making of the Representative for Planet 8* (Cape, London).

Lewis, C. S. (1938), *Out of the Silent Planet* (Bodley Head, London).

— (1954), *The Silver Chair* (Bles, London).

Lindsay, D. (1974), *A Voyage to Arcturus* (Pan, London). First published in 1963.

Long, A. A. (1974), *Hellenistic Philosophy* (Duckworth, London).

Lovelock, J. (1974), *Gaia: a New Look at the Earth* (Oxford University Press, Oxford).

MacIntyre, A. (1981), *After Virtue* (Duckworth, London).

Mackie, J. L. (1982), *The Miracle of Theism* (Clarendon Press, Oxford).

Madell, G. (1982), *The Identity of the Self* (Edinburgh University Press, Edinburgh).

Malcolm, N. (1977), *Thought and Knowledge* (Cornell University Press, Ithaca, New York).

Mao Tse-Tung (1967), *Thoughts of Chairman Mao* (Foreign Language Press, Peking).

Marcel, G. (1949), *Being and Having* (Black, London).

Martin, P. S. & Wright, H. E. (1967), (eds.), *Pleistocene Extinctions* (Yale University Press, New Haven/London).

Mathews, G. (1978), 'Animals and the unity of psychology', *Philosophy* 53, pp. 437 ff.

Mayr, E. (1968), *Principles of Systematic Zoology* (McGraw-Hill, New York).

McGonigle, B. (1982), 'Evolution and intelligence from the standpoint of comparative psychology': paper to Thyssen Symposium (forthcoming in volume edited by C. Hookway).

Midgley, M. (1981), 'Why Knowledge Matters' in D. Sperlinger (ed.), *Animals in Research* (John Wiley and Sons, Chichester), pp. 319 ff.

Monod, J. (1972), *Chance and Necessity*, tr. A. Wainhouse (Collins, London).

Mugford, R. A. (1981), 'The social skills of dogs as an indication of self-awareness' in Woodgush *et al.* (1981), pp. 40 ff.

Nagel, T. (1974), 'What is it like to be a bat?', *Philosophical Review* 83, pp. 435 ff: reprinted in Nagel (1979).

— (1979), *Mortal Questions* (Cambridge University Press, Cambridge).

Nasr, S. H. (1981), *Knowledge and the Sacred* (Edinburgh University Press, Edinburgh).

Neuhaus, R. (1971), *In Defence of People* (Macmillan, New York).

Newman, J. H. (1906), *The Grammar of Assent* (Burns & Oates, London). Third edition.

O'Riordan, T. (1976), *Environmentalism* (Pion, London).

Otto, W. F. (1954), *The Homeric Gods*, tr. M. Hadas (Thames & Hudson, London).

Palmer, G. E. H., Sherrard, P., and Ware, K. (1979), (eds.), *The Philokalia* I (Faber, London).

Pascal, B. (1966), *Pensées*, tr. A. J. Krailsheimer (Penguin, Harmondsworth).

Pearsall-Smith, L. (1933), *All Trivia* (Constable & Co., London).

Peirce, C. S. (1931-60), *Collected Papers*, eds. C. H. Hartshorne, P. Weiss, and A. W. Burks (Harvard University Press, Cambridge, Mass.).

Perry, R. B. (1904), 'Conceptions and misconceptions of consciousness', *Psychological Review* 11, pp. 282 ff.

Pirsig, R. M. (1974), *Zen and the Art of Motorcycle Maintenance* (Bodley Head, London).

Plotinus (1969), *The Enneads*, tr. S. Mackenna, ed. B. S. Page (Faber, London). Fourth edition.

Powys, J. C. (1974), *In Defence of Sensuality* (Village Press, London). Reprint of 1930 edition.

Primatt, H. (1831), *The Duty of Humanity to Inferior Creatures* ed. A. Broome (Whitmore & Fenn, London). First published in 1776.

Proudhon, P. J. (1970), *What is Property?*, tr. B. J. Tucker (Dover, New York). Reprint of 1890 edition.

Raine, K. (1981), *Collected Poems* (1935-80) (Allen and Unwin, London).

Ramsey, F. P. (1931), *Foundations of Mathematics* (Kegan Paul, London).

Ritchie, D. G. (1916), *Natural Rights* (Allen & Unwin, London).
Rorty, R. M. (1973), 'Genus as matter' in E. N. Lee, A. P. D. Mourelatos, and R. M. Rorty (eds.), *Exegesis and Argument* (Van Gorcum, Assen), pp. 393 f.
Rosenfield, L. C. (1968), *From Beast-Machine to Man-Machine* (Octagon Books, New York).
Royce, J. (1885), *The Religious Aspect of Philosophy* (Houghton Mifflin & Co., Boston, Mass.).
— (1913), *The Problem of Christianity* (Macmillan, New York).
Rubinoff, M. L. (1974), 'Violence and the retreat from reason' in S. M. Stanage (ed.), *Reason and Violence* (Blackwell, Oxford), pp. 73 ff.
Russell, B. (1918), *Mysticism and Logic* (Longman, Green, & Co., London).
Russell, J. B. (1977), *The Devil* (Cornell University Press, Ithaca, New York).
Satprem (1968), *Sri Aurobindo: The Adventure of Consciousness*, tr. Tehmi (Aurobindo Ashram, Pondicherry).
Schnackenburg, R. (1968), *The Gospel according to St. John*, tr. K. Smyth (Burns & Oates, London).
Searle, H. C. (1980), 'Minds, brains and programs' in *Brain and Behavioural Sciences* 3 (Cambridge University Press, Cambridge). Reprinted in Hofstadter and Dennett (1981), pp. 353 ff.
Sextus Empiricus (1933), *Works*, tr. R. G. Bury, Loeb Classical Library (Heinemann, London).
Shea, W. R. (1972), *Galileo's Intellectual Revolution* (Macmillan, London).
Sheldrake, R. (1981), *A new Science of Life: the Hypothesis of Causative Formation* (Blond & Briggs, London).
Sober, E. (1980), 'Evolution, population thinking and essentialism', *Philosophy of Science* 47, pp. 350 ff.
Spencer, H. (1870), *The Principles of Psychology* (Williams and Norgate, London/Edinburgh). Second edition.
Sperry, R. W. (1969), 'A modified conception of consciousness', *Psychological Review* 76, pp. 532 ff.
— (1970), 'Reply to D. Bindra', *Psychological Review* 77, pp. 585 ff.
Spiegelberg, H. (1971), *The Phenomenological Movement* (Mouton, The Hague).
Sprigge, T. L. S. (1979), 'Metaphysics, physicalism and animal rights', *Inquiry* 22, pp. 101 ff.
Staal, F. (1975), *Exploring Mysticism* (Penguin, Harmondsworth).
Stapledon, O. (1961), *The Star Maker* (Berkeley, New York). First published in 1937.

— (1963), *Last and First Men* (Penguin, Harmondsworth). First published in 1930.

Steiner, G. (1978), 'Has Truth a Future?', *Listener* 99, pp. 42 ff.

Strehlow, T. G. (1934), *Aranda Traditions* (Melbourne University Press, Carlton).

Suzuki, D. T. (1960), (ed.), *Manual of Zen Buddhism* (Grove Press, New York).

Swinburne, R. G. (1979), *The Existence of God* (Clarendon Press, Oxford).

Symmachus, Q. Aurelius (1883), *Opera Quae Supersunt*, ed. O. Seeke (Weidmann, Berlin).

Tax, S. and Callender, C. (1960), (eds.), *Evolution after Darwin*, III (University of Chicago Press, Chicago).

Tevoedjre, I. *et al.* (1980), *Minority Rights Group Report 47: Female Circumcision, Excision and Infibulation* (MRG, London).

Tolkien, J. R. R. (1966), *The Lord of the Rings* (Allen & Unwin, London). Second edition.

Traherne, T. (1960), *Centuries* (Clarendon Press, Oxford).

Uexkuell, J. von (1926), *Theoretical Biology*, tr. D. L. Mackinnon (Kegan Paul, London).

— (1957), 'A stroll through the worlds of animals and men' in *Instinctive Behaviour*, ed. C. H. Schiller (International University Press, New York).

Unger, P. (1975), *Ignorance* (Clarendon Press, Oxford).

Waddell, H. (1934), *Beasts and Saints* (Constable & Co., London).

— (1952), *Mediaeval Latin Lyrics* (Penguin, Harmondsworth). First published in 1929.

Wallace-Hadrill, D. S. (1968), *The Greek Patristic View of Nature* (Manchester University Press, Manchester).

Washburn, M. L. (1917), *The Animal Mind* (Macmillan, New York).

Westphal, M. (1974), 'Hegel's theory of religious knowledge' in F. G. Weiss (ed.), *Beyond Epistemology* (Mouton, The Hague), pp. 30 ff.

White, R. J. (1971), 'A defence of vivisection', *American Scholar* 40: reprinted in P. Singer and T. Regan (eds.), *Animal Rights and Human Obligations* (Prentice-Hall, Englewood Cliffs, New Jersey), pp. 163 ff.

White, T. H. (1939), *The Sword in the Stone* (G. P. Putnam's Sons, New York).

— (1954), *The Book of Beasts* (Cape, London).

Wigner, E. P. (1964), 'Two kinds of reality', *Monist* 48, pp. 248 ff.

Wiles, M. (1960), *The Spiritual Gospel* (Cambridge University Press, Cambridge).

Williams, C. (1950), *He Came Down from Heaven* (Faber. London).

Williams, L. (1971), *Challenge to Survival* (New York University Press, New York). Revised edition published in 1977.

Willis, R. (1974), *Man and Beast* (Hart Davis MacGibbon, London).

Wilmot, J. (1964), *Rochester's Poems*, ed. V. de Sola Pinto (Routledge & Kegan Paul, London).

Wilson, E. O. (1975), *Sociobiology: A New Synthesis* (Harvard University Press, Cambridge, Mass.).

Wisdom, J. (1953), *Philosophy and Psychoanalysis* (Blackwell, Oxford).

Wittgenstein, L. von (1961), *Tractatus Logico-Philosophicus* tr. D. Pears and B. F. McGuinness (Routledge & Kegan Paul, London).

Wodehouse, P. G. (1957), *The Mating Season* (Penguin, Harmondsworth).

Wolff, K. H. (1970), 'The Sociology of Knowledge and Social Theory', in J. E. Curtis and J. W. Petras, (eds.), *The Sociology of Knowledge* (Duckworth, London), pp. 545 ff. First published in 1959.

Woodgush, D. G. M., Dawkins, M., and Ewbank, R. (1981), *Self-Awareness in Domesticated Animals* (UFAW, Potters Bar).

Yampolsky, P. (1971), *The Zen Master Hakuin* (Columbia University Press, New York).

# Index